Alexander Grant Ruthven
of Michigan

Alexander Grant Ruthven of Michigan

BIOGRAPHY OF A UNIVERSITY PRESIDENT

BY

Peter E. Van de Water

WILLIAM B. EERDMANS PUBLISHING COMPANY

Library of Congress Cataloging in Publication Data

Van de Water, Peter E
  Alexander Grant Ruthven of Michigan.

  Includes bibliographical references and index.
  1. Ruthven, Alexander Grant, 1882– 2. College
presidents—Michigan—Biography. I. Title.
LD3275 1929.V36   378.1'12'0924 [B]   76-45094
ISBN 0-8028-3493-0

TO BECKY

Contents

Foreword

In *Alexander Grant Ruthven of Michigan: Biography of a University President* we meet a zoologist who soon becomes a teacher and researcher, earns his doctorate and becomes Professor of Zoology and director of the Museum of Zoology early in his career.

His abilities were more fully realized as president of the university. By sharing responsibility and authority with the deans he established an administration in which both the deans and the faculties could function efficiently. One of the most satisfying results of this system occurred during the Depression. The president, the deans, the faculties, and all members of the business staffs received salary reductions. However, the salaries of instructors and assistant professors were reduced proportionately less than the salaries of full professors. These actions came after all concerned had met together and had worked out an acceptable solution.

In *Naturalist in Two Worlds,* President Ruthven noted that "University administrators are worth their salt to the degree to which they delegate *authority without shirking responsibility"* [italics mine]. "This principle," he added, "applies to boards in control as well as to presidents, deans, business managers, and other college officers" (p. 36).

In consequence, the "kitchen cabinets" which had been appointed by the deans when they were responsible only to the president, gave way to an elective system in which college officers were elected by professors and instructors and then recommended to the president for approval. Dean Edward H. Kraus of the College of Literature, Science, and the Arts was the first dean to be elected by his faculty. The system soon had general university acceptance.

From his early years as president, Dr. Ruthven took a special interest in the alumni. He wrote this brief creed:

We believe that the student should be trained as an Alumnus from matriculation; he enrolls in the University for life and for better or

9

worse he will always remain an integral part of the institution.

We believe that the relations between the alumnus and his University should be beneficial to both, and that the mutual assistance provided by the graduates and by the institution should be limited only by their powers for service.

We believe that to the person who has obtained what he should from his alma mater, Michigan is the actual expression of a practical idealism—government, religion, and the state supported education being inseparable. . . .

We believe that to the University the alumnus is a member of a brotherhood bound by the spiritual tie of faith in the ideals of education.

The alumni returned such affection in many ways. When their president retired in 1951, the Board of Directors of the Alumni Association conferred on him the title "Dean of Alumni." He prized this honor above any other that he received.

Peter E. Van de Water has written a complete account of the university's seventh president. He deserves high praise for his work.

Erich A. Walter

Preface

The University of Michigan is known as "the mother of state universities" and, as such, has always enjoyed a position of eminence in American higher education. Much of any institution's history is the story of its presidents; Michigan is remarkable in that, over its lifespan of approximately 150 years, only nine men have held its presidency. Some, such as Henry P. Tappan, James B. Angell, and Harry B. Hutchins have been the objects of considerable biographical study. Surprisingly, Alexander G. Ruthven, the president who had the second longest tenure of office—during what was undoubtedly the most trying period in the institution's history—has remained virtually unacknowledged by historians of the university. This biography, I hope, will correct that oversight.

I became interested in Alexander G. Ruthven when, with typical graduate student despair, I sought a dissertation topic. At that time, I knew only that the topic must be historical, and I preferred that it encompass the fascinating subject of academic freedom. "Why don't you immerse yourself in the history of the University of Michigan?" asked my advisor, and this chance question led me to two important discoveries. First, the Michigan Historical Collections on the Michigan campus is a rich reservoir of university history , for its depositories contain most of the primary source material still available. Second, I read Ruthven's *Naturalist in Two Worlds,* an enchanting little collection of the random reminiscences of Michigan's seventh president. The value of my discoveries was enhanced when I discovered that the Michigan Historical Collections had recently been given eighty-seven boxes of Ruthven's presidential papers, and that these papers were as yet virtually unexplored. Further, I found that Dr. Ruthven, then eighty-eight years old, but still lucid and lively, was living in Ann Arbor.

Once the topic was agreed upon, it seemed important to supplement the written record by interviewing Dr. Ruthven and a selected few of his contemporaries. The Michigan Historical Collections and the Horace H. Rackham School of Graduate Studies generously provided a grant for an "Alexander G. Ruthven Oral History," and eighteen key faculty, regents, and administrators, most of whom had experienced the Ruthven years in their entirety, were asked for interviews. Eleven responded affirmatively. In most cases the interviews with them were taped, transcribed, and then edited. Interviews varied in length from forty-five minutes to three hours. Those interviewed were Professor Robert Cooley Angell, former chairman of the sociology department; Professor Harold Dorr, former chairman of political science; Miss Hazel ("Doc") Losh, professor of astronomy; Professor Wesley Maurer, former chairman of the journalism department; E. Blythe Stason, former provost and dean of the Law School; Edward H. Kraus, former dean of the College of Literature, Science, and the Arts; Marvin Niehuss, former Vice President in Charge of University Relations; Walter B. Rea, former Dean of Men; Erich Walter, former associate dean of the College of Literature, Science, and the Arts and Dean of Students; and Regent Emeritus Alfred B. Connable. With three exceptions (Kraus, Niehuss, and Rea preferred not to have their reminiscences recorded for posterity) these interviews are now on file at the Michigan Historical Collections. This distinguished assemblage of Michiganders was most cooperative and extremely generous in sharing their recollections of the Ruthven years.

Five men have died since our interviews in 1970: Rea, Kraus, Dorr, Stason, and Ruthven.

I was indeed fortunate to have my interviews with Dr. Ruthven. I looked forward to those weekly interviews with keen anticipation, and I like to think he did too.

The Ruthven biography is an outgrowth of my earlier research and interviews.

I should mention two items for anyone who may be inclined toward further research on the Ruthven era at Michigan. The Michigan Historical Collections, which house the Ruthven Papers, has been moved from the Rackham Building to a magnificent new home, the Bentley Library on North Campus. Secondly, since I first researched the Ruthven papers in 1969–70, they have been catalogued. Accordingly, some of the box numbers may be different from those cited in my footnotes. Any confusion may be remedied by simply relying on dates, for the Ruthven Papers are catalogued chronologically.

I owe acknowledgements to many people.

Dr. Robert Warner and Mary Jo Pugh of the Michigan Historical Collections were always gracious, helpful, and professional. I use the latter word even though they relaxed their standards to permit this researcher the rare privilege of sharing the staff coffee room.

President Frank Piskor of St. Lawrence University believes that administrators, like faculty, can profit from leaves of absence, and he encouraged me to complete this project.

Alan and "Til" MacCarthy, now of Naples, Florida, introduced me to Dr. Ruthven at a dinner in their home. Both were instrumental in seeing this project to fruition.

Two former teachers, my father-in-law, Thomas H. Blaisdell, of South Westerlo, New York, and my father, John Van de Water, of Canton, New York, read the manuscript for grammatical errors.

Dr. David Madsen, now at the University of Washington, was my dissertation chairman and a strong source of support.

Bryant and "B" Ruthven, now retired to the family cottage at Frankfort, Michigan, were most helpful. They shared with me their home, their reminiscences, and their photo albums; and Bryant wrote a number of wonderful letters, parts of which I incorporated in the text. With his flair for writing he rather than I should have written his father's biography.

Professor Laurence C. Stuart, in his letters from Guatemala, provided some family insights not otherwise available.

President Robben Fleming of Michigan, who read the original manuscript, supported completion of the project by agreeing to underwrite the author's expenses for two months in Ann Arbor.

I interviewed many people not directly associated with the University of Michigan who knew Dr. Ruthven in non-university settings. Mrs. Julie Furstenberg Owens, Mrs. Donald Bacon, and Mr. Joseph Hooper were particularly helpful.

Robert G. Forman, Director of the Michigan Alumni Association, and Richard H. Emmons, Editor of *The Michigan Alumnus,* volunteered secretarial assistance in typing the final manuscript.

My own secretary, Elaine White, has been a constant help.

Deserving of special thanks are those many loyal friends of Michigan—especially Dr. Harry Towsley—who supported the Ruthven project with their finances and their written reminiscences.

Alexander G. Ruthven of Michigan

And, more than anyone, I thank Dr. Erich Walter. This kind and gentle man knows Michigan history like few others. It was his initiative which kept interest in the Ruthven biography alive, and his guidance which saw it to completion.

Peter E. Van de Water
Canton, New York

1

Beginnings

THE SETTLERS

The settlers called their lumbering Conestoga wagons "prairie schooners," for the canvas that covered their ribs billowed in the breeze like sailcloth on a ship. Families from Wisconsin, Indiana, and Illinois rode them, searching restlessly for richer dirt and cooler water. The wagons were their transitional homes. They contained all of an uprooted household's tools and furnishings—resources for a new beginning in the promised land further west.

Soon after the Civil War, these intrepid pioneers came into the northwest corner of Iowa, a flat, windswept plain bereft of trees.[1] Prairie grass stretched endlessly. The earliest families settled near a grouping of six shallow lakes. Those who were closest to the lakes built log cabins from the sparse number of trees growing near the shore. Those further from the lakes dug the sod of the prairie for their homes.

After the rough homes were finished, a shelter was erected for the livestock. Tall prairie grass was firmly packed in a frame of light posts for sides and ends, and grass was used for a thatched roof. Each settler made a firebreak around his buildings by plowing a strip of land for protection against prairie fires—a never-ending source of anxiety to the early settlers.

Deer and wolves were plentiful, but the herds of buffalo and elk had moved further west. Occasionally, Indians were sighted. They were feared, for the pioneers were expropriating the hunting lands of the Sioux and anticipated retribution.

Still, the prairie air was quiet except for the croaking of frogs and the chirping of birds. The marshy lowlands near the lake and the endless prairie were abundant with wild flowers. Pussywillows, violets, buttercups, and marsh marigolds came and went in seasonal splendor.

Alexander G. Ruthven of Michigan

Many of the settlers who came to the Iowa frontier were enticed by the Homestead Act of 1862. It provided that any person over twenty-one who was the head of a family and either a citizen or an alien who intended to become a citizen could obtain the title for 160 acres of public land if he lived on the land and improved it. In 1870, the Homestead law was changed. Civil War veterans were given sections of land; others paid fifty dollars for a homestead of 160 acres.

One of the earliest of the pioneers in this northwestern corner of Iowa was Alexander Ruthven, a Scotsman who came to this country in 1868.

Alexander Ruthven and his wife, née Margaret Geddes, had reared eight children in Stanerigg House, Shotts Parish, an industrial area halfway between Glasgow and Edinburgh. Mrs. Ruthven's brother, John, was employed by the Glasgow shipyards, and his duties carried him to many countries, including America. He had become aware of the opportunities presented by the Homestead laws and fascinated his brother-in-law with tales of the American West. Alexander, with his sons Alexander, Jr. and Robert, sailed for America, pushed into northern Iowa, and claimed their individual homesteads. The following year another son, John, sailed across the Atlantic to join his father and brothers. When the father and brothers had staked their claims and turned their initial sod shanties into more substantial homes, Mrs. Ruthven and two daughters, Minnie and Margaret, were sent for—probably in 1874.

John Ruthven was more railroader than homesteader.[2] As a boy he had watched the construction of the Caledonian railroad from Glasgow to Edinburgh; railroading thrilled him. After claiming a homestead west of present-day Ruthven, John, age twenty-four, became a construction superintendent for the railroads, then beginning their inexorable march westward. He spent the first ten years of his life in America with the Chicago, Milwaukee, and St. Paul and the Canadian Pacific railroads, working as far west as Manitoba. One can imagine the skill, strength, and stamina needed to oversee the brawny, brawling railroad crews of that era. John Ruthven had these qualities in good measure; he was, as well, shrewd enough to take advantage of the liberal land acquisition policies of the railroads, for when the Chicago, Milwaukee, and St. Paul came to the northern Iowa area that the Ruthven family had homesteaded, John purchased

16

several tracts of rich prairie loam from the railroad at bargain-basement prices.

John's lands were near the farms that his father and brothers had established. In fact, when the railroad came in 1878 to the area occupied by the Ruthven farms, Alexander, Jr. and his wife, Carrie, and Robert and his wife, Clara, donated the necessary thirty acres of land for a depot. A town was platted around the depot and called Ruthven in honor of Alexander Ruthven, Sr.

That same year, 1878, John Ruthven decided, at age thirty-three, that it was time to marry. During his railroad contracting he had met Katherine Rombough, daughter of a pioneer family who had moved to Hull, Iowa, from Rome, New York, in 1870. Katherine was only seventeen but, like John, she was a sturdy, God-fearing individualist.

In her twentieth year, Katherine Rombough Ruthven was with her parents in Hull when the first child was born, April 1, 1882. The baby was given his grandfather's name, Alexander. The middle name Grant was added as a tribute to Ulysses S. Grant, a folk-hero despite his scandal-rocked presidency just concluded.

John, in partnership with his brother Robert, continued to contract for the Chicago, Milwaukee, and St. Paul. In addition, the brothers operated a general store in the hamlet of Ruthven. In concert with his father and brothers, John began to work his lands. The old patriarch, Alexander Ruthven, Sr., and his energetic, robust sons were among the most substantial citizens of the nascent community. Their large farms produced an abundance of corn and cattle and, before long, there were "regularly assigned hired hands."[3] The town prospered, too, and by 1880 the population exceeded one hundred.

The leading citizen of Ruthven, however, was not John but his brother Alex, Jr., who was the first man in Ruthven to replace the wooden boardwalk in front of his house with a cement walk—a sure mark of distinction! In addition to his farms he operated the first lumber yard in the area. He was a director of two banks, president of the first school board in 1881, one of the first trustees of the Methodist church, and mayor of Ruthven from 1904 to 1910. Indeed, Alex, Jr. was so prominent that he warranted one of two biographical sketches included in the local history of Ruthven.

The description of Alex, Jr. from that local history is interesting, for very likely the characterization would fit his brother John as well:

17

Alexander G. Ruthven of Michigan

John Ruthven

Alex Ruthven was a man of few words and some regarded him as harsh and unfeeling. Those who had the occasion to penetrate that quiet personality saw a beautiful character beyond that mask of reserve. His friendship was not extended freely, but once extended, it was found to be the staunch old dependable brand that counts for more than an easy smile and a free hand shake. A friend who proved himself worthy found Alex Ruthven always standing by in reserve and ready to back him to the limit in worthy enterprises, but those who proved unworthy found no place in his friendship.

One surmises from this that Alex, Jr. was a "dour old Scot." Indeed, those same words were used by Alexander Grant Ruthven to describe his father, John, who was also a successful businessman and

18

Katherine Rombough Ruthven

farmer.[4] He, too, served on the bank board. He was a domineering, austere father to Alexander Grant and the children who followed: Beatrice ("Bea") and Bernard ("Bernie"). John was over forty when the younger two were born; Katherine, his wife, was still in her twenties. It is easy to imagine that the children in the John Ruthven family were not encouraged to be frivolous. One can see John and Katherine, dressed in their Sunday finery, sternly shepherding their growing family to weekly services in the Methodist church. Katherine Ruthven, in particular, was a pillar of the church and a staunch supporter of community causes. Except for Sunday, the days were filled with the chores of farm, home, and business. The family worshiped the Lord and the Puritan ethic in full measure.

19

CHILDHOOD

As soon as he was old enough, young Alexander Grant was expected to help, especially with farm chores. The happiest moments of his childhood probably followed his introduction to horses. Riding skills were needed on the farm, and he became proficient at herding cattle and breaking horses. At age eight he was already riding, and this new mobility opened his inquisitive mind to the wide outdoors. Years later, in one of his rare references to his youth, he wrote: "Riding a cowpony over the sunlit, wind-swept prairie, trampling over the black loam of plowed fields under dull autumn skies, listening to the calls of the wild fowl as they dropped into sloughs swollen with floods from melting snows . . . a small boy dreamed of knowing wild animals, studying their habits, and being associated with them in a museum or zoological garden."[5]

Compared with the freedom and excitement of the marshes, lakes, and prairies, school must have seemed dull. The schoolhouse was a two-story frame building, heated by a furnace and supplied with water from a well on the lot. There were two rooms on the first floor, and an assembly room, recitation room, and a library on the second. This small wooden structure was undoubtedly bulging with village youth, for the census reveals that Ruthven's population grew from

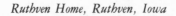

Ruthven Home, Ruthven, Iowa

150 in 1881, when the school was built, to 920 in 1897.[6] There were seven teachers, including the principal, many of whom were graduates of only the eighth grade. The high school courses offered were: grammar, arithmetic, physiology, history, physical geography, rhetoric, algebra, botany, civil government, etiology, geometry, physics, literature, and economics. There is nothing to remind us of Alexander Grant Ruthven's grades in secondary school, for all of the Ruthven school records were consumed by fire in 1944 and, mischievously, he never told.[7]

There was evident, however, the beginning of a consuming interest in the study of natural history. He recalled this vividly many years later:

> A remarkable event occurred when I was twelve years old which I cannot fully explain. I mentioned in my mother's hearing one day that I would like to have a copy of a book I had heard about, the *Origin of Species* by Darwin. Much to my surprise I received a copy as a Christmas present. My mother was a disciplinarian with a strict code of ethics, but apparently she was not a fundamentalist. At that time not only his book but the very name Charles Darwin was anathema to most churchgoers.
>
> Darwin's epoch-making work is hard going even for an adult, but I absorbed the contents of every page, even though I had to read some pages many times. From then on I knew I must, if possible, become a biologist of some kind.[8]

MORNINGSIDE COLLEGE

Following high school in Ruthven he was, as he later recalled, "shipped off to Morningside College, outside of Sioux City."[9] This was extraordinary in itself because at the turn of the century only one in a hundred went to college and no one in the Ruthven family had ever attended. It could have been that young Ruthven, as the scion of the town's ranking dynasty, was expected to enroll at college, but it seems more likely that he was eager to pursue his passion for natural history.

When Alexander G. Ruthven began classes, Morningside was only five years old. A board of Methodist ministers had resurrected it from the remains of a defunct college called the "University of the Northwest" by its hopeful founders. There were only about two hundred students when Ruthven attended Morningside; classes were held in the two college buildings—one inherited from the University of the Northwest and a new one called, inevitably, "Main Hall."[10]

In later years Ruthven would remember college life at Morningside as a "pleasant and rewarding experience." He makes reference to student-arranged entertainment and athletics and recalls wistfully that "everyone knew everyone."[11] Reviewing his "random recollections," one gets the impression that he was a full participant in the fin de siècle "college life" so graphically portrayed by Henry Siedel Canby.[12]

Probably the fact was less than the remembrance. Ruthven was, after all, the product of an austere heritage. His experience was limited to his own observations, for he hadn't traveled beyond his home environs, he had no acquaintance with others educated at college, and books were scarce in his hometown. In all likelihood young Ruthven moved inconspicuously among his college confreres. He remembers that he played on the football team, and college records indicate participation in tennis and the science club as well. Certainly there was no evidence of the leadership qualities he demonstrated later. Nor is there any indication that Ruthven became entangled in any romantic alliances while at Morningside; surprisingly, he made no lasting friends of either sex during college days.

Ruthven gave mixed accounts of the intellectual stimulation he received from Morningside. *Naturalist in Two Worlds,* his reminiscences, tells of R. B. Wylie, "one of the most inspiring teachers I have ever known," and makes reference to laying the foundations for a career in science.[13] We do know that Ruthven's work at Morningside included a heavy dosage of science courses: Inorganic Chemistry, Chemistry, Physics, College Physics, Scientific German, Human Physiology, Scientific French, Algae and Fungi, Zoology, Plant Ecology, Field Zoology, Morphology of Spermatophytes, and Arthropoda.[14] On the other hand, he was to tell his museum colleagues at Michigan, "College offered nothing for three years except botany, which proved to be an unsatisfactory substitution."[15] Probably he absorbed more from his academic exposure at Morningside than he cared to admit, for somewhere—and it wasn't in his home or his high school—he received a basic grounding in the sciences which permitted his immediate success as a graduate student.

On balance, however, Morningside was a bittersweet experience

22

for Ruthven at best. If one measures the meaning of a college experience by alumni allegiance to alma mater, it can be said that for Ruthven close ties with Morningside did not exist after he graduated. He did not return to the campus for years; there is no record of financial support; and he did not become a leader in the college's alumni affairs. It was a chapter in his life, and the chapter was finished.

UNIVERSITY OF CHICAGO

Following his third year at Morningside—so the family story goes—Alexander G. Ruthven was given the task of supervising the sale of a carload of his father's cattle. The cattle were to be shipped to the stockyards at Chicago and young Ruthven was charged with seeing that they were delivered and that his father was compensated.[16]

Ruthven used the opportunity to enroll for summer classes at the University of Chicago. "During this summer," he wrote years later, "I had the greatest advantage of becoming personally acquainted with such distinguished scientists as Cowles, Whitman, Tower, Williston, and Counter; and in particular with Charles C. Adams."[17]

Inspired by Adams and excited by the promise of a scholarship at Chicago, Ruthven returned to his last year at Morningside. Following graduation, he would enroll at Chicago and become a scientist.

His newly found goal caused great alarm in family councils. He was the eldest of a prominent yet provincial family; he was the first Ruthven to complete college, and his parents had plans for him. His son relates:

It was apparently . . . understood, as far as his parents were concerned, that Dad would go into the bank in which his father had acquired an interest. This kind of an arrangement, however, was clearly not what my dad had in mind.

Dad was not what I'd term a venturesome person, so we can imagine what a big decision it was for him to defy the wishes of his strong-willed parents, turn his back on an assuredly comfortable future in Ruthven, and enroll at the University of Chicago—a giant step into the unknown. And, in taking this step, he effectively severed relationships with his family and, as far as we were concerned, drew a veil across his youth.[18]

23

Alexander G. Ruthven of Michigan

It took unusual courage. The young man's resolve was bolstered, no doubt, by two factors. First of all, one senses a yearning to flee the nest, for although Ruthven respected his parents there was little affection or easy communication between them. He saw them infrequently and there is no indication that he was a regular correspondent. In later life his feelings toward them were more dutiful than loving.[19] Secondly, Ruthven was afflicted with the "tunnel vision" common to young scientists. He referred to his Chicago experience as the "glorious summer" and there can be no question that he was determined to follow science wherever it led. His parents' wishes were repudiated; he could hardly wait to begin his graduate work at Chicago.

NOTES

1. The descriptions of Ruthven, Iowa, and environs that follow are taken from *Ruthven Town and Country,* an undated booklet (ca. 1966) compiled by the Town and Country Study Club of Ruthven, passim.

2. The account that follows is from the *Ruthven Free-Press,* ca. May 8, 1939, and from the *Spencer Daily Reporter,* February 26, 1936.

3. Bryant Ruthven, letter, November 26, 1974.

4. Interview, Bryant Ruthven, December 17, 1974.

5. Alexander G. Ruthven, *A Naturalist in a University Museum,* privately printed, 1931, from the preface.

6. Ruthven has never exceeded the 1897 population.

7. "My academic performance as a student will forever be a secret. In afteryears to prod my children to do well in school I could boast of a perfect record. Both my offspring and my secretary were skeptical. When they connived to check my class records, however, they were disappointed to discover there were none extant. My high school had burned. My college records had been destroyed by fire. I had been admitted to Michigan on diploma, and in my time graduate students were not graded on classwork—they passed or flunked. I cannot prove I was always a model student, but no one can prove I was not." Alexander G. Ruthven, *Naturalist in Two Worlds* (Ann Arbor: University of Michigan Press, 1963), p. 8. For the record, Ruthven was Phi Beta Kappa.

8. Ruthven, *Naturalist in Two Worlds,* p. 2.

9. *Ibid.*

10. "Chronological History of Morningside College," mimeographed.

11. Ruthven, *Naturalist in Two Worlds,* p. 2.

12. See Canby, *Alma Mater: The Gothic Age of the American College* (New York: Farrar and Rinehard, 1936) and *College Sons and College Fathers* (New York: Harper and Brothers, 1915).

Beginnings

13. Ruthven, *Naturalist in Two Worlds*, p. 2.
14. A. W. Buckingham, letter, Morningside College, September 9, 1974.
15. Ruthven, *A Naturalist in a University Museum*, from the preface.
16. Bryant Ruthven, letter, November 26, 1974.
17. Ruthven, *Naturalist in Two Worlds*, p. 4.
18. Bryant Ruthven, letter, November 26, 1974.
19. Interview, Bryant Ruthven, December 17, 1974. Ruthven's younger brother, "Bernie," left home as a young man and was not heard from for many years. Eventually he contacted his sister, "Bea," and it was learned that he had been working in menial tasks for the Chicago, Milwaukee, and St. Paul Railroad.

2

The Museum

STUDENT AND TEACHER

In the summer of 1903 the nascent scientist received a telegram from his former teacher at the University of Chicago, Charles C. Adams. Ruthven learned that Adams had been appointed curator of the Museum of Natural History at the University of Michigan. Adams asked if Ruthven would accept a graduate assistantship to continue his study at Michigan and, because of his high regard for Adams, Ruthven promptly accepted. The salary was 150 dollars a year, less than he would have received at the University of Chicago.[1]

Adams was the heart and soul of the little museum at Michigan. He was brilliant, egotistical, and restless. He had a consuming love for his scientific work and little patience with students or faculty who didn't share his dedication. His nimble mind constantly sought new people who might match his scientific zeal, and he was a frequent investigator of new professional opportunities for himself and his students.

Adams found Ruthven to be a promising pupil and became friend and confidant as well as mentor to the twenty-one-year-old graduate student. They took long walks together and shared wide-ranging discussions. Adams was full of advice, which the eager Ruthven absorbed gratefully. In addition to chairing Ruthven's dissertation committee, Adams suggested books for his protégé's personal library, told him which professional meetings he should attend, and showed him how to prepare his scientific papers. As an example of his commitment to science and to Ruthven, Adams lent his young friend personal monies so that he might attend professional meetings throughout the country.[2] In addition, Adams offered the gratuitous advice that young scientists should not marry, for family obligations precluded full devotion to the profession.[3]

Ruthven blossomed under Adams's astute tutelage. He was com-

26

pletely engrossed in his work. He led the expeditions to the Porcupine Mountains of the Upper Peninsula and to Isle Royale in Lake Superior during the summers of 1903 and 1904 and, for his efforts, received a commendation in the curator's annual report.[4] He contributed snakes, frogs, fish, and shells in abundance to the museum inventories. His first publication, on the rare Butler's garter snake, appeared in 1904 and, in 1906, his doctoral dissertation on the garter snakes of North America was accepted.

During these formative years, Ruthven absorbed Adams's principles for museum work; he would never deviate from his mentor's precepts. Adams taught that a museum must constantly engage in aggressive exploration and acquisition. Field work and research were to be the sine qua non of the museum. Above all, a museum must be constantly changing and expanding. Adams was fond of quoting G. Brown Goode to anyone who would listen: "A finished museum is a dead museum, and a dead museum is a useless museum."[5]

Not surprisingly, Ruthven expressed the same sentiments in *Naturalist in Two Worlds*. "I learned," he wrote, "that a museum of zoology is not a 'dead circus,' not a gallery of elaborate exhibits to astound the public, and not a storehouse to demonstrate material for professors and students to tear to pieces. It is a teaching and research institution akin to a library. Its proper function is to gather intelligently and to preserve carefully specimens for research and to maintain exhibits illustrating biological facts and principles."[6]

Under the aegis of the museum Ruthven pursued his scientific interests. He was an herpetologist, or specialist in snakes, and within this discipline he began to break new ground. His research was to become instrumental in relating the geographical distribution of reptiles to their ecological adaptation.

CURATOR

When the peripatetic Adams left Michigan in 1906, Ruthven succeeded him as instructor in zoology and curator of the museum. It was hardly a coup for the twenty-four-year-old scientist. The nominal director of the museum, Professor Jacob Reighard, had little interest in promoting its activities. In addition to Ruthven, the staff consisted only of a taxidermist and a general assistant. The annual fund appropriated by the regents for the museum was $800.[7] The museum building, erected in 1880–81, was concurrently occu-

Ready for the Field, Before

pied by classes in geology, paleontology, and zoology and housed, in addition, the Stearns collection of musical instruments.[8] Ruthven's salary was $1200.[9]

The new curator, however, was undaunted by such limitations and happily set himself to his new task.

In his first full year as curator, Ruthven taught a course in animal ecology, rearranged the reptile collection, led an expedition to northern Iowa, and published six articles in professional journals. He became chief field naturalist for the Michigan Geological and Natural History Survey in 1908.[10] Ruthven relished this period when he was at liberty to pursue his interests in research, later referring to it as "one of the most pleasant and rewarding parts of my life."[11]

The pleasures and rewards for Ruthven were not purely scientific, for he was also courting during this period. Florence Hagle's father, Peter, had received his medical degree in 1867 from the University of Michigan, but had died of tuberculosis when she was only eight. Soon after his death the widow moved with her two daughters to Albion, Michigan, where she could take in student boarders for

Ready for the Field, After (1964)

income. Florence began her college studies at Albion, and when her mother moved to Ann Arbor to take in student boarders once again, Florence transferred to Michigan.[12] It was at the university, while assisting in a zoology class, that Ruthven met Florence Hagle. As he said later: "In one of my classes I was particularly annoyed by a coed who sat near the lantern. When I was in trouble, she would look my way and grin at my discomfiture. I finally got even with her—I married her."[13]

Ruthven courted Florence for at least three years, during which time she taught science in the high school at Chelsea, Michigan. An acquaintance from those days recalls that Ruthven and a friend, George Ellsworth, would board the "Interurban" trolley from Ann Arbor to Chelsea on Saturday evenings to visit Florence and her friend, Edith Shaw, at the Bacon home where both women boarded. Occasionally the two swains lingered, and the midnight Interurban rattled back to Ann Arbor without them. It was the last trolley, and the understanding Bacon family would take them in for the night.[14]

What attracted the handsome, brilliant young scientist to his former student? She was quite slim and did not possess striking features. It seems probable that during their extended courtship Ruthven learned to appreciate her vivacious manner, strong mind, interest in zoology, and—above all—her devotion to him. After his austere and parochial upbringing he had found someone who would understand his passion for his life's work, and who would love him unfailingly in the bargain. The young professor's influence on Florence even affected her classroom; she encouraged her students to collect specimens so that Chelsea High School might have a museum of its own.[15]

They were married in September, 1907, at a friend's home on Mackinac Island. After a short honeymoon the newlyweds returned to Ann Arbor where they moved into Mrs. Hagle's boardinghouse on Oakland Avenue. The bridegroom lost no time in returning to his museum.

Ruthven's correspondence during the years as curator indicates that he was a young man on the move. He was busy, and his letters frequently complained of too little time to accomplish his objectives. He was a scientist absorbed in his work; there was no time for "small talk." His letters to his colleagues were almost always short and businesslike to the point of being terse. He worked in earnest, for he knew he had a great deal to accomplish.

Ruthven's old master, Adams, kept a watchful eye on his young pupil. The two corresponded regularly, and some of Adams's ideas found a ready audience in Ruthven. Adams complained that his museum superiors wouldn't listen, but there was a way: "I have about decided to make the first move to some of the wealthy members for a few hundred dollars for storage cases for skins, insects, fossils. . . . If I can get this within a few weeks—the money—it will clear a way with these people for my ideas—over their own—as theirs have produced no results."[16]

Ruthven was well aware that Adams's museum and other collections profited from the largesse of wealthy patrons with avocational interests in museums. Even during Adams's time at Michigan it was not uncommon to ask benefactors to supplement the museum's limited budget, particularly in financing field expeditions. In 1909, Ruthven began to expand and enrich the work of his museum by incorporating interested patrons into the museum staff. Dr. William W. Newcomb, a physician, and Bryant Walker, a lawyer, both of Detroit, became Honorary Curators. Both of these men were superb amateur naturalists; both were instrumental in expanding the museum collections; both contributed generously. Ruthven frequently protested that Walker and Newcomb were too generous, but he never hesitated to tell them exactly what the museum needed and how much it would cost.[17]

In 1911 Miss Crystal Thompson was added to the staff as scientific assistant and Miss Helen Thompson was placed in charge of the library and photographic work. Ruthven became Assistant Professor of Zoology. He continued his prolific writing in professional journals.

Despite the rapid growth of the museum staff and collections, and his growing reputation as a scientist, Ruthven was uneasy. The museum director, Professor Reighard, viewed the museum as strictly an adjunct to the Department of Zoology, and Ruthven had no assurances that President Harry Burns Hutchins would support the museum's continued growth. Ruthven began trying to convince others that the university museum should be the museum for the state of Michigan.[18] Concurrently, he began to look for opportunities to leave Michigan.

"I will let you know if some museum position turns up . . . but I really think a few years more work where you are . . . will put you into one of the larger museums," Adams wrote.[19]

In 1910, Ruthven told Bryant Walker that he was contemplating a position at the Carnegie Museum in Pittsburgh.[20]

He was offered an opening at the University of Washington by a former professor at Morningside College, but turned it down with uncharacteristic arrogance: "A careful reading of your letter leads me to believe that you people don't know what a museum should be."[21]

Ruthven's frustration was solved, at least temporarily, when the regents raised his salary to $1600 and granted increases to the members of his staff.[22] The museum was humming with activity. "We are so busy that my brain feels like a merry-go-round," Ruthven told Bryant Walker, "but I am thoroly [sic] glad of it. We are working on things that count. . . . My assistants are a delight to me. . . . We have 16 papers in press at this minute."[23]

Still, Ruthven's letters to Walker indicate that as early as 1909 he wanted to direct the museum.[24] He wrote to Walker suggesting that letters to Harry Burns Hutchins might call the president's attention to the needs of the little museum and—one assumes—to the good work of its curator as well![25]

By December, 1912, Ruthven's frustration and ambition prompted an extraordinary letter sent directly to the regents of the university. He requested that the Museum of Natural History become the Museum of Zoology and that he become its director. He argued that the geological collections should be removed, for they were supervised by the Department of Geology and required valuable space that could better be used for a separate Museum of Zoology. He asked the regents to recognize the fact that Reighard, the director, had done little with the museum for years and that Ruthven was preparing the budget and the annual report for Reighard's signature.[27] Surprisingly, the regents agreed to these changes.[27]

"Hurrah for you! Free from Jake [Reighard]!! This will give you a chance to go ahead now as a free man. Hearty congratulations," wrote Charles C. Adams.[28]

DIRECTOR

The directorship was the opportunity Ruthven had been waiting for. He was strong, energetic, and enthusiastic. Thirty-one years old, he was recognized as one of the most promising young scientists in the country. He was developing into a skillful administrator; he knew what he wanted for his museum, and he knew how to get it. The regents' acquiescence with his reorganization plan was an indication of their confidence in him. The museum would go full speed ahead.

Within a year he added three Associates to the staff. Associates, like the Honorary Curators, were amateur naturalists. And, like the Honorary Curators, the associates were in a position to be of great assistance to the museum, both in terms of scientific expertise and financial support. During the 1912–13 academic year, Ruthven authored or co-authored ten papers for national publications.[29] His burgeoning annual reports indicate that the museum staff was attaining a new peak of productivity. During this time, the staff began a series entitled "Occasional Papers of the Museum of Zoology." These papers—publication of which continues to the present—were an attempt to share short scientific studies with other libraries and museums. The Occasional Papers were well received in the scientific community.

Bryant Walker, for years a friend of the museum, became a personal angel to Ruthven. Theirs was a special relationship. As curator, Ruthven had occasionally asked for Walker's financial support in an emergency. Now, as director, he called regularly on Walker for substantial support for a wide variety of museum enterprises. Walker never refused a Ruthven request. After 1913, when Walker gave $1,000 to finance a Ruthven expedition to South America, the museum could count on at least this amount for the annual expeditions; in addition, Walker subsidized museum publications and any other special projects requested by the director. Ruthven was not reluctant to ask for assistance. Frequently he would write to Walker, describing a pressing museum project, lamenting the absence of money to cover it, and noting that he was prepared to finance the project out of his own pocket if need be. He must have known that Walker would not call his bluff, for there was always a check in the return mail.

Walker opened his pocketbook cheerfully, for he shared Ruthven's vision of a great scientific museum at the university and—perhaps more important—Ruthven was like a son to the elderly lawyer. Walker was a house guest of the Ruthvens whenever he was in Ann Arbor, and Ruthven stayed with Walker in Detroit.

Walker lent Ruthven money so that he might buy land for a new home and, during the 1920s, Walker sent an annual check to Ruthven and asked him to be "Santa Claus" for the three Ruthven children. "I am very glad you are interested in the Museum," Ruthven wrote, "but quite apart from this and to me much more valuable is the inspiration of your personal friendship and my association with you. My personal friends in Ann Arbor know that I consider this to be the most important factor in my life since I came to Michigan."[30]

Whenever he could, Ruthven paid tribute to his benefactor. He must have been pleased when, in 1912, the regents granted Walker an honorary degree in recognition of his classification of mollusks. The library in the museum became the Bryant Walker Library, and when the last Ruthven child was born in 1919, he was named Bryant because, as the proud father wrote, "You are the best friend we ever had."[31] There is no question that Ruthven's rise at Michigan would have been less likely without the largesse of his elderly friend.

Under Ruthven's direction the field work of the museum staff increased. Except for a Ruthven expedition to Vera Cruz, Mexico, in 1910, all of the museum field trips had been in the United States. In 1913, Ruthven, his assistant Frederick M. ("Dick") Gaige, and Arthur S. Pearse, Honorary Curator of Crustacea, planned an ambitious expedition to the Santa Marta mountains of Colombia, South America. Their journey to South America was by rail and ship, and the expedition stayed from June to September. Ruthven estimated the cost for one person at $370, almost half of which went to pay for the round trip from New York to Colombia.[32] After the little party arrived in Colombia, the means of travel was uncertain. As Ruthven explained later:

> The usual way of taking side trips is to settle down for a few days and argue with the natives about the price of mules. After agreeing on the price, which is half of the first price asked or less, one generally takes the mules with the feeling that one has been cheated, and starts for an objective, putting up at the villages encountered on the way. About all one needs in the way of equipment is a hammock, tho' one has to make up his mind to live as the natives do, and not be particular about bunking with twenty-five to thirty mule drivers.[33]

There were comforts to be found, however, at the coffee haciendas, where the plantation owners competed in offering their hospitality to the intrepid visitors from North America.[34] The haciendas provided welcome relief from the rigors of the jungle and the bites of the "wretched Garrapatas," a tropical tick.[35] In *Naturalist in Two Worlds* Ruthven tells the amusing incident of a climb from a coffee hacienda to the summit of Mount San Lorenzo to study animal life above the timberline. The party was accompanied, against their wishes, by "a mysterious German count and countess." As Ruthven remembered the story:

> We reached the summit of·San Lorenzo after a stiff climb above the spot where we left our mules. As it was late and getting cold when we arrived at the summit, we set up a canvas lean-to, built a fire, had supper, and rolled ourselves in blankets under the protection of the shelter.
>
> The next morning when I awakened I saw the men in the party standing in front of the lean-to with a camera taking a picture of the Countess and me sleeping the sleep of the just. I have tried to buy or steal this picture for years without success. My companions claim to be holding it for blackmail on some appropriate occasion. I have tried to explain the whole occasion many times to Mrs. Ruthven, but all she will say is: "Well, sometime let me see the picture."[36]

Although Ruthven's memoirs tend to debunk the dangers of the field expeditions to South America, they were, in fact, a threat to life and health. Prior to his second expedition to Santa Marta, Ruthven told Bryant Walker: "If anything happens to me, I want the honorary curators (including the associates) to meet at once, and agree on a successor."[37] The 1914 expedition to British Guiana was perhaps the most hazardous. Even Ruthven, by then a rugged veteran, admitted: "This is truly a pretty tough country to work. Mud everywhere but the sand reef, and rain every blessed day. We go wading about in the mud cursing the sand flies and wiping the perspiration from our eyes."[38] During this field trip, when Ruthven was trying to capture several bushmasters (a venomous snake that grows to a length of eleven feet) he discovered that he had been trailed for at least half a day by a large jaguar.[39] The British Guiana expedition was concluded prematurely, not because of natural hazards, but because World War I had begun and Americans were summoned home.[40]

Both Ruthven and Gaige, his faithful assistant, suffered from malaria after these South American journeys. Ruthven, particularly, was badly afflicted. In his correspondence there is frequent mention of being "down and out" with the fever. These recurring bouts with malaria continued for many years.

During the teens and early twenties the museum flourished as never before in its history. The collections could not be contained within the archaic museum building and were housed in temporary quarters in the Natural Science building, two frame houses, two rooms in Angell Hall, two rooms in the Medical building, and two rooms in University Hall. By 1925, the staff had grown to twenty-five people, and had been organized into nine divisions: mammals, birds, reptiles and amphibians, fish, insects, mollusks, crustaceans, parasitic worms, and protozoa. The director's annual report to the regents was forty pages long. During the academic year 1925–26, 226,491 specimens and 1,786 books and reprints were received by the museum. "Chief," as his staff fondly called Ruthven, was in frequent correspondence with the leading museums in the country. The museum at Michigan was becoming one of the very best. A chatty, informative museum newsletter, dubbed *The Ark,* was begun in 1922. It was published once a month by "THE ONLY RESEARCH MUSEUM IN THE MIDDLE WEST." A. G. Ruthven was listed on the masthead as "Chief Humorist." In actual practice, however, it was the editors of *The Ark* who took great delight in teasing their popular director.

It was a marvelous time for the Ruthven gang. Morale was high. Ruthven's success did nothing to alienate him from others on his staff. On the contrary, the letters received from faculty and students in absentia indicate great respect and affection for the Chief. He was a world-renowned scientist and an able administrator. When the need arose, he would crusade for improved staff salaries; he chose competent and hard-working associates; he seemed to care about his staff as people; and he had a wonderfully subtle sense of humor. In the museum, he was idolized.

Two letters to Ph.D. candidates whose committee he chaired illustrate something of Ruthven's relationship with his students. Frank N. Blanchard, later a renowned scientist, was anxiously preparing his dissertation defense and asked what to expect. "I will probably content myself with asking you leading questions about your thesis and some general questions on zoogeography," Ruthven responded.

36

"I do not believe that you will be questioned in detail on subjects you have not pursued. . . . I have known of this being done but if it is ever done in one of my examinations . . . some one besides the candidate will get mussed up."[41]

With A. I. Ortenburger, whose thesis he had just reviewed, Ruthven was not as solicitous. "If you have any hope of a life hereafter, for God's sake spend all of the time you can spare from playing golf on revising your punctuation. . . . There are still a lot of sentences that would make a teacher of English curl up and die. One thing in particular—try to get your modifiers somewhere within a gun shot of the words modified."[42]

Ruthven obviously enjoyed working with graduate students and continued to chair graduate committees long after he became president of the university. He has been credited with training a large proportion of the herpetologists in America.[43]

In assessing Ruthven's rapid rise, one must ask if he "used" others for his own purposes—if his road to glory was paved with the broken bones of defeated rivals. There is little evidence that this was so, but there is considerable evidence to suggest that Ruthven was shrewd in advancing his own interests. He was acquainted with the power brokers of the state early in his career, for in 1909 he knew Governor Chase Osborn well enough to recommend the appointment of R. C. Allen as state geologist.[44] Through Bryant Walker he had ready access to regent Harry C. Bulkley, for Walker and Bulkley were close associates in Detroit. As a guest at the Huron Mountain Club, where Walker was a member, Ruthven became acquainted with many of the corporate leaders in the state. Ruthven made sure that President Hutchins, as well as presidents Burton and Little—who succeeded Hutchins—knew of every gift coming to the museum, and it seems probable that his own standing with the administration rose with every evidence of support for his museum. Ruthven worked closely with the Michigan Department of Conservation and, because of this, knew many state legislators. He became acquainted, indirectly, with Horace H. Rackham of Detroit when Bryant Walker induced Rackham to give the university museums $10,000 a year for three years to support the acquisition of Chinese pottery in the Philippines.[45] The Ruthven name was frequently before the regents, both in the annual reports that he prepared so carefully, and in his communications announcing still other gifts to the museum.

Alexander G. Ruthven of Michigan

In a letter to Walker there are some insights into Ruthven's thinking during this time. His mother had bought him a new car which he proudly drove about the campus.

> The other day the President's secretary phoned that I was wanted at the President's Office. I jumped into the car and drove up, and I arrived just as a group of Regents came up. Secretary [of the University Shirley] Smith said, "Ruthven has a new car; he doesn't need any more budget," and a Regent spoke up: "Yes he does. I like to see a man stick his chest out. Ruthven, keep it up; he who has gets." . . . Smith told me afterwards that many of the faculty come sobbing to the Regents on every pretext, and that I had made a hit by making them realize that we are doing things and believe in ourselves.[46]

Ruthven related this little story with relish, for he was confident of his ability and anxious that those in high places recognize it.

Soon after he became director, Ruthven was approached by the American Museum of Natural History which had an opening for a curator of herpetology. He was very interested in this opening because the salary was $5,000 and the American Museum represented additional prestige. "For the life of me I cannot decide what to do,"[47] he confided to Walker. Then, to cover his flank, he wrote directly to Regent Bulkley, telling him of the offer and his dilemma.[48] Ruthven was probably sincere in his interest, but if he used the American Museum offer as a ploy for more recognition at home, it worked. Bulkley and Bryant Walker were distressed that Ruthven might leave Michigan, and Bulkley resolved to ask his fellow regents to raise Ruthven's salary immediately.[49] The regents agreed not only to a salary raise (to $2500) but jumped Ruthven from assistant professor to professor.[50]

The regents continued to regard Ruthven as their "fair-haired boy," and he, in turn, continued to relish their confidence. "The Regents called me over Saturday," he reported to Walker. "They should have known better. I in turn got Regents Murfin and Gore to visit the museum. The results are as follows:

> They gave me $450 more than I asked for
> They raised every salary in the Museum 30%
> They increased my salary to $3500
> They granted in full the increases I asked for current expenses
> Our total budget will be over $13,000."[51]

In retrospect, Ruthven's personal ambition was healthy, without being machiavellian. His ambition for his museum, however, knew no bounds.

"I have only one ambition, and that is to put this department on the map," he told his friend Edgar M. Ledyard. "I won't stop short of crime to do this."[52] His commitment to the museum he was building consumed his energies. He was "enshrouded in gloom" over all that remained to be done.[53] Yet he was proud of his staff, the collections, and the museum's expanding reputation. There were precious moments of exhilaration, as when the Harvard Museum of Comparative Zoology sent the skeleton of a rare Great Auk as a gesture of friendship.[54]

FAIR OAKS

There was hardly time enough to be husband and father to his growing family. The first child, Katherine ("Kate"), was born in 1909, and Peter followed in 1912. Bryant ("Bud") was added in 1919. Whenever he could, Ruthven took Peter with him on his travels, and the children sometimes joined the museum staff at weekly "brown bag" lunches. Ruthven's letters indicate that he was a warm, considerate father, and affectionate—perhaps even a bit patronizing. He encouraged his children to share his interest in collecting and riding. After a family trip to South Dakota he told Bryant Walker with amusement that "Pete and Bud have decided to be cowboys."[55] Later, he reported, "We now have 1 parrot, 1 parakeet, 1 canary, 2 love birds, 3 salamanders, 2 telescope fish, 742 gold fish, 1 alligator, 1 turtle, and 1 dog." "I am thinking of charging admission," he added.[56]

The burgeoning household and his increased station in the university prompted a search for a new home. Land was purchased by installments on Fair Oaks Parkway, a pleasant, wooded area only a brisk walk from the campus. The new house at 1220 Fair Oaks, a spacious white colonial, cost $12,000 to build; the finished structure was a delight to the new owner, who considered himself "general contractor, supervising architect, and painter on the job."[57] To ensure long life, all boards in the house were painted front and back—perhaps a measure of Ruthven's Scotch frugality, and certainly an indication that the family intended to stay at Fair Oaks indefinitely.[58]

Except for an occasional cursory reference to "Mrs. R.,"

Ruthven's letters do not offer any insight into his relationship with his wife. Evidently no slight was intended, for despite her frail frame, those who knew Florence Hagle Ruthven considered her an unusually "strong" person who became a pillar of support for her husband right from the beginning.[59] "We children came a long second after Mother," her son recalled. "Mother and Dad, in a sense, were a closed corporation. As long as she lived, they were socially self-sufficient. They nourished and sustained each other. And there can be no doubt about it: Mother was a power source. Physically diminutive, socially unobtrusive, Mother was solid steel, tough as hell."[60]

Such a description does not imply that Florence Ruthven was a strict disciplinarian in the home (she wasn't) or that she made the telling decisions in her husband's career. He "wore the pants" in the

Florence Hagle Ruthven, Katherine, and Peter (1912)

40

1220 Fair Oaks (c. 1922)

family and career decisions were his to make, but she was a valued sounding board and, once her husband reached a judgment, she would defend it fiercely against any criticism.

A favorite family story illustrates both Florence Ruthven's toughness and her devotion to her husband. Sometimes, when family obligations permitted, she would accompany the museum field expeditions. "On an expedition to southern Vera Cruz," Alexander G. Ruthven recalled, "the Indians brought in two boa constrictors about ten or eleven feet long just before our departure. We placed them in a suitcase in our stateroom. During the voyage home, it became quite cold, and we feared the boas would not live to reach Ann Arbor. Mrs. Ruthven . . . solved the problem. She placed them in her berth. All three got along very comfortably."[61]

Life at Fair Oaks was good. The Ruthvens were a happy, close-knit family; they enjoyed the high regard of their neighbors; and they entertained university colleagues frequently. Florence Ruthven's culinary limitations were readily forgiven, for she was a gracious and thoughtful hostess. "Alex" Ruthven would help out occasionally, mixing his favorite drink—martinis—or grilling

41

steaks on the patio. Particularly good friends were Dick and Helen Gaige, neighbors and long-time associates on the museum staff. The Ruthvens enjoyed typically suburban leisure pursuits: he was proud of his yard and plantings, and she shared his interests in flowers and animals and enjoyed her knitting.

THE NEW MUSEUM

As the Roaring Twenties began, Ruthven, age thirty-eight, had one major, unaccomplished goal: a new museums building. He introduced the subject to the regents in his annual report submitted in 1918. He told them that the present museum building would no longer do, for it was not fireproof and it was "congested to such an extent that by no shifting and rearrangements of the collections can more space be provided." Ruthven told them bluntly that "by far the best solution of the problem would be a modern fire-proof building designed for museum purposes."[62]

The following year the director warned the regents: "It may be said conservatively that if a new building is not constructed within the next three years, the growth of the Museum and all of its activities will be seriously retarded."[63] Ruthven went on to say that he was submitting a plan for the regents to consider. "If you believe in the efficacy of prayer now is the time to pray," Ruthven advised Bryant Walker.[64]

Despite Walker's prayers it was to be some time before Ruthven realized his dream of a new museum. There was great anticipation, as when "the president and three regents told me last Thursday that a new building is a certainty."[65] There was also disillusionment and despair when the regents decided in 1921 that they could not build the museum. Ruthven's annual reports from 1921 to 1924 speak plaintively of the pressing need for a new museum but, to his dismay, it became a "back-burner" project for the administration and the regents.

This change in attitude was in part due to the change in presidents. President Harry B. Hutchins thought highly of Ruthven and was considered to be a staunch supporter of a new museum. When Hutchins resigned and Marion LeRoy Burton became president in 1920, Ruthven must have been apprehensive, for Burton had been a minister and his scientific sympathies were suspect. He was temporarily relieved when Burton "made the statement yesterday that the museum would be built at once."[66] His relief was short-lived. At the end of the 1921 legislative session $4,800,000 was voted for capital funds for the East Medical College, literary building, East Engineering building, model high school, new physics laboratory, continuation of the University Hospital, addition to the dental building, and additional land.[67] There was nothing for the new museum, and for the moment Ruthven's dream was shattered, perhaps by President Burton. "The whole situation has upset all my plans," Ruthven told Walker. "I propose that you write a letter to the President expressing your regret that the Regents have decided not to build the Museum."[68] Ruthven then wrote directly to President Burton saying that if there was a reasonable prospect that the university would build a museum in the near future, members of the museum staff should be sent to Washington, D.C., to study the methods of the United States National Museum and the various federal departments.[69] There is no recorded response other than Burton's scrawled note in the margin of Ruthven's letter: "Inform Walker candidly." This could only mean that plans for the immediate construction of the museum had gone awry. Ruthven received occasional assurances from the administration that his museum would eventually be built, but he must have fretted as he watched the new structures rise around the archaic building that he and his staff occupied. When Marion LeRoy Burton died in February of 1925, Ruthven was not altogether respectful. "As you know, le roi est mort," he wrote Walker.[70] The poor pun probably indicated the depth of Ruthven's frustration. Commenting on Burton's successor he noted: "For the first time we have an honest and intelligent president who understands what a museum is."[71] The correspondence between Ruthven and Burton, the Burton Papers reveal, was perfunctory and lacking in the warmth common to each man.[72]

After Burton's premature death on February 9, 1925, Dean Alfred H. Lloyd of the Graduate School was appointed acting president. It was during his interregnum in 1925 that the Michigan legislature appropriated $310,000 for land and $900,000 for the first unit of a new museum building. Governor Groesbeck signed this legislation on May 26, 1925. "Hallelujah! 'tis done! Hip Hip Hurrah!" Bryant Walker exulted. "Now you can sleep peacefully and dream of the museum that is to be."[73] The museum newsletter,

The Ark, printed a special edition called the *Jubilee Number.* [74] Meanwhile, Michigan was searching for a new president. No doubt Ruthven wished ardently for a supportive chief executive.

When C. C. Little was elected president in September, 1925, Ruthven welcomed a fellow scientist. Little was an interesting character. He came to Michigan from the presidency of the University of Maine, a position he had accepted when he was only thirty-three years old. He had established a reputation at Maine as a progressive educator and a brilliant biologist whose expertise was in the area of cancer research. He was tall, handsome, and charming and, initially, his appointment was greeted with approbation at Michigan. Ruthven liked him right from the start. "He is simply a fine chap . . . he and I are very close personally, and I know we can trust him," the museum director told Walker. "This is the happiest time I have had at the University."[75]

Little backed Ruthven and his plans to the hilt. When Ruthven was offered the directorship of the New York State Museum in Albany, "Little . . . sent me word by Mrs. Ruthven that the Regents would do anything to keep me," Ruthven wrote Walker. "The most powerful reason for my decision [to stay at Michigan] is, however, that you would be disappointed," he added.[76]

In 1926, when Governor Fred W. Green tried to persuade a reluctant Ruthven to become director of the State Department of Conservation, Ruthven and Little used "all of [their] diplomacy to sidetrack him without offending him."[77] In his reminiscences, Ruthven referred to Green's offer:

> He took me up on a high mountain and showed me the scenery. The party had been in power for years. The leaders were in agreement on my appointment. If I could accept and hold the post for a period, I would advance to the legislature. From there I could choose one of two routes, to the governorship or to Congress. I was not tempted, but I had to have the help of the President of the University to remain free.[78]

When Ruthven became embroiled in a lively dispute with the Department of Zoology concerning jurisdiction over budgets and collections as well as supervision of graduate students, Little never hesitated. He named Ruthven chairman of the Department of Zoology in addition to his duties as museum director and told him to straighten out the "mess." Ruthven wasn't reluctant. "It is not egotistical for me to say that no one else could straighten it out. I know all the ins and outs," he told his confidant Bryant Walker. "Before I get through I am going to have zoology at Michigan well organized, and a staff working at peace and harmony. . . . My motto is 'make the University safe for the Museum.' "[79]

With the welcome backing of a new chief executive, Ruthven's considerable energies were directed toward his long-awaited museum building. He wrote his friend, Dr. Howard Kelly: "The Regents told me to go ahead and build it, selecting the architect, the building materials, etc. I have not been able to share the responsibility, so that I have been swamped with details."[80] The evidence indicates that Ruthven did assume the major responsibility for planning the building, although he had help from a building committee of Regent Clements and the architect, Albert Kahn, of Detroit. When one considers that Ruthven had no experience in planning buildings, the project must have appeared overwhelming to him. *The Ark* indicates that Ruthven worked closely with his staff in soliciting their suggestions and reactions to the architect's plans. Apparently, all was not harmony between architect Kahn and Director Ruthven. By the time plans for the museum were underway, Kahn had established himself as perhaps the preeminent architect in Detroit. Compared with other buildings he had designed, the museum was a rather minor project and Kahn became annoyed by Ruthven's attention to detail.[81] Ruthven, in turn, thought that "Albert Kahn is a jack-ass and I am glad I will soon be through with him."[82]

The formal opening for the museum was June 14, 1928, and the main speaker was one of Ruthven's dearest friends, Dr. Thomas Barbour, director of the Museum of Comparative Zoology at Harvard.

Ruthven's museum is an impressive edifice even today. Its two brick wings have been joined by a formless modern addition, but the building can still be considered the "artistic triumph" the editor of *The Michigan Alumnus* declared it to be when it was built.[83] The large lettering over the main entrance bears Louis Agassiz's admonition: "Go to nature, take the facts into your own hands, look and see for yourself." Above the entrance doors is the inscription: "Truth conquers by itself," variously ascribed to Antoninus and Epictetus. It can be safely assumed that Ruthven selected both mottoes.

Indeed, Agassiz was a special hero to Ruthven and his papers

The Museum (1928)

contain Agassiz's 1861 report to the Committee of Overseers of
Harvard College with the floor plan for the Harvard Museum of
Comparative Zoology.[84] No doubt Ruthven scrutinized these plans
as his own building progressed.

J. Speed Rogers, who became museum director in 1947, summed
up Ruthven's accomplishment:

> The new building was finally ready for occupancy in 1928, and the
> Museums of Zoology, Anthropology, and Paleontology and the Uni-
> versity Herbarium were housed in a functionally planned and admi-
> rably appointed building. Ruthven had given many years of thought
> to a university museum and the role it should play. He and his staff
> had carried on the researches and amassed the carefully selected and
> pertinently documented collections that were bringing the Museum
> an international reputation. The University Museum's attainment of
> academic status and financial support was pre-eminently his accom-
> plishment, and the new building reflected both his concept of what a
> university museum should be and the detailed planning that only a
> trained museum staff could provide. The excellence of this planning
> is perhaps best shown by the fact that today, twenty-five years after

46

completion, the Museums Building remains a model for the combined storage and active use of large research collections.[85]

Ruthven's labors left him exhausted. His doctor suggested a complete rest, and he and Mrs. Ruthven left for Scotland and England. Before he could leave Ann Arbor, however, new responsibilities were thrust upon him. The *Proceedings of the Board of Regents* for the annual June meeting in 1928 disclosed that Ruthven was to become Dean of Administration, at a salary of $10,000. He was to retain his other titles and duties.[86] Ruthven accepted the administrative appointment, which corresponded to an executive vice presidency, with ambivalence. He termed the switch to administrative life "a distinct shock" and he knew that his scientific work would suffer; on the other hand, he was flattered by the recognition and the salary, and he felt obligated to help his friend, C. C. Little, by now sinking in a sea of troubles. His museum staff was concerned that they would lose his leadership forever. He assured his colleagues that his interest in the museum would continue "as long as I can toddle to it."[87]

NOTES

1. Alexander G. Ruthven, *Naturalist in Two Worlds* (Ann Arbor: University of Michigan Press, 1963), p. 4.

2. Charles C. Adams to Alexander G. Ruthven, December 4, 1906. Ruthven Papers, box 51–1, Michigan Historical Collections, University of Michigan (hereafter referred to as MHC). This occurred after Adams had become director of the Cincinnati Society of Natural History. For the Adams-Ruthven correspondence, see the Ruthven Papers, boxes 51–1 and 51–2, MHC.

3. Ruthven, *Naturalist in Two Worlds,* pp. 5–6.

4. "Report of the Curator of the Museum to the Board of Regents," July 1, 1903–July 1, 1904, *University Bulletin,* vol. 7, no. 3, December, 1905, p. 9.

5. *Ibid.* Also quoted in Ruthven, *Naturalist in Two Worlds,* p. 7.

6. Pages 6–7.

7. "Report of the Curator," July 1, 1907–July 1, 1908, p. 7.

8. *The University of Michigan: An Encyclopedic Survey,* vol. 4 (Ann Arbor: University of Michigan Press, 1958), p. 1436.

9. Adams to Ruthven, July 30, 1906, Ruthven Papers, box 51–1, MHC.

10. "Report of the Curator," July 1, 1907–July 1, 1908.

11. Ruthven, *Naturalist in Two Worlds,* p. 8.

12. From *Io Triumphe,* the Albion College alumni magazine, vol. 16, no. 3, May, 1951, pp. 323–24.

13. Ruthven, *Naturalist in Two Worlds,* p. 6.

14. Telephone conversation with Mrs. Edith Zapf, Frankfort, Michigan, December 17, 1974.

Alexander G. Ruthven of Michigan

15. Harlan A. DePew to Erich Walter, November 27, 1974. DePew was one of Miss Hagle's students.

16. Adams to Ruthven, September 12, 1906, Ruthven Papers, box 51–1, MHC.

17. For example, Ruthven to Dr. W. W. Newcomb, June 17, 1912, Ruthven Papers, box 52–2, MHC.

18. Ruthven to Bryant Walker, September 13, 1909, Ruthven Papers, box 52–17, MHC. See also "The Report of the Curator," July 1, 1910–June 30, 1911, pp. 7–9.

19. Adams to Ruthven, February 8, 1909, Ruthven Papers, box 51–2, MHC.

20. Ruthven to Walker, October 20, 1910, Ruthven Papers, box 52–17, MHC.

21. Ruthven to Theodore C. Frye, August 22, 1911, Ruthven Papers, box 51–20, MHC.

22. *Proceedings of the Board of Regents,* July meeting, 1911, p. 240.

23. Ruthven to Walker, December 12, 1912, Ruthven Papers, box 52–18, MHC.

24. Ruthven to Walker, September 2, 1909, Ruthven Papers, box 52–17, MHC.

25. Ruthven to Walker, undated (probably 1910), Ruthven Papers, box 52–17, MHC. Walker, on at least two occasions, did write directly to Hutchins.

26. Ruthven to Hon. Harry C. Bulkley, December 2, 1912, Ruthven Papers, box 52–18, MHC.

27. *Proceedings of the Board of Regents,* March meeting, 1913, p. 681.

28. Adams to Ruthven, April 2, 1913, Ruthven Papers, box 51–2, MHC.

29. "Report of the Director of the Museum of Zoology to the Board of Regents," July 1, 1912–June 30, 1913, pp. 18–19. In all, Ruthven authored or co-authored 137 professional papers and articles.

30. Ruthven to Walker, December, 1913, Ruthven Papers, box 52–18, MHC.

31. Ruthven to Walker, April 8, 1919, Ruthven Papers, box 52–21, MHC.

32. Ruthven to Arthur S. Pearse, January 22, 1913, Ruthven Papers, box 52–5, MHC.

33. Ruthven to Dr. F. C. Newcombe, June 1, 1927, Ruthven Papers, box 52–2, MHC. For additional descriptions of the Santa Marta expedition see Ruthven's *The Amphibians and Reptiles of the Sierra Nevada de Santa Marta, Colombia,* published by the University Museum of Zoology, 1922.

34. See correspondence with Orlando Flye, Ruthven Papers, box 51–18, MHC. Ruthven and Flye corresponded frequently after Ruthven returned to Ann Arbor, and Ruthven was able to engage a Michigan student who went to South America as a tutor for the Flye children.

35. Orlando Flye to Ruthven, October 28, 1913, Ruthven Papers, 51–18, MHC.

36. Pages 12–13.

37. Ruthven to Walker, May 12, 1920, Ruthven Papers, box 52–22, MHC.

38. Ruthven to Walker, August 10, 1914, Ruthven Papers, box 52–19, MHC.

39. Ruthven, *Naturalist in Two Worlds,* pp. 10–12.

40. For an account of the return voyage, see *Naturalist in Two Worlds,* pp. 13–14.

The Museum

41. Ruthven to Frank N. Blanchard, May 28, 1919, Ruthven Papers, box 51–11, MHC.

42. Ruthven to A. I. Ortenburger, September 24, 1924, Ruthven Papers, box 52–4, MHC.

43. *The University of Michigan: An Encyclopedic Survey,* vol. 4, p. 1512.

44. R. C. Allen to Ruthven, undated, Ruthven Papers, box 51–2, MHC.

45. Walker to Ruthven, May 24, 1922, Ruthven Papers, box 52–22, MHC. Rackham gave this gift to the university anonymously.

46. Ruthven to Walker, June 17, 1918, Ruthven Papers, box 52–21, MHC.

47. Ruthven to Walker, undated (probably April, 1915), Ruthven Papers, box 52–19, MHC.

48. Ruthven to Bulkley, May 14, 1915, Ruthven Papers, box 52–19, MHC.

50. *Proceedings of the Board of Regents,* May meeting, 1915, p. 167.

51. Ruthven to Walker, June 23, 1919, Ruthven Papers, box 52–21, MHC.

52. Ruthven to Edgar M. Ledyard, February 27, 1927, Ruthven Papers, box 51–32, MHC.

53. Ruthven to Walker, February 11, 1920, Ruthven Papers, box 52–22, MHC.

54. Ruthven to Walker, December 5, 1919, Ruthven Papers, box 52–21, MHC.

55. Ruthven to Walker, August 30, 1924, Ruthven Papers, box 53–1, MHC.

56. Ruthven to Walker, January 14, 1926, Ruthven Papers, box 53–3, MHC.

57. Ruthven to Walker, September 21, 1921, Ruthven Papers, 52–22, MHC.

58. Interview, Bryant Ruthven, December 17, 1974.

59. Interviews with Mr. and Mrs. Bryant Ruthven, December 17, 1974 and Mrs. Julie Furstenberg Owens, December 18, 1974.

60. Letter, Bryant Ruthven, November 26, 1974.

61. Ruthven, *Naturalist in Two Worlds,* p. 9.

62. "Report of the Director," July 1, 1917–June 30, 1918, pp. 8–9.

63. "Report of the Director," July 1, 1918–June 30, 1919, pp. 7–8.

64. Ruthven to Walker, May 13, 1919, Ruthven Papers, box 52–21, MHC.

65. Ruthven to Walker, October 21, 1920, Ruthven Papers, box 52–22, MHC.

66. Ruthven to Walker, April 19, 1921, Ruthven Papers, box 52–22, MHC.

67. See Howard H. Peckham, *The Making of the University of Michigan* (Ann Arbor: University of Michigan Press, 1967), pp. 140–41.

68. Ruthven to Walker, April 19, 1921, Ruthven Papers, box 52–22, MHC.

69. Ruthven to M. L. Burton, April 25, 1921, Burton Papers, box 4–5, MHC.

70. Ruthven to Walker, February 21, 1925, Ruthven Papers, box 53–2, MHC.

71. Ruthven to Walker, December 23, 1926, Ruthven Papers, box 53–3, MHC.

72. The Burton Papers are on file in the Michigan Historical Collections.

73. Walker to Ruthven, May 3, 1925, Ruthven Papers, box 53–2, MHC.

74. *The Ark,* April, 1925.

75. Ruthven to Walker, December 23, 1926, Ruthven Papers, box 53–3, MHC.

76. Ruthven to Walker, December 8, 1925, Ruthven Papers, box 53–2, MHC.

Earlier Ruthven told Walker that "three of the men declare they will resign if I do" (Ruthven to Walker, December 3, 1925). At the weekly colloquium of the museum staff a portrait of Ruthven was presented to the director "as a result of the fear by some that he would accept a position elsewhere, but which he declined" (Ann Arbor *Times-News*, March 5, 1926).

77. Ruthven to Walker, December 20, 1926, Ruthven Papers, box 53–3, MHC.

78. Ruthven, *Naturalist in Two Worlds*, p. 20.

79. Ruthven to Walker, undated (probably November, 1927), Ruthven Papers, box 53–4, MHC.

80. Ruthven to Howard Kelly, April 24, 1926, Ruthven Papers, box 51–30, MHC.

81. Interview, Dr. Edgar Kahn [son of Albert Kahn], December 8, 1974.

82. Ruthven to Walker, February 27, 1928, Ruthven Papers, box 53–4, MHC. This discord, evidently, was not permanent, for Kahn's firm has continued to provide architectural services for the university to the present.

83. Volume 34, no. 31, May 26, 1928.

84. Ruthven Papers, box 51–8, MHC.

85. *The University of Michigan: An Encyclopedic Survey*, vol. 4, p. 1440.

86. Page 609.

87. Ruthven to Carl L. Hubbs, August 29, 1928, Ruthven Papers, 51–25, MHC.

The Making of a
University President, 1929

Upon his return from England, Ruthven plunged into his new duties as Dean of Administration. He became President Little's "right hand man." He was given the responsibility of preparing and presenting the university's annual budget for approval by the Michigan legislature, a task he performed skillfully. He learned to deal cautiously with the deans of the various colleges, for they were powerful figures, as likely to communicate directly with the regents as with the president and the Dean of Administration.

Ruthven viewed his brief term as Dean of Administration as "learning to sink or swim." With typical understatement, he remembered the fall of 1928 and the spring of 1929 as "a time of confusion."[1] It was at least that.

LITTLE'S LEGACY

The fact of the matter was that the four tempestuous years of C. C. Little's presidency were building to a climax. Little had strong convictions, often contrary to the public consensus, and he had expressed himself forcefully and frequently right from the start.[2]

Within a month after his inauguration he had spoken to the Illinois Birth Control League, the Chicago Women's Club, and a Michigan state convention of public health officers and nurses on the subject of birth control. He advocated sterilization of certain types of criminals and mentally defective persons while also supporting more conventional types of birth control. The Detroit League of Catholic Women, eight thousand strong, censured Little and filed a formal protest with the regents.

Before he had been in office three months, he had demanded that the fraternities stringently police their houses for any violations of

Prohibition regulations. If they refused to comply within two days, he told them, university proctors would search for bootleg liquor. Two hundred representatives of forty campus fraternities passed a resolution condemning the president for his hasty action.

President Little was anxious to improve living conditions of students, and he was exasperated to discover that a number of landladies engaged in "rent profiteering." Under his direction a faculty study committee recommended that the university build a series of dormitories and residential colleges which would eventually house all but fraternity and sorority members. *The Michigan Alumnus* reported, "Petitions signed by several thousand householders of Ann Arbor, protesting the action of the University in erecting student dormitories, have been presented to Governor Fred W. Green."[3]

The young president's major educational innovation was the University College, a separate administrative unit that would enroll all university freshmen and sophomores. The University College would stress individual differences; yet all students would receive wide exposure to cultural courses and introductory courses in the sciences and arts. At the end of two years, comprehensive examinations would determine which students would continue in the university. The university senate agreed that individual colleges could exercise the option of not affiliating with the University College. The College of Engineering and the Literary College chose not to affiliate. The ensuing debate was acrimonious and many felt that the entire plan should be abandoned, but the regents were convinced by the president and agreed that the University College would be operative on September 1, 1929.

Another difficulty for Little involved Claude Van Tyne, distinguished chairman of the Department of History, who was being beleaguered by Mr. and Mrs. Alfred Brousseau because he had delivered a series of lectures on the American Revolution that were not uniformly complimentary to some of the founding fathers. The Brousseaus were wealthy benefactors of the university, and Mrs. Brousseau was president-general of the Daughters of the American Revolution. In defending Professor Van Tyne, Dr. Little became embroiled in a public debate with the Brousseaus during which he declared that the DAR was "un-American" because it refused to hear views contrary to its own.

All of these contentions stirred public interest because Little continued to express his views in frequent speeches, and he called weekly press conferences to discuss university affairs.[4] Sometimes the regents agreed with his stand; at other times they disagreed; at all times they wished that Little would exhibit more tact and patience.

As if these difficulties were not enough, Little's marriage was on the rocks. The Littles had been married for eighteen years; yet people noticed that Mrs. Little was seldom seen at university functions with her husband.[5] There were whisperings among campus insiders.[6]

The last straw in the rapidly deteriorating situation involved the Law School and its major benefactor, W. W. Cook. Cook, an individualist with eccentric tendencies, had donated the major buildings of the Law Quadrangle. A number of riders that accompanied these gifts had seemed unreasonable to Henry M. Bates, dean of the Law School, and since Bates was not the conciliatory sort, he and Cook had become estranged. Cook's unpredictability upset the regents, too, but they also knew that over $14 million of Cook's remaining fortune was earmarked for the University of Michigan. The regents knew that Cook was dying, and they were certain that his estate would soon be available if they could but mollify Bates and humor Cook a little longer. President Little thought differently. After a series of frustrating attempts to placate Cook, Little became convinced, as Bates had, that Cook's whims compromised university principles. He proposed that the regents scrap their hopes of obtaining Mr. Cook's estate and instead ask the state legislature for the needed funds. The regents were aghast to think that their valuable catch, nearly in the boat, might now shake off the hook.

At this point a majority of five regents concluded that President Little and the University of Michigan must part company. Regent Murfin told the president of the board's decision, and Little—who had by now concluded that he was not meant to be a university president—soon announced his resignation.

The story found in the University of Michigan annals is that C. C. Little resigned voluntarily, but Van Eyck's dissertation on Little's presidency paints a different picture. Four regents wanted Little dismissed; four did not; Regent Walter Hulme Sawyer was undecided. Sawyer was due for reelection, and Governor Green, a resolute Little antagonist, controlled the convention that would nominate Sawyer.

It was suggested to Sawyer that he would face an uphill convention struggle unless he agreed that Little must go. Sawyer got the message.[7]

A review of the record indicates that Van Eyck was only partially justified in his conclusion. Regent J. O. Murfin wrote to his colleagues that "at the request of *five* [italics mine] of my associates" he had had an interview with President Little and expected him to present his resignation on January 21.[8] *After* this Murfin-Little meeting, Dr. Sawyer did receive subtle pressure from the governor's office.[9] However, this pressure must be weighed in the light of several facts: Sawyer must have been one of the five referred to in Murfin's letter; the hints from the governor's office were gentle; and Sawyer refused to meet with the governor until after Little resigned because "I would at once be charged with conniving to sacrifice the President to my own personal ends. I think you will appreciate that I would not put myself in that position for anything."[10]

Little was never again associated with higher education; he remained in Ann Arbor as titular president until June 20, when he began an official leave of absence. He then returned to Maine, where he directed cancer research for the Roscoe B. Jackson Memorial Laboratory.

Little's resignation caused a commotion in the college world. *The Nation* editorialized that Little's innovations were anathema to "one of the most rigid of our great State educational institutions. . . . The lesson of it is that here is another place where a man of charm, distinction, intellectual courage, and advanced thought is not wanted . . . he paid the price in this reactionary age."[11] *Time* magazine, in a cover story featuring Little, spoke of the "inevitable personal dislike" between the president and Michigan Governor Fred Green.[12] Wilfred B. Shaw, editor of *The Michigan Alumnus,* alluded to the elderly regents: "It is the eternal conflict between the progressive and vigorous expression of youth and the conservatism and more cautious thought of mature years."[13] *The Michigan Daily* sprang to Little's defense in an editorial entitled, "Michigan Turns Its Back on a Genius." The student writer lamented, "Michigan loses, with his passing, a man who had greater potentialities as one of the foremost educators of the world than any other man at present in the educational field in the United States." *The Daily* wistfully called for the reinstatement of the young president.[14]

It was too late. Despite Little's acknowledged brilliance and charm, he was out and the search was on for a successor. As Dean of Administration, Ruthven carried out the duties of the chief executive until a new appointment could be made.[15]

THE REGENTS

The final decision would, of course, be the province of the regents.[16] In 1929 the men who would make Michigan's decision were veterans, men of acknowledged stature, dedicated to the university, and compatible as a group.[17] To a man they were Republicans.

Dr. Walter Hulme Sawyer was the senior member, and probably the most influential.[18] "He was respected wherever he went," wrote Shirley W. Smith, "and wherever he stayed he was loved."[19] Candid, yet moderate and magnanimous, he considered everyone on the board to be his friend.

William L. Clements had been a regent since 1910. His avocation was early Americana, and the Clements Library on the Michigan campus was his gift. He was thoughtful, deliberate, and diplomatic, a man who could "finesse" the legislature when the occasion demanded. He was very wealthy and very generous.

Junius E. Beal had held the traditional post of local regent since 1908. His Ann Arbor residence put him in the center of every campus concern. He had bulldog tenacity, and "sought to be right the first time because it was so hard for him to change."[20]

Lucius Lee Hubbard was the oldest member of the board. His health was poor; he spent his winters in Florida and the Caribbean and did not usually attend the regents' meetings. He was a kind, gentle, and philosophical man who was regarded with affection by his colleagues.

Benjamin S. Hanchett was a self-made man, and the only regent without college training. He was sensitive about this, and was also deeply affected when the university was criticized by the legislature or the press. He was concerned with student welfare, and had been a major proponent of the health service.

Victor M. Gore was known to his fellows as a clear thinker and an appealing orator. His opinions and convictions were highly regarded, but poor health caused his influence to wane in his final years on the board.

James O. Murfin was the youngest regent in both age and service.

Smith's description of him is appropriate: "Here was a colorful character. Tall, slender . . . impetuous, a hard fighter for what he wanted but surprisingly without rancor if he lost, if he had had eyes in the back and sides of his head the University of Michigan would have been the apple of every one of them."[21]

Ralph Stone was a Detroit attorney. The president of the Detroit Trust Company, he became the fiscal expert on the board. He was a close friend of Regent Murfin, and their views were usually in harmony.

These were the central actors in the drama about to be staged. The faculty, whose committee of professors Reeves, Huber, and Sadler had participated actively in the selection of Dr. Little, was not to be involved this time. Both regents Clements and Stone believed that faculty participation in the selection process was desirable.[22] However, Regent Beal held that the previous faculty committee was partially responsible for the mistake of selecting Little. Besides, he argued, the faculty was prejudiced against educators and might overlook someone otherwise eminently qualified.[23] Beal was adamant, and the regents proceeded without faculty assistance. In 1929 nobody even thought of suggesting student participation in the selection process.

Beal and Sawyer, along with Regent Clements as chairman, were named the committee to screen candidates and make a final recommendation to the entire board.

SPECULATION OVER LITTLE'S SUCCESSOR

Speculation arose immediately concerning Little's successor. *The Ann Arbor Daily News* reported, "Michigan's faculty is discussing, almost without exception, possibilities... from within its own number and from men recently on the campus."[24]

Many names were proposed. Paul V. McNutt, commander of the American Legion and dean of Indiana University Law School, was publicly recommended by Governor Green.[25] *The Michigan Daily* thought that only one man was big enough to replace Little: Alexander Meiklejohn of Wisconsin.[26] It was suggested in the newspapers that ex-President Calvin Coolidge was being considered.[27] Some felt that Edmund Ezra Day, a former Michigan Dean of Administration who was then with the Rockefeller Foundation, was a logical choice. Others suggested Owen D. Young, then chairman of the board of General Electric and also chairman of the Board of Trustees of St. Lawrence University. The "outsider" most frequently mentioned was Walter A. Jessup, President of the University of Iowa. The "insiders" supposedly receiving consideration were Jesse S. Reeves, chairman of the political science department, Dean Henry M. Bates of the Law School, Edward H. Kraus, dean of the College of Pharmacy and director of the summer session, and Alexander G. Ruthven, Dean of Administration.

RUTHVEN'S DILEMMA

It is difficult to determine what went through Ruthven's mind at this time. Forty-one years later he recalled the uncertainties of the spring and summer of 1929 as "some kind of Hell."[28] He had been distressed at Little's fall, for he believed that if only Little had had more patience he would have been the greatest university president in America.[29] Ruthven also noted that he was not an active candidate in any way, and took no part in the intrigues that swirled around him. His first love was science, and both he and his colleagues were distressed to think that his scientific pursuits might cease.[30] He again assured his friends that he would never give up his museum and that the "God-awful, thankless" job as Dean of Administration was only temporary.[31]

On the other hand, Ruthven was an insider and very loyal to his alma mater. He knew he was an able man at the peak of his powers, and his endeavors had always met with success. He recognized that the university was in a "terrible mess," and he thought he knew what to do about it.[32]

As early as January, 1929, he had written a long letter to Ralph Stone to "acquaint you with the general situation here." "The morale of the faculty is very low," the dean told the regent. "Like vultures grouped around a dying dog other universities are picking off . . . our best men." Ruthven went on to say that a new form of centralized reorganization was needed, for he and a General Motors vice president had discussed Michigan's organization vis-à-vis General Motors and the comparison was "enough to make the angels weep."[33] Stone wrote back that he was "very much impressed by what you say," and expressed the hope that Ruthven would also communicate his views to the other regents.[34]

Ruthven did this from time to time. To Dr. Sawyer he explained that "several of Dr. Little's policies . . . are of doubtful importance." He specifically suggested one Dean of Women to replace Little's three Advisors to Women and proposed that the controversial University College plan be replaced by a plan acceptable to all the faculties.[35] To Regent Murfin he outlined his plan for a group of vice presidents to remedy "an outworn form of organization."[36]

Dr. Ruthven's opinions were discussed among the regents, as he must have known they would be. It could easily be said that his letters revealed the "platform" on which he hoped to gain election. On the other hand, his book, *Naturalist in Two Worlds,* records that he did not aspire to the position, had not been approached by the regents, and was surprised by their eventual decision.[37]

In fact, Ruthven had discussed his own resignation as Dean of Administration with Regent Stone soon after Dr. Little resigned. Stone had told him not to resign, for "things may happen between now and June which we cannot now foresee."[38] Ruthven also told Stone at this time that he was considering the offer of another position.[39]

In mid-May Ruthven wrote again to Regent Stone, this time telling him that he firmly intended to resign as Dean of Administration after the June commencement. He told Stone plaintively that he was "actually putting in from sixteen to eighteen hours a day, and [had not] this year at any time had more than seven hours sleep. . . ." With all his duties, he had not "been able to give the staff the help which it needs."[40] The regents were upset; and Clements, Murfin, Gore, and Stone urged him to reconsider.[41]

It may very well be that Ruthven did not know his own mind during the summer of 1929 and took a fatalist's posture. He knew he was the acknowledged front-runner in the presidential sweepstakes, but he was not sure the position, if offered, was right for him. Nor did he have any insights into the regents' reasoning. Like Will Rogers, all he knew was what he read in the papers. Ruthven had to wait it out. Meanwhile, the regents, faced with the single most important responsibility of any governing board, followed their own twisted path to a decision.

RUTHVEN'S APPOINTMENT APPEARS CERTAIN

By July the regents had formed definite opinions. Murfin, the youngest, promptly decided that Ruthven was his man. "The more

I see of Ruthven the better I like him," he wrote Regent Sawyer.[42] In a letter to Regent Gore later in the summer, Murfin enumerated his reasons:

(1) He comes from our own group and will not be compelled to be educated as to Michigan policies, plans, and traditions.
(2) He has shown, as Dean of Administration, a firmness and tact and an executive ability that I think could only be called outstanding.
(3) He is ultra-conservative and the day of storm and stress will be over for the present.
(4) The overwhelming majority of the deans and the faculties are for him.
(5) Professor Hobbs is against him.[43]

Ralph Stone, Murfin's colleague from Detroit, had also become a firm proponent of Dr. Ruthven. Stone was committed to the general practice of promoting from within the organization.[44] He wanted Ruthven's appointment for the same reasons as Murfin, but in addition he was much impressed with the "very unusual financial and business sense" that the Dean of Administration had demonstrated.[45]

William L. Clements was initially opposed to Ruthven's appointment, but C. C. Little and Claude Van Tyne convinced the regent of Ruthven's merits.[46] By July, Clements was ready to vote for Ruthven. However, he admitted to Ralph Stone that he had nagging doubts about Ruthven's ability as a speaker and would have favored Jessup of Iowa had Jessup been a Michigan man.[47]

Regent Gore believed that Ruthven's "essential soundness" was "a guaranty of stability in University affairs." Gore predicted that Ruthven would "*grow* into an able and worthy president," and announced his willingness to act immediately.[48]

Lucius L. Hubbard, while not active in these deliberations, was known to favor Dr. Ruthven.

Benjamin Hanchett was in a quandary. He had indicated to Regent Murfin that he was ready to vote for Ruthven, but he had also told Dr. Sawyer that he regarded Ruthven with suspicion because Dr. Little, whom Hanchett despised, was promoting him. Furthermore, he thought Ruthven's friends were guilty of "logrolling" with the regents.[49]

Dr. Sawyer was also undecided, but inclined to support Dean Ruthven. As early as March he had expressed a preference for

Ruthven.[50] Three months later he wrote to Ralph Stone, "Ruthven has grown with me. I think he is a good deal of a man, and we might do much worse while trying to do better. He has a faculty of putting his finger on the weak spots and pointing a remedy."[51]

Regent Beal's initial choice was Dean Edward Kraus.[52] Beal liked Ruthven personally, but he was opposed to his selection. For one reason, he was afraid that Ruthven would carry out ex-President Little's policies. "I doubt if we desire these past fights to be perpetuated by those already committed to them," he warned Ralph Stone.[53]

Beal also doubted that Ruthven could ever be "a great spiritual, scholastic leader," and felt that Ruthven "might be a 'good' President, but not one who can keep Michigan up at the head of hard competition."[54] When it became apparent that Beal's enthusiasm for Dean Kraus's presidency was not shared by the faculty or any of the other regents, Beal centered his attention on President Jessup of Iowa.[55]

On the campus, some heavy artillery wheeled into line behind Ruthven. The biggest, despite the hopes of many that he had been forever spiked, was ex-President Little. It was understood on the campus that Little backed Ruthven. Others fired off letters of support to the regents. John R. Effinger, dean of the Literary College, wrote Regent Murfin that Ruthven's appointment would lead to "a quiet administration in which the faculties and the President might work together from the start."[56] The venerable Van Tyne endorsed Ruthven as a man of "hard work and good honest brains."[57] "I know of *no one* here I should prefer to Dr. Ruthven," wrote Shirley W. Smith, secretary of the university.[58]

Off campus, it became known that Governor Green, ex-Regent Harry Bulkley, and ex-Governor Chase S. Osborn favored Ruthven's appointment.

Regent Murfin scented victory for his candidate and he pressed the attack. "I am informed that every Dean but two would enthusiastically welcome him as President and he would not be objectionable to the other two," he wrote Clements. "I have never before seen such a near-unanimity of opinion on the campus as there seems to be in favor of Dr. Ruthven."[59] Murfin felt that action was warranted, and he fretted over the sluggish deliberations of his colleagues. By July he confidently assured Dr. Sawyer that every regent except one was prepared to vote for Dean Ruthven.[60] Only Regent Beal held out.

Despite the recalcitrant Beal, Ruthven's selection seemed certain. The appointment was expected on August 2 because a special session of the regents had been announced.[61] The waiting appeared to be over.

THE TABLES TURN

Suddenly, only two weeks before the special session, *The Ann Arbor Daily News* reported that Ruthven's selection was not as certain as it had appeared. The paper speculated that the regents lined up five to three in favor of the "home talent." The article mentioned support, both on campus and among the regents, for President Jessup of Iowa, and concluded that "by tradition" election of the Michigan president was unanimous.[62]

If the paper was to be believed, the regents' views had shifted. In fact, they had. One cause was Regent Beal. His intransigence was having an effect on regents Hanchett, Clements, and Sawyer, all lukewarm supporters of Ruthven. Beal sent frequent letters to the triad, and reported that a small, but influential group of faculty leaders "do not think [Ruthven] is Presidential timber."[63] There was enormous respect for Beal among the regents. Clements wrote to Stone, "I think so highly of Junius, and he has been such a good friend for so many years, and has been of such great use to the University, that I for one hesitate to override him...."[64]

Regent Sawyer also felt that way about Junius Beal. Sawyer, it will be recalled, was probably the most influential member of the board. Had he stood foursquare for Ruthven, Clements and Hanchett would almost certainly have followed his lead and Ruthven would have been elected on August 2, as expected. But at this crucial juncture Dr. Sawyer was swayed by his medical colleague, Dr. James P. Bruce. Dr. Bruce, professor of postgraduate medicine at the university medical school, was treating Sawyer's ailing wife. In addition, he was a trusted friend, and he became Sawyer's campus confidant. Bruce did not want Ruthven to become president. During June and July Bruce sent at least ten letters and telegrams to Regent Sawyer warning him of a campus conspiracy whose principals were Ruthven, Little, and Dr. Hugh Cabot, dean of the Medical School. Bruce intimated that these three had initiated a skillful campaign on campus, among the regents, and even in the newspapers, aimed at placing Ruthven in the presidency. Although Bruce, like Regent Beal, thought well of Ruthven personally, he both disliked and distrusted Little and Cabot. If Ruthven was to become president, Bruce told Sawyer, Sawyer should enact a price: the understanding that Ruthven would dismiss Cabot as dean of the Medical School.[65]

Dr. Sawyer was unsettled by the reports from Bruce. In mid-July he responded to a letter from A. S. Whitney, retiring dean of the School of Education. "I have a very high opinion of Dean Ruthven," Sawyer wrote, "but his choice is now rather doubtful in view of the opposition which has developed."[66] "If I had to make a choice at this time it would be Jessup," Sawyer told Allen Schoenfield of the *Detroit News* a few days later.[67]

At this very time, Regent Clements released a bombshell. In a copyrighted article, the *Bay City Daily News* reproduced an interview with Clements in which he stated that the regents would vote on August 2 and Ruthven would be the choice by a seven to one margin. Regent Beal, he said, was the only regent opposed. *The Summer Michigan Daily* was quick to point out that such a pronouncement by a regent was not cricket.[68] Nevertheless, the story was carried by the press throughout Michigan and most assumed that Clements was stating facts. *The Ann Arbor Daily News,* strongly pro-Ruthven, responded immediately with a large front-page photograph and a banner headline entitled, "Practical Man, Equipped with Energy but Also Patience, Is Dr. Ruthven."[69] The following day, Editor R. Ray Baker, a Ruthven friend, wrote a lengthy, laudatory page-one piece headlined, "Ruthven's Prospects Attract Attention to His Probable Policy."[70]

The unfortunate Clements had been duped. A reporter had, by conjecture, written an article purporting to show the various attitudes of the regents as fact, and asked Clements to comment on its veracity. The reporter's guesswork was close enough to the truth to entice some statements from Clements and, unhappily, he found himself in print.[71]

The presidential speculators buzzed over the Clements interview. Regent Beal wrote Regent Sawyer that on the campus some took it "as a political move intending to bludgeon us into the Ruthven camp, but I know Will [Clements] better than that. They just cunningly hooked him."[72] The regents forgave their errant brother, and thereafter referred to the incident discreetly as "Clements' mistake." Clements, chagrined at being fooled and crestfallen because he had exposed his friend Beal to public ire, decided that he should placate Beal by withdrawing his support from Ruthven.[73]

Regent Gore suddenly remembered that there were certain things he would like to know about Ruthven. "Is Dean Ruthven a Pacifist? Is Dean Ruthven a Socialist? Is he committed to the Little creed of Birth Control?" he demanded of Regent Murfin.[74]

The tables had turned. Beal, Clements, and Sawyer, the three members of the selection committee, did not favor Ruthven. Gore and Hanchett were uncertain. The long-awaited August 2 special session was approaching. Dr. Sawyer decided to take a vacation. From San Diego he sent a telegram to Murfin:

> We must not be torn asunder by dissensions among ourselves. Advise that we drop all discussion of names now under consideration and start anew or appoint a new committee. Cannot be home for August second meeting.[75]

The meeting was cancelled.

MURFIN AROUSED

James O. Murfin was not known for being prudent, and he was indignant over the sudden turn of events. He sent a heated letter to Dr. Sawyer:

> I think you should arrange with Regent Clements for a meeting of our Board at once. I have reached the point where I care not how nearly unanimous we may be. . . . We have become the laughing stock of the State of Michigan by our hesitation and vacillation. If Ruthven was good enough for seven of us before Mr. Clements burst into print he is certainly good enough yet.[76]

Murfin hammered away. He told each of the regents that he had been corresponding with James R. Angell, President of Yale, who had told him that after their experience with Little the regents should not consider a young man from another institution. When the deadlock continued, Murfin threatened to resign from the board. He wrote Regent Hanchett:

> I am thoroughly disgusted with the efforts of some members of the Board to please Regent Beal rather than choose the best man available for the Presidency. I am seriously thinking of leaving the Board if . . . Dean Ruthven is not chosen. If I do leave I will tell the public in no uncertain terms why I reached such a decision.[77]

Murfin's threatened resignation was probably a bluff, but Murfin's ally, Ralph Stone, was earnestly considering his own resignation from the board. He told Dr. Sawyer that he was in a state of nervous exhaustion, and would use his increasing responsibilities at the Detroit Trust Company as a "cover" for his resignation.[78]

With these threats hanging over their head the selection committee of Beal, Clements, and Sawyer searched frantically for a compromise candidate who would be acceptable to all regents. Dr. Robert A. Milliken of the California Institute of Technology was approached, but was unavailable.[79] The committee hurried to New York to consult with Frederick P. Keppel, President of the Carnegie Corporation. Keppel's advice was to select Dean Ruthven, but he suggested some other names, among them Harry Woodburn Chase, President of the University of North Carolina.[80] When the committee decided to approach Chase, Murfin wrote to Stone, "It seems peculiar that our associates should go to Mr. Keppel for advice and then not follow it."[81] Undaunted, the selection committee opened negotiations with President Chase.[82]

Early in September, the committee met with Chase in New York. The committee's impression was most favorable, and Regent Beal expressed the group opinion, "We think he is just the man for us."[83] There was one catch: Chase's wife was in Europe and he would not guarantee his availability until discussing the matter with her. It wasn't until September 30 that Chase told the committee that he was available, but he added that it was "doubtful whether I could come to Michigan before the end of this academic year."[84]

The regents had expected this response and decided that, with the academic year approaching, someone would have to be in charge of the university. Regents Clements and Stone conferred in Detroit and proposed that the regents "delegate to the Dean of Administration the powers and duties of President of the University until further action by the Regents."[85] All of the regents except Hubbard and Murfin agreed to this, and Dean Ruthven became, in effect, acting president, although that title was avoided by the regents.[86] *The Ann Arbor Daily News* again ran the big Ruthven picture with a banner headline, "Ruthven Is Appointed Acting President."[87] However, at least one regent viewed the board's decision as an agreement that Ruthven would not be named president, at least until after he had once again proved himself in his new role. "Poor Ruthven!" Hanchett wrote to Murfin, "It was tough on him and he has been so faithful and loyal under most trying circumstances, that he deserved anything but that."[88]

By late September if regents Murfin and Stone (who was following

Murfin's lead) had been persuaded to drop their support of Ruthven, there is no question that the board would have united behind Chase of North Carolina. Even Regent Hubbard, who had not wavered in his backing of Ruthven, agreed that his "mind [was] open to the recommendation of the committee."[89] Murfin and Stone refused to yield. Dr. Sawyer admitted, "We must concede as much to Stone and Murfin as we have to Beal, and I think every one would be in accord with Ruthven's appointment, except perhaps Beal."[90]

One final event occurred late in September that strengthened the Murfin-Stone position. Benjamin Hanchett resigned on September 23. Although Hanchett had backed Ruthven, his support was neither constant nor committed, and it seems probable that he would have voted with the majority. His resignation was ostensibly for reasons of physical health.[91]

To the disgust of the remaining regents, Governor Fred Green decided to break precedent and appoint a woman to succeed Hanchett. Flint alumna Mrs. Esther Marsh Cram, described by Green as "in every sense a cultured and capable lady," was chosen.[92] It seems likely that Green, a Ruthven advocate, made certain that his new appointment would steadfastly favor Ruthven's selection. In fact, Ruthven's *Naturalist in Two Worlds* describes an amicable meeting in Governor Green's office between Mrs. Cram and himself just prior to her appointment as regent.[93] With the addition of Mrs. Cram to the board, the balance of support once again shifted to Ruthven.

The next regents' meeting was scheduled for October 5. *The Ann Arbor Daily News* urged the regents to act. The public, the editor stated, "believes the time has arrived . . . to give the University a permanent president."[94]

On October 5, the regents named Alexander Grant Ruthven as the seventh president of the University of Michigan.

Murfin, victorious, was elated. He wrote C. C. Little:

> I made the motion after two hours of alleged oratory including a charming speech by Madame Regent Cram. Whereupon the three members of the committee went into a huddle in the hall. When they came back Regent Sawyer asked me to withdraw my motion. I inquired why and he said in order that Regent Beal might make it. Whereupon Regent Beal made the motion and the action was unanimous.[95]

"Good work and congratulations," "Pete" Little had written. "It was worth waiting for."[96]

NOTES

1. Alexander G. Ruthven, *Naturalist in Two Worlds* (Ann Arbor: University of Michigan Press, 1963), p. 27.

2. Soon after arriving in Ann Arbor, during one two-week interval in September and October, Little spoke before a different group each night. See Daniel Van Eyck, "President Clarence Cook Little and the University of Michigan" (Ph.D. dissertation, University of Michigan, 1965), p. 66. Much of the discussion of Little's problems that follows is based on the Van Eyck dissertation, pp. 93–219, passim.

3. Volume 35, no. 6 (1928), p. 133.

4. Interview, Alexander G. Ruthven, January 20, 1970.

5. *Detroit Free Press*, June 25, 1929, p. 1.

6. On June 26, 1929, Little sued for divorce on the basis of "legal desertion." On September 1, 1930, he married Beatrice Johnson, who had served as President Little's lab assistant and as one of three Advisors to Women while at Michigan. *The Michigan Alumnus*, vol. 36, no. 36 (1930), p. 751. Little's philanderings became the subject of a thinly disguised novel, *Wings of Wax*, by Janet Hoyt (New York: J. H. Sears and Company, 1929).

7. Van Eyck, "President Clarence Cook Little and the University of Michigan" (Ph.D. dissertation, University of Michigan, 1965), pp. 225–26.

8. J. O. Murfin to "The Members of the Board of Regents," January 12, 1927, Sawyer Papers, vol. 18, MHC.

9. Junius E. Beal to Walter H. Sawyer, January 12, 1929, Sawyer Papers, vol. 18, MHC; Perry F. Powers to Beal, January 18, 1929, Sawyer Papers, vol. 18, MHC; Benjamin Hanchett to Sawyer, January 17, 1929, Sawyer Papers, vol. 18, MHC.

10. Sawyer to Hanchett, January 16, 1929, Sawyer Papers, vol. 18, MHC.

11. Volume 128, no. 3318 (1929), p. 149.

12. Volume 13, no. 5 (1929), p. 38.

13. Volume 35, no. 16 (1929), p. 340.

14. January 22, 1929, p. 4.

15. Regent Ralph Stone later claimed that the appointment of Ruthven as Dean of Administration was a "tryout" for the presidency. (Stone to Alexander G. Ruthven, June 6, 1951, Stone Papers, box 1, MHC.)

16. Article XI, Sec. 5, Constitutional Provisions, 1908: "The regents of the university shall as often as necessary, elect a president of the university." See Lucius L. Hubbard, *University of Michigan: Its Origin, Growth, and Principles of Government* (Ann Arbor: University of Michigan Press, 1923), p. 37.

17. The writer suggested to Dr. Ruthven that his first board of regents was probably his best. He replied, "*Nobody* ever had a better board than that one." (Interview, January 20, 1970.)

18. Dr. Ruthven was of the opinion that Clements had the most influence. (Interview, January 20, 1970.) Shirley W. Smith, author of *Harry Burns Hutchins and the University of Michigan* (Ann Arbor: University of Michigan Press, 1951), thought that "no member of the Board exceeded [Sawyer] in influence" (p. 123).

19. Smith, *Hutchins and the University of Michigan*, p. 123. The descriptions of the regents that follow are from Smith, pp. 120–47, passim.

20. *Ibid.*, p. 122.

21. *Ibid.*, p. 147.
22. Stone to Sawyer, February 23, 1929, Sawyer Papers, vol. 18, MHC.
23. Beal to Sawyer, February 22, 1929, Sawyer Papers, vol. 18, MHC.
24. January 23, 1929, p. 1.
25. *The Michigan Alumnus,* vol. 35, no. 18 (1929), p. 383.
26. January 22, 1929, p. 4.
27. *The Ann Arbor Daily News,* January 25, 1929, p. 4.
28. Interview, Alexander G. Ruthven, January 20, 1970.
29. Dinner with Alexander G. Ruthven, Mr. and Mrs. Alan MacCarthy, and Mrs. Elizabeth Van de Water. Ruthven said of Little: "He wanted everything done yesterday."
30. Interview, Alexander G. Ruthven, January 20, 1970. Dr. Ruthven told the writer that all of his colleagues in zoology signed a plea urging him to decline any invitation to the presidency.
31. Ruthven to Edgar M. Ledyard, January 28, 1929, Ruthven Papers, box 85, MHC.
32. Interviews, Alexander G. Ruthven, January 20 and January 23, 1970.
33. Ruthven to Stone, January 3, 1929, Ruthven Papers, box 1, MHC.
34. Stone to Ruthven, January 4, 1929, Ruthven Papers, box 1, MHC.
35. Ruthven to Sawyer, June 3, 1929, Ruthven Papers, box 1, MHC.
36. Ruthven to Murfin, May 21, 1929, Ruthven Papers, box 1, MHC.
37. Ruthven, *Naturalist in Two Worlds,* pp. 28–29.
38. Stone to Ruthven, February 23, 1929, Ruthven Papers, box 1, MHC.
39. During the months before he became president, Dr. Ruthven had museum offers from Harvard and the Smithsonian. (Interview, Alexander G. Ruthven, January 20, 1970.)
40. Ruthven to Stone, May 16, 1929, Stone Papers, box 1, MHC.
41. Ruthven Papers, May, 1929, box 1, MHC.
42. Murfin to Sawyer, March 6, 1929, Murfin Papers, box 6, MHC.
43. Murfin to Victor M. Gore, July 31, 1929, Murfin Papers, box 6, MHC. Hobbs was a world-renowned geologist whose strong opinions irritated the regents at times.
44. Stone to Alfred B. Connable, Jr., February 14, 1951, Stone Papers, box 1, MHC.
45. Stone to Murfin, June 20, 1929, Murfin Papers, box 6, MHC.
46. Sawyer to Murfin, March 7, 1929, Murfin Papers, box 5, MHC.
47. Clements to Stone, July 19, 1929, Murfin Papers, box 6, MHC.
48. Gore to Clements, June 20, 1929, Murfin Papers, box 6, MHC.
49. Hanchett to Sawyer, June 11, 1929, Sawyer Papers, vol. 19, MHC.
50. Sawyer to Murfin, March 7, 1929, Murfin Papers, box 5, MHC.
51. Sawyer to Stone, June 5, 1929, Sawyer Papers, vol. 19, MHC.
52. Beal to Sawyer, January 4, 1929, Sawyer Papers, vol. 18, MHC.
53. Beal to Stone, May 9, 1929, Sawyer Papers, vol. 19, MHC.
54. Beal to Sawyer, June 24, 1929, Sawyer Papers, vol. 19, MHC.
55. Regents Clements, Beal, and Sawyer went to Iowa City to interview Jessup on May 2, 1929. He expressed his availability, saying "I am convinced that you have the outstanding opportunity in the country." Letter of W. A. Jessup to Clements, May 3, 1929, Sawyer Papers, vol. 19, MHC.

56. John R. Effinger to Murfin, May 16, 1929, Murfin Papers, box 6, MHC.
57. C. H. Van Tyne to Sawyer, February 9, 1929, Sawyer Papers, vol. 18, MHC.
58. Shirley W. Smith to Sawyer, April 15, 1929, Sawyer Papers, vol. 18, MHC.
59. Murfin to Clements, May 28, 1929, Murfin Papers, box 6, MHC.
60. Murfin to Sawyer, July 3, 1929, Murfin Papers, box 6, MHC.
61. *The Ann Arbor Daily News*, June 28, 1929, p. 1.
62. July 18, 1929, p. 1.
63. Beal to Sawyer, June 24, 1929, Sawyer Papers, vol. 19, MHC.
64. Clements to Stone, July 19, 1929, Murfin Papers, box 6, MHC.
65. J. Bruce to Sawyer, June 25, 1929, vol. 19, Sawyer Papers, MHC. The Bruce-Sawyer correspondence is found in the Sawyer Papers, MHC. There is no evidence that Ruthven's subsequent dismissal of Dean Cabot was the result of any "deal."
66. Sawyer to A. S. Whitney, July 15, 1929, Sawyer Papers, vol. 19, MHC.
67. Sawyer to Allen Schoenfield, July 20, 1929, Sawyer Papers, vol. 19, MHC.
68. July 19, 1929, p. 2.
69. July 19, 1929, p. 1.
70. July 20, 1929, p. 1.
71. Clements to Murfin, July 19, 1929, Murfin Papers, box 6, MHC.
72. Beal to Sawyer, July 25, 1929, Sawyer Papers, vol. 19, MHC.
73. Clements to Lucius L. Hubbard, August 13, 1929, Hubbard Papers, box 7, MHC.
74. Gore to Murfin, July 30, 1929, Murfin Papers, box 6, MHC.
75. Telegram of Sawyer to Murfin, July 22, 1929, Murfin Papers, box 6, MHC.
76. Murfin to Sawyer, August 13, 1929, Murfin Papers, box 6, MHC.
77. Murfin to Hanchett, September 14, 1929, Murfin Papers, box 6, MHC.
78. Stone to Sawyer, August 14, 1929, Sawyer Papers, vol. 19, MHC.
79. Sawyer to Ralph Jenney, August 20, 1929, Sawyer Papers, vol. 19, MHC. Jenney was a Sawyer friend who acted as an intermediary for the board.
80. Clements to Stone, September 4, 1929, Murfin Papers, box 6, MHC.
81. Murfin to Stone, September 6, 1929, Murfin Papers, box 6, MHC.
82. Clements to "Members of the Board of Regents," September 13, 1929, Murfin Papers, box 6, MHC.
83. Beal to Hubbard, September 14, 1929, Sawyer Papers, vol. 19, MHC.
84. H. W. Chase to Clements, September 30, 1929, Murfin Papers, box 6, MHC.
85. Telegram of Smith to Murfin, September 20, 1929, Murfin Papers, box 6, MHC.
86. Telegram of Smith to Murfin, September 21, 1929, Murfin Papers, box 6, MHC.
87. September 21, 1929, p. 1.
88. Hanchett to Murfin, September 12, 1929, Murfin Papers, box 6, MHC.
89. Hubbard to Beal, September 18, 1929, Hubbard Papers, box 7, MHC.
90. Sawyer to Gore, September 26, 1929, Sawyer Papers, vol. 19, MHC.
91. Mystery surrounds the Hanchett resignation. It seems unlikely that he resigned for "ill health" during the climax of the search for the new president. In

fact, a letter from Dr. James D. Bruce to Regent Hanchett (August 27, 1929, Hanchett Papers, MHC) shows that Dr. Bruce had given Hanchett a complete physical examination and at that time he was not unhealthy. The letters of other regents make veiled reference to public knowledge of sexual deviancy as the cause for Hanchett's hasty resignation.

92. Fred W. Green to R. Perry Shorts, September 30, 1929, Shorts Papers, box 1, MHC.

93. Ruthven, *Naturalist in Two Worlds,* pp. 45–46.

94. October 3, 1929, p. 4.

95. Murfin to Little, October 15, 1929, Murfin Papers, box 6, MHC.

96. Little to Murfin, October 5, 1929, Murfin Papers, box 6, MHC.

4

The Ruthven Platform

The appointment was greeted favorably. The regents agreed that any past differences would be forgotten. "Everyone will now fall in line," Dr. Sawyer predicted. "Junius [Beal] took his medicine with a wry face but he will recover from his disappointment. . . . Jim [Murfin] held himself pretty well which lessened the trouble I feared."[1] Regent Beal wrote soothingly to Regent Murfin: "I want to tell you how glad I am that we came through the recent differences of opinion in harmony. . . . Everything is all right."[2] Beal demonstrated the regents' solidarity by agreeing to act as toastmaster at a banquet in Ann Arbor at which 900 friends honored President Alexander G. Ruthven. It was the largest function of its kind ever held in the city.[3]

The Ann Arbor Daily News called him "the logical choice" and claimed that "the citizens of Michigan . . . would have been satisfied with nobody but Ruthven in the president's chair."[4]

The Michigan Daily recognized the enormity of Ruthven's task: "Today there descends on his shoulders the full weight of a university that is not a well-oiled, smoothly working piece of machinery." The *Daily* editorialized, "We have great faith in the ability of his calm personality and quiet efficiency to put Michigan back where she belongs in the front rank of American universities."[5]

The faculty of the College of Literature, Science, and the Arts adopted a unanimous resolution stating its pleasure that "for the first time in the history of the University of Michigan, one of its members has been elected to the Presidency. . . . Dr. Alexander Grant Ruthven . . . commands our admiration and respect."[6] Interviews with faculty members who were on campus at the time confirmed that this feeling was general.

The campus, unaware that within the past two weeks the regents had narrowly failed to unite behind another prospect, calmly accepted the appointment. Ruthven was "the least disturbed of all."[7]

"KEEP IT OUT OF THE NEWSPAPERS"

One thought dominated President Ruthven's mind. He must steady the university, "keep it out of the newspapers," and restore harmony among its many discordant elements.[8]

He called a press conference. The university under President Little had proved to be such a source of headlines that newspapers from Detroit, Grand Rapids, and Chicago had assigned reporters to Ann Arbor. Little had reveled in the repartee with these reporters at weekly press conferences. Ruthven, however, told the disappointed newsmen that there would be no more press conferences, and that he would call them individually when something newsworthy occurred.[9] He suggested that the university would profit from a "highly trained news editor" who would interpret the university to "the papers of the state and other mediums of publication."[10]

T. Hawley Tapping's editorials in *The Michigan Alumnus,* which had freely and frankly commented on campus controversies, were suddenly replaced by the bland "Conning the Campus" column. "I told Tapping that he was getting as bad as the *Michigan Daily,*" Dr. Ruthven recalled in explaining why he had ordered the change to more affable prose.[11]

"The office of the president has been unduly exalted," Ruthven remarked, and to insure that the presidency remained out of the public eye he decreed that there would be no formal inaugural ceremonies.[12] He told the University Senate that he would have no inauguration, but instead wished his first meeting with them to mark the real beginning of his work.[13]

THE PLATFORM STATEMENT

Ruthven balanced this "low profile" by releasing what was later known as his "platform statement." He had given considerable thought to the various problems of the university and had prepared a complete summary of his views for distribution as soon as his selection was announced. His modest disclaimers to the contrary, Ruthven must have had some inkling that he would be Michigan's seventh president or he would not have prepared an elaborate "platform statement" beforehand.[14] The "platform statement" set forth the guidelines for his administration; thus, it deserves careful attention.

Alexander G. Ruthven of Michigan

The state university, Ruthven said, must recognize that its function includes both technical training and liberal education. The first must never develop without regard for the second, since "no student should be considered properly educated unless he has come to appreciate good pictures and other forms of art, to love good music more than jazz, to prefer drama in higher forms than represented in the movies. . . ."

The first purpose of the university must be the instruction of students, and the "service function" cannot be allowed to detract from the regular academic purposes of the university. While the university would cooperate with the people of Michigan in providing services, Ruthven warned that "the cost . . . should be paid by the person, firm, or state department receiving it."

He said that large size was not an asset, and could lead to "excessive expansion of curricula and multiplication of departments." "Expansion in the way of new units," Ruthven stated, "should be encouraged only when the need is great and funds are available. . . ." As a correlative of size as a quality control, Ruthven wanted the university to accept "only those students evidently qualified to pursue advanced studies." If the university attempted to raise the general level of culture by admitting the maximum number of high school students, "the result would be a lowering of standards to the dull level of mediocrity. . . ."

The student must recognize that a degree of "in loco parentis" is necessary, for he is transitory. Furthermore, the student will face laws not of his own choosing upon graduation. "Above all, the student wants and has a right to know just what he can do," Ruthven affirmed. "He will not object to discipline administered expeditiously and justly." However, the president recognized that rules and regulations must not be "immutable laws," but rather "experimental and subject to change" by faculty and students.

"In a very real sense the university is its faculty," he declared. "Administrators who fully appreciate the fact that a university can be no better than its faculty will see to it that available funds are first used to secure for its staff the best scholars and teachers available, that once secured the faculty is kept happy and contented, and that no sacrifice of staff is permitted because of an expressed need for other facilities."

Ruthven noted that the alumni should become an integrated and meaningful segment of the university. Courses, either on the cam-

72

pus or at university extension centers, should be made available to the alumni so that they can keep abreast of developments in their professions. While discussing the general topic of alumni, Ruthven warned that benefactors must not control the university through restricted gifts, and that both donors and the university would profit from discussions that included the faculties of the units concerned.

Ruthven attacked the university's organization as "the curiously antiquated and cumbersome machinery with which the routine work is performed. . . ." He suggested that increased efficiency could be obtained if the various administrators, deans, and department heads were given "authority in proportion to the responsibility which is theirs." The executive officers should collectively determine broad university policies, he said. The president should not, Ruthven reasoned, initiate projects such as the University College and force them on the faculties. Rather he should be supportive of whatever sound educational ideas the faculties sought to develop.

He stated that the traditional "town and gown" dichotomy was "unfortunate" and assured the troubled Ann Arbor landladies that, while the university was committed to dormitories, it would not build them so rapidly that the landladies would be deprived of needed income.

The "platform statement" demonstrated that the new chief executive was the proper medicine for the ailing institution. He was, in effect, telling the various segments of the university that he was one of them and understood their difficulties for, after all, he had been on the campus for nearly thirty years. He was telling them that he was not reactionary (many had feared that the regents' choice would be), for he forcefully urged some progressive ideas of his own. Neither would he follow the Little line, since he had no commitment to the University College and wished to revamp the present organizational structure completely. The "platform statement" was clearly the work of a faculty man, one who believed that the administrator's role was to serve the faculty in its vital functions of teaching and research, and one who was willing to acknowledge the faculty responsibility for much of the educational innovation and decision making. Above all, the statement was considered, balanced, carefully reasoned, and stimulating without being inflammatory.

Ruthven's statement was heartily accepted just as his appointment had been. The president of Johns Hopkins wrote: "As a document I think it is unique and really cannot help admiring the spirit and wisdom shown."[15]

The Michigan Alumnus called the statement a "master stroke."[16] Greek professor Campbell Bonner told his colleague, Latin professor John G. Winter: "Ruthven made an admirable statement of his plans and policies . . . so that even some of the disappointed ones were greatly pleased."[17] The statement showed "a disposition and ability to give the University of Michigan a tactful, firm, just, forward looking, wide awake administration," according to *The Detroit Free Press.*[18]

TOWARD A NEW STABILITY

On the same day Ruthven assumed office, the Regents announced that former governor Chase S. Osborn had presented the university with over 3,000 acres of land on Sugar Island and Duck Island (between Lake Huron and Lake Superior) as well as his library of several thousand volumes. Soon afterward, W. W. Cook died and the university received his estate of almost $15 million, a sum which was severely reduced later by litigation and the stock market crash, but which, nevertheless, was the largest single gift in university history. Over $300,000 in additional gifts to the university were announced in the first year of Ruthven's presidency.[19] These beneficences were not directly attributable to Ruthven, for the spadework had been done by others, but no doubt they enhanced his reputation at a crucial time.

Dr. Sawyer wrote:

Again, I want to say to you how happy we are over the way things are going at the University. From every quarter I hear the kindest, most encouraging reports. It seems to me that this is rather an unusual condition of things, to deal with such a mixed up affair and bring order out of it which all approve.[20]

Ruthven was not a typically dour Scot as his father had been, and he occasionally delighted the regents with flashes of wit. When Regent Beal invited the "Regential Golf Experts" to a match, he suggested that non-player Ruthven referee.[21] Ruthven responded by prescribing a series of rules which outlawed Regent Beal's cigars ("the smoke, to say nothing of the aroma, tends to persist") and "scurrilous comments . . . on the game, stance, or approach of any player. . . ."[22] Beal enjoyed the president's levity so much that he wrote back in kind, and sent Ruthven's letter to all the other players.

Another time Regent Clements wondered how it was that his favorite Jersey cow had presented him with twin black and white calves. He called upon Ruthven "as a specialist in zoology" to explain such an event.[23] "As a biologist and not as a college president," Ruthven responded, "may I say that there must have been a hole in the fence."[24] It is easy to understand, after the tension of the Little years, how readily the regents welcomed this easy camaraderie.

Buoyed by this climate of support, Ruthven decided on two bold strokes. In February, 1930, he fired Dr. Hugh Cabot as dean of the medical school and the following month he appointed Alice C. Lloyd Dean of Women.

Cabot was a Boston Brahmin who had been appointed dean in 1919; he was a friend of fellow Harvardian C. C. Little. Many medical school faculty members, as well as university administrators, believed that Cabot's administrative techniques were slipshod at best. Ruthven recalled that Dr. Cabot had a disconcerting habit of neglecting to include the salary request for a faculty member or two when submitting his budget. When the mistake was discovered, adjustments would have to be made from other items in the medical school budget.[25]

This was only one of many administrative difficulties which led to alienation between the dean and his faculty. Besides, there was a policy dispute over whether medical school faculty should teach full time or be allowed to supplement their salaries by lucrative private practice. Cabot held the former view, believing that the university hospital should be open to private patients with fees paid to the university. The faculty disagreed and, naturally, the Michigan State Medical Association sided with the faculty. The intensity of the conflict escalated until eleven key members of the medical school faculty together demanded Dr. Cabot's resignation.[26] The Board of Regents wanted this solution all along, but was reluctant to act because of the furor that they were sure would ensue. Furthermore, there were no established precedents for firing a dean; by custom "deans were deans until they died."[27] The regents agreed, however, that if Dr. Ruthven dared to dismiss Cabot they would support the president in any showdown. Ruthven immediately relieved Dr.

President Ruthven (1929)

Florence Hagle Ruthven (1929)

Cabot of his duties as dean and department chairman, but he was allowed to remain as a member of the medical school faculty. An executive committee, chaired at the outset by Ruthven and later by Dr. Frederick Novy, was formed until a new dean could be appointed. To Ruthven's vast relief, the dismissal of Dr. Cabot met with general approval, "even by the interns."[28] *The Ann Arbor Daily News* viewed the dismissal as "inevitable" because of the "chronic condition of inharmony" in the Medical School. "We are convinced, with the administration, that Dean Cabot's removal was in the best interests of the University," the local paper editorialized.[29]

Another surprising but sagacious decision was to name Alice Lloyd Dean of Women. Miss Lloyd was the daughter of former graduate school dean Alfred Lloyd and, although some considered her too young for this assignment, she quickly proved to be a highly capable and respected member of the administration. Her appointment brought to an end the Little system of three Advisors to Women which Dr. Ruthven had considered "terrible."[30]

SWORDS INTO PLOWSHARES

Early in his regime Ruthven displayed a surprising talent for turning potential detractors into allies. Jesse S. Reeves was influential among the faculty, and he would not have been at all averse to accepting the university presidency for himself.[31] A few months after Ruthven became president, Reeves appealed to him for aid in securing Reeves' appointment to the World Conference on International Law at The Hague. Dr. Ruthven, as he often did in matters of this sort, asked his friend Arthur Vandenberg to intercede, and the senator was able to secure the prestigious appointment for Reeves. Reeves sent the president a pipe in gratitude.[32] In 1931 Reeves filled a new chair as W. W. Cook Professor of American Institutions, and concurrently became chairman of the political science department.

Also in 1931, James D. Bruce (who had earlier so vigorously opposed Ruthven's appointment as president) was offered the newly-created post of vice president in charge of university relations. He found the offer "tremendously stimulating," Bruce told Ruthven, and he hastened to accept "without any reservation of either heart or mind."[33]

Edward H. Kraus, the dean of the College of Pharmacy and director of the summer session, was a name frequently mentioned in the presidential sweepstakes of 1929. He was unusually able and extremely strong willed, and there is some evidence that Kraus may have wanted the Michigan presidency for himself.[34] During the uneasy summer of 1929, Kraus had been one of two deans who were opposed to Ruthven's presidency, yet when Dean John R. Effinger of the Literary College died in 1933, Ruthven considered Kraus for this sensitive post. The Literary College at that time enjoyed notoriety for its elitist posture, a posture nourished by the presence of a small cluster of academic celebrities, men whose national reputations made any conflicts with them risky. Ruthven is supposed to have remarked, "Ed Kraus is just the man to tame those wildcats," and Kraus was appointed.[35]

The men chosen for these assignments proved to be respected, able, and loyal. One could argue that these appointments resulted more from beginner's luck than from political adroitness—for

The Ruthven Platform

Ruthven was not by nature a political manipulator—but, at the outset of his presidency, he was able to win the services and the support of three of the most critical members of the faculty. Ruthven's next challenge came from off campus. Former governor and regent and recent benefactor Chase S. Osborn was covertly maneuvering for reappointment as a regent, for Lucius L. Hubbard had announced his intention to resign.[36] This alarmed the regents, because Osborn, though unusually able and a man of great personal charm, was also mercurial and could be abrasive. Regent Murfin, in particular, had been bloodied by past political battles with Osborn and thought the prospect of his being on the board "horrible."[37] The regents' papers reveal that the other members of the board shared Murfin's concern and agreed that the only way to avert the threatened disruption of their cordial relationships was to persuade Hubbard to remain on the board.[38] They unanimously agreed to do this; Ruthven conveyed the board's request to Hubbard, who replied that he would "reluctantly consent to hold [his] formal resignation in abeyance for some further time."[39] The unpredictable Osborn changed his mind and told Governor Green that he would not accept the appointment even if it were offered.[40] Nevertheless, he knew about the regents' reaction and it had galled him. He wondered if Ruthven could be to blame. Osborn decided that he would try Ruthven out, he would "test . . . the blood pressure and the metabolism" of the new president, as he put it later.[41] He wrote to Ruthven (who did not know that Osborn had withdrawn from regental consideration) to tell the president that his [Osborn's] appointment as a regent was being considered.[42] Ruthven, who must have been as upset as the regents, replied unconcernedly: "You know, I am sure, that I could work with you as a Regent and as a matter of fact it seems to me to be my business to work with the Regents whoever they are."[43] Osborn told Ruthven that his tone was "cold and petulant," and Osborn further suggested that since he was "persona non grata to the regents and to you perhaps it is my duty to turn in my honorary doctorate. . . ."[44] Still Ruthven refused to rise to Osborn's bait. "It was kind and thoughtful of you to keep me informed," he wrote to the former governor, "We have been friends too long . . . to be estranged now by the tone of a letter."[45] Osborn gave up. "NOW after reading your most gracious letter I KNOW I WAS WRONG in my interpretation of yours, Dear President ALEXANDER GRANT RUTHVEN. . . . If you 'hendle' everybody as you have me in this matter you may be confident that your regime as President shall be brilliant."[46] From then until his death in 1949 the crusty old "Iron Hunter" regarded Ruthven as a close friend and one of the three greatest University of Michigan presidents.[47]

The absence of corrosive publicity, the considered rhetoric of the "platform statement," the beneficence of donors, the favor of the regents, the bold action with Deans Cabot and Lloyd, and the gratification of potential opponents set the Ruthven regime on solid footing. Even the former dean of the education school, A. S. Whitney, who had bitterly opposed Ruthven's selection as president, confessed to Murfin: "You were right and I was wrong. I now think he has the makings of a great President and the University seems to be functioning as though every joint was doubly greased."[48] The Depression brought new challenges but, after a long absence, stability had returned to the Ann Arbor campus.

NOTES

1. Walter H. Sawyer to Ralph Stone, October 7, 1929, Sawyer Papers, vol. 19, MHC.

2. Junius E. Beal to James O. Murfin, October 17, 1929, Murfin Papers, box 6, MHC.

3. *The Washtenaw Tribune,* November 19, 1929, p. 1.

4. *The Ann Arbor Daily News,* October 5, 1929, p. 4.

5. *Michigan Daily,* October 5, 1929, p. 4.

6. *The Michigan Alumnus,* vol. 36, no. 3 (1929), p. 57.

7. *The Michigan Alumnus,* vol. 36, no. 2 (1929), p. 2.

8. Interviews, Alexander G. Ruthven, January 20 and 23, 1970.

9. Interview, Alexander G. Ruthven, January 20, 1970.

10. "Platform Statement," *The Ann Arbor Daily News,* October 5, 1929, and *The Michigan Alumnus,* vol. 36, no. 2 (1929).

11. Interview, Alexander G. Ruthven, January 23, 1970.

12. *Proceedings of the Board of Regents,* November meeting, 1929, p. 96.

13. Speech of Alexander G. Ruthven to the University Senate, November 11, 1929, Ruthven Papers, box 77, MHC.

14. The writer asked Dr. Ruthven to explain the genesis of the "platform statement." He said that there had been no precedent for it. "Just say I was inspired," he added with a twinkle in his eye. Interview, Alexander G. Ruthven, January 23, 1970.

15. Joseph S. Ames to Ruthven, December 26, 1929, Ruthven Papers, box 1, MHC.

16. *The Michigan Alumnus,* vol. 36, no. 3 (1929), p. 60.

17. Letter of Campbell Bonner to John G. Winter, October 15, 1929, Winter Papers, box 1, MHC.

18. *The Detroit Free Press,* October 7, 1929, p. 6.

19. *The University of Michigan: An Encyclopedic Survey,* ed. by Wilfred B. Shaw, I (Ann Arbor: University of Michigan Press, 1942), p. 111.

20. Sawyer to Ruthven, November 29, 1929, Ruthven Papers, box 2, MHC.

21. Letter of Junius Beal to "Regential Golf Experts," September 11, 1930, Ruthven Papers, box 3, MHC.

22. Ruthven to Beal, September 12, 1930, *ibid.*

23. Clements to Ruthven, April 3, 1931, *ibid.*

24. Ruthven to Clements, April 6, 1931, *ibid.*

25. Interview, Alexander G. Ruthven, January 23, 1970.

26. *The Michigan Alumnus,* vol. 36, no. 18 (1930), p. 352.

27. Interview, Alexander G. Ruthven, January 23, 1970.

28. *Ibid.* The controversy over Cabot's dismissal has not yet been forgotten by a few senior faculty in the medical school. Interviews with Dr. Edgar Kahn, December 8, 1974, and Dr. H. Marvin Pollard, January 13, 1975.

29. February 9, 1930, p. 4. After leaving Michigan Cabot joined the Mayo Clinic as a surgeon and concurrently held an appointment as professor of surgery at the University of Minnesota. He died in 1945. *Who Was Who in America, 1943–1950.*

30. Letter of Ruthven to Sawyer, June 3, 1929, Ruthven Papers, box 1, MHC.

31. Letter of Walter S. Penfield to Jesse S. Reeves, June 7, 1929, Reeves Papers, box 25, MHC.

32. The Reeves-Ruthven-Vandenberg correspondence is found in the Ruthven Papers, box 2, February-May, 1930, MHC.

33. Letter of James D. Bruce to Ruthven, August 7, 1931, Ruthven Papers, box 5, MHC.

34. Dr. Ruthven remembered that during the summer of 1929 Kraus had let it be known that "Ruthven has a mistress in Ypsilanti." Ruthven promptly scotched the rumor, saying, "I can't afford a mistress, and if I could I certainly wouldn't keep her in Ypsilanti." (Interview, January 20, 1970.)

35. Interview, Walter B. Rea, February 12, 1970.

36. The Hubbard Papers, box 7, MHC, show that Hubbard was corresponding with Governor Green about resigning even before Ruthven became president.

37. Murfin to William L. Clements, October 30, 1929, Murfin Papers, box 6, MHC.

38. *Ibid.*

39. Lucius L. Hubbard to Ruthven, November 5, 1929, Hubbard Papers, box 8, MHC.

40. Fred W. Green to Hubbard, November 29, 1929, *ibid.*

41. Chase S. Osborn to Ruthven, January 20, 1930, Ruthven Papers, box 2, MHC.

42. Osborn to Ruthven, undated, 1929, *ibid.*

43. Ruthven to Osborn, November 11, 1929, *ibid.*

44. Osborn to Ruthven, January 20, 1930, *ibid.*

45. Ruthven to Osborn, January 27, 1930, *ibid.*

46. Osborn to Ruthven, January 30, 1930, *ibid.*

47. "There have been three great Presidents of Michigan: Angell, Burton, and yourself. That is a triad no other university can equal." Osborn to Ruthven, May 13, 1939, Ruthven Papers, box 28, MHC.

48. Letter of A. S. Whitney to Murfin, March 20, 1934, Murfin Papers, box 8, MHC.

5

The Michigan System

In his letters to the regents and again in his "platform statement" Dr. Ruthven voiced his dissatisfaction with the university's form of organization. As a student of ecology he had long been interested in the order in which living things related to each other. As he surveyed the university, its structure appeared to him archaic, aimless, and amorphous.

PAST ORGANIZATION

In fact, the university's organizational pattern had changed little from President Angell's era. The president was expected to initiate educational policies, adjudicate disciplinary cases, address alumni, student and civic groups, plan and present the budget, entertain notables, woo the legislature, hire the faculty, and set the moral standards for the campus. It did not seem too much to expect because, after all, President Angell had performed these tasks until he was over eighty years old. To be sure, Michigan's presidents no longer addressed weekly chapel sessions, answered correspondence in longhand, and personally enrolled Literary College students as Angell had done, but what assistance they had was largely in the performance of routine tasks in specialized areas. Dr. Ruthven, after assuming office, found that his executive support consisted mainly of Secretary and Business Manager Shirley W. Smith.

Ruthven viewed the administrative plan as "militaristic," and "one in which there is a continuous line of authority . . . all problems being routed along much the same course, and most of the executives having too little authority and responsibility." It was a form of governance, Ruthven predicted, which would "soon be as dead as the Dodo."[1]

However, it was the form used in virtually all American colleges and universities at the time Ruthven took office. In fact, in 1930 the

United States Office of Education (USOE) was urging a "systematic plan . . . for the routing of business." The USOE contended:

> The most efficacious line of procedure is from the individual staff member to the head of the department to the dean or director, and from the dean or director to the president. . . . All administrative authority is thus centered in the president's office.

This was the plan in all but four of sixty-nine land-grant colleges and universities surveyed, the USOE noted approvingly. Were the four exceptions more democratic? Not at all, for in these institutions the department heads simply bypassed the deans to get to the president. The USOE report noted that a few of the institutions surveyed had executive committees and, in some cases, faculty legislative procedures designed to advise the president, but it urged the president to "exercise the right of veto over . . . their decisions."[2]

At Michigan the regents themselves had come to be largely responsible for the administration of educational matters. It was common in the 1920s for a regent to select the school or college which corresponded with his particular expertise and become, in effect, a committee of one to advise—and often to actually administer—that unit. Thus Dean Henry M. Bates and Regent James O. Murfin, a lawyer, would jointly make policy for the law school. Regent Walter Sawyer had as his bailiwick the medical school, and advised the dean in the preparation of its budget. Regent William L. Clements' province was the library. The number of regents' committees approximated the number of schools and colleges.[3]

Under this arrangement, individual deans wielded enormous power. Mortimer Cooley in engineering, John R. Effinger in the Literary College, Henry M. Bates in law were legendary leaders whose empires were sacrosanct—provided, of course, that the pipelines to their guardian regents were intact. The deans hired their own faculty, prepared their budgets, and usually ran their empires in the fashion of benevolent despots.

When concerns pertaining to the entire faculty of the university were raised, the University Senate, which included all faculty above the rank of instructor, assembled in time-honored town-meeting style.

In President Angell's era this organizational pattern worked, for when he took office in 1871 Michigan—with Harvard the largest university in the land—had only 1100 students.[4] By 1929, however, the student enrollment was over 12,000; courses had proliferated; departments, schools, and colleges had been added; and Michigan had established the growth pattern which would lead to its emergence as a full-fledged multiversity.

DEMOCRATIC REORGANIZATION

Dr. Ruthven witnessed this emergence, and he considered both the set oligarchies of the deans and the disordered growth alien to his nature. His boyhood on the Iowa frontier, where he rode cow ponies and saw the covered wagons moving westward, and his scientific expeditions in the jungles of South and Central America, had taught him that intelligent men were resourceful and capable of guiding their own destinies.

He was a democrat who believed in the intrinsic worth of all men. A favorite campus story relates that Ruthven was seen walking along the "diag" chatting amiably with a campus janitor. One of the most senior of professors, a classics man, later admonished Ruthven that this kind of fraternizing was beneath the dignity of a university president. Ruthven replied that his friends were from all classes of society and he would be seen with whomever he pleased.

As a young scientist, he had been taught to respect the careful presentation of facts in the search for new truths; one did not forge ahead unless it seemed justified by prior evidence. His concern for the environment fostered a respect for order and the interdependency of all organisms.[5] As a long-standing member of the faculty, he understood the pride, aspirations, and prejudices of that group.

Through his efforts to raise funds for the university museums, Dr. Ruthven had become a friend of Ormand Hunt, a vice president of General Motors, and Regent Ralph Stone, President of the Detroit Trust Company.[6] He was also acquainted with Michigan alumnus Chester Lang, a vice president of the General Electric Company. The Ruthven Papers reveal that in 1929 and 1930 both Dr. Ruthven and his assistant, Frank E. Robbins, were very much interested in the organizational charts of corporations. Ruthven recognized that the university's organization was no longer appropriate for its magnified functions and he turned to his corporate friends for suggestions. Their ideas, coupled with his own predilection for democratic yet orderly governance gave birth to the plan of university organization which eventually became widely accepted throughout the United States and was sometimes referred to as "The Michigan System."[7]

Ruthven started with the Board of Regents. He reasoned that their role was not to make basic educational decisions, for they were primarily "captains of industry" and had had no experience in the ways of academia. Rather, as "guardians of a public trust" the regents were obliged to insure that the university was able to secure funds from the legislature and private donors adequate to carry out the ongoing educational program. Regents, Ruthven thought, should educate themselves to the broad needs of the university in order to judge the merits of proposals brought to them by the president from the faculties.[8]

During Marion Burton's presidency the regents of Michigan had been formed into eight working committees and Burton had tried with limited success to have each regent take an interest in all facets of university operation. Ruthven further reshuffled the regents' committees, so that by 1933–34, in addition to the Executive Committee, the only remaining committees were Finance, Plant and Equipment, Educational Policies, Student and Alumni Relations, and Public Relations.[9] This meant that key regents would sit on more than one committee, and President Ruthven impressed upon the group that their interests must no longer remain parochial.[10]

As the regents became generalists, Dr. Ruthven felt that regents' meetings could be shortened, and even expressed the view that the customary monthly meetings were too frequent.[11] Dr. Ruthven recalls that the regents surrendered their administrative chores gladly, but the record shows that Regent William L. Clements, for one, complained to Ruthven that the regental committees no longer took "a detailed part in administration." He declared that he "did not care to be on a non-functional committee."[12]

The president's own role, Ruthven decided, should be:

Chairman of the faculties, . . . representative of the staff before the Board of Regents, . . . the interpreter to the faculty of the actions of the Board of Regents, and . . . coordinator of the interests, problems, and policies of the several units. As an overseer of the University [the president] will be expected to suggest broad lines of policy to the Regents and faculty, as a moderator and budget director, he will . . . digest and harmonize the claims and interests of departments and schools; and as chief personnel officer he will concern himself with the problem of developing the staff.[13]

86

THE VICE PRESIDENTS

In March, 1930, Shirley W. Smith and Clarence Stone Yoakum were named Vice President and Secretary, and Vice President in Charge of Educational Investigations, respectively. Smith's new title did not mean a change in duties, for he continued to have responsibility for finance and physical plant, but Yoakum's appointment was an innovation of major proportions. *The Michigan Alumnus* described the new office as "experimental" and supposed that its purpose was to aid the faculties in proposing new teaching methods and curriculums.[14] Soon after these appointments, Lewis M. Gram became Director of Plant Extension, which corresponded to a vice presidential post. Gram's duties were concerned with the building program and space allocations, for Ruthven told the regents that too often university buildings had been built with only "financial and mechanical" considerations in mind. He proposed to build them "from the inside out," and therefore one of Gram's primary duties was to assess the academic needs of the faculties when new buildings were proposed.[15] Next, Dr. Ruthven appointed Dr. James D. Bruce to a position of Vice President in Charge of University Relations. In this post Bruce was to coordinate the university's extension work, adult education, alumni activities, and all other matters relating to the people of the state. In 1933 Henry C. Anderson became Director of Student-Alumni Relations; his responsibilities were auxiliary enterprises such as the Women's League, the Michigan Union, and the dormitories. This position, too, was regarded as vice-presidential. Thus, as the academic year 1933 began, the president had a cabinet of five officers of vice-presidential rank.

Each vice president was to be responsible for his own area and each was given the authority to make binding decisions in his area. The president, of course, did not relinquish his constitutional responsibility for the entire operation of the institution, but in actual practice vice presidents were given "carte blanche." The vice presidents acted as consultants to the president on matters affecting total university policy. Ruthven hoped that the vice presidents would relieve him of many of his peripheral duties and free him for more direct contact with deans, department chairmen, and faculty committees. The president, however, did continue with the back-breaking responsibility of preparing the budget and presenting it to the legislature. It was carefully pointed out to the faculty that the vice-presidential coterie was not to be a barrier between them and the president.[16]

THE DEANS

This was especially important to the deans, since they were concerned that Ruthven's new organizational scheme would diminish their powers. Their concern was justified, for one of Ruthven's objectives was to curtail the customary "empire building" of the deans. In his first appearance before the University Senate, the new president referred to the deans as "old barons," and this jibe drew an appreciative chuckle from the assembled faculty.[17] Ruthven insisted that all correspondence with the regents be done through his office; no longer would deans and regents jointly prepare budgets and discuss faculty appointments. To improve communication a "deans' conference" consisting of the president, the vice presidents, the deans of the schools and colleges, the librarian, and the student service deans met weekly. At these conferences, frequently held in the president's home, matters of general university policy were discussed. But these were informal gatherings and the "deans' conference" had no legislative powers.

Early in his regime Ruthven offered his personal message to each dean in turn. He wrote to the dean of the education school: "You know, I am sure, that I am very much interested in your School. I will assist you in every possible way to make its work successful. To this end permit me to criticize and comment freely (to you), and please keep me informed of the progress and ideals of your department."[18] He urged the dean of the Graduate School to get additional help, for he was "a fiend for work" and was trying to do too much.[19] The president complimented Dean Effinger on the revised curriculum in the Literary College.[20] However, he had a slap on the wrist for Dean Bates, the old monarch of the Law School. When Bates proposed certain changes in building structure to the architect of the Law School, Ruthven reprimanded him: "In my opinion, the faculty should confine its criticism to the arrangement and the amount of space in class rooms and offices . . . the decision as to the size of the building and possible methods of construction should be decided by the administration."[21] From the engineering dean he requested a statement of policy regarding the nature and amount of consulting done by engineering faculty. Dean Sadler piously assured the president: "It is considered desirable for all members of the Staff to adhere rigidly to the ethics of the profession, and particularly to avoid the active solicitation of outside work."[22] "There is apparently some discrepancy between your statement of policy and the practice of certain men on your staff," Ruthven retorted. "May I ask you now to give me a report upon the status of the work of Professors Hoad, Decker, and Menefee...."[23]

It is doubtful that President Ruthven's badgering had any ameliorating effect on old warhorses like Bates and Sadler, but he had served notice that it was a new system and, like it or not, the deans would have to get used to it.[24]

THE FACULTY REORGANIZED

In 1930 the university faculty conducted its business through the University Senate, a group which was comprised of 531 faculty members. President Ruthven realized that the University Senate was too large for legislative deliberations and encouraged the formation of the smaller, representative University Council, which consisted of twenty-two deans and other administrators and thirty-four elected members of the faculty. The University Council was empowered to legislate, but it was agreed that the entire University Senate might review any of the Council's actions. At the outset the major work of the University Council was done by its Committee on Program and Policy. This committee, chaired by President Ruthven and consisting of the chairman and vice chairman of the Council and the chairmen of the four standing committees, initiated discussions of any academic policies affecting the general faculties.[25] When some faculty complained that the presence of all of the top level administrators inhibited discussion, the representation was revised so that about one-third of the Council was administration and the other two-thirds were faculty.[26]

Within the schools and colleges executive committees were established to aid the dean in budget preparation, promotion and tenure, and faculty recruitment. These committees assumed a good deal of the decision-making which had previously fallen to the dean. The first executive committee was appointed in the medical school upon the dismissal of Dr. Hugh Cabot. The second executive committee was formed in the College of Literature, Science, and the Arts following Dean Effinger's death in 1933. Thereafter, executive committees were formed periodically at the request of the faculties of the individual schools and colleges. In most cases members of the executive committees were appointed by the president from a list submitted to him by the faculty of the school or college. Members of the executive committees were regarded as major executive officials by the regents, and that body refused to allow the faculties final authority for the selection of executive committee members.[27]

Individual departments, too, were encouraged to establish executive committees, and these also served to aid the chairman in budget preparation, faculty appointments, and salaries. Since departments varied in size from two to more than fifty members, it was recognized that executive committees would not be feasible in the smaller departments. Within some departments the foundation for more democratic governance had already been established, for in the early 1920s it became the practice to do away with the autocratic title of "department head" and replace it with "chairman."[28]

One further organizational procedure was promoted by the Ruthven administration, although the term used to describe it had originated a few years earlier. To foster better communication between units of the university with similar interests, "divisions" were established. Because divisions were not intended as administrative units, there was some confusion as to their function. A division was officially defined as:

> a grouping of units and departments for the purpose of coordinating various allied activities, and of developing the general field therein. . . . Its specific duties of advice and recommendation concern the interrelations of its several curricula, the encouragement of individual research, and the promotion of cooperative investigations.[29]

The purpose, then, was simply to promote common goals and avoid overlap. The Ruthven Papers show that the president, through Vice President Yoakum, worked doggedly to bring about a Division of Fine Arts, a grouping consisting of the College of Architecture, the Department of Fine Arts, the Department of Landscape Design, and the play-production courses in the Department of Speech.[30] When this grouping was finally secured, it pointed the way for similar groupings in other disciplines.

One final coordinating body was named. This was the faculty personnel committee, chaired by the president. Its function was to review all academic appointments to insure that equal standards would exist throughout the university.

CONSEQUENCES

These changes brought manifold results; one of the most striking was the shifting of responsibility and authority from the deans to the faculties. After all, Ruthven reasoned, the faculties are the "educational experts" and the university should utilize their expertise. Not only would the institution profit, but self-government would lead to greater individual dignity and job satisfaction. Ten years after his installation as president, Ruthven spoke at the National Alumni Dinner. "The University," he said, "requires for efficient administration both wholehearted cooperation and decentralized responsibility; a democratic way of life is the inclusive purpose of American education, and our schools cannot assist in the achievement of this purpose if they encourage autocratic administration, permit a spirit of uncertainty, fear, rivalry, or suspicion to prevail among staff members...."[31] He spoke earlier of a "faculty copartnership in administration," and expressed his hopes that the new plan would "promote harmony between administration efficiency and the human value of self-determination and self-respect."[32] "No distinction should be made between faculty opinion and administrative opinion," he once told the University Senate. "In the University of Michigan there is no administrative view, only a University point of view."[33] It seems significant that faculty members from the Ruthven years are unanimous in agreeing that Michigan has been a democratically administered university. Obviously, as executive committee memberships rotated, practically all senior faculty had the opportunity to participate extensively in governance. Ruthven, reminiscing, was sure that the extent of faculty participation in decision-making had a salutary effect, although he recalled that change, when it was the responsibility of the faculty, was apt to come slowly.[34] Ruthven could wait, since he typically allowed the machinery established for academic governance to grind along until it produced a decision. Ruthven seldom looked for rapid solutions to complex problems, nor did he often interfere with either the method or results of a faculty or regental committee.

Another outcome of the Ruthven reorganization was increased daily contact between the president and the faculty. The Ruthven Papers indicate that he regularly attended, ex-officio, the meetings of most of the major committees on campus, including such divergent groups as the Board in Control of Athletics and the Board of Governors of the Student Religious Association. He frequently stressed that the vice presidents were not to stand between him and the faculty; they were "out at the side to keep them out of the functional line. . . . We are definitely subordinating administration," he told the faculty in a speech that must have warmed their scholarly hearts.[35]

The introduction of the vice presidents, the plan which Ruthven borrowed from his corporate friends, also made an impact. A review of the American Council on Education publication, *American Universities and Colleges*, reveals that in 1928 the term "vice president" was used in only a half dozen American colleges and universities. Major universities, in listing "administration," would name their president and, usually, academic deans and, sometimes, their registrar, Dean of Men, and Dean of Women. The University of Chicago was the only institution at that time to list more than one vice president, for Chicago had designated a Vice President and Dean of Faculties and a Vice President and Business Manager.[36]

Ruthven's methods of using vice presidents was antedated in print by President Raymond M. Hughes of Iowa State College. Hughes suggested to the Governing Boards of State Universities and Allied Institutions that those universities with 10,000 students should be prepared, when selecting a new president, to allow him to name one or two vice presidents of his own choosing. "It is impossible for one man to do all that the president of a great university should do," Hughes concluded.[37]

There is no doubt that Ruthven, in command of a university of over 12,000 students, exhibited great foresight in establishing the vice-presidential structure which provided the administrative manpower to help the university survive the Depression and, soon after, World War II.

TRAILBLAZER

The Michigan system combined elements of many types of administrative organization and is therefore not easy to categorize. The plan for vice presidents charged with executive authority for designated areas has come to be known as a "cabinet" form of organization. The emphasis on faculty executive committees with shared administrative responsibilities in schools, colleges, and departments appears as a precursor of the group participation techniques of the modern management experts.[38] The president's relationship with the regents and the deans maintained elements of traditional line-staff organization.

When considered in toto it seems probable that the Michigan system introduced by President Ruthven was a trailblazer in American higher education. More than any other plan or organization it anticipated the needs of a large modern university. Even though the Board of Trustees of the University of Chicago had authorized the title of "vice president" as early as 1923, Chicago's plan did not give the executives set areas of responsibility and real authority as Michigan's did. By 1932, only one other major university—the University of Pennsylvania—had established a group of vice presidents who functioned in a somewhat similar manner to those at Michigan.[39]

There were, of course, varying degrees of faculty participation in governance in evidence when the Michigan system was introduced. Antioch College, for example, had gone so far as to establish an Administrative Council of three faculty elected by the faculty, three faculty appointed by the president, and the president and dean ex officio. Antioch's Council met weekly to "determine general policies and to advise the president and dean."[40]

A 1919 study of written statements by ninety-three college and university presidents showed that at twenty-eight institutions the faculty "practically" determined educational policy. However, at twenty-two other institutions the faculty had no voice whatsoever in the matter. Surprisingly, a follow-up study in 1929 revealed that in these ninety-three institutions there had been a slight decrease in faculty governance during the decade.[41]

In 1930 one of the most authoritative sources on the subject of governance was one by E. E. Lindsay and E. O. Holland, *College and University Administration.*[42] Lindsay was Head of the Department of Educational Administration at the University of Pittsburgh, and Holland was President of the State College of Washington.[43] Prior to publication their manuscript had been reviewed by Presidents Lowell of Harvard, Aydelotte of Swarthmore, Sproul of California, and Frank of Wisconsin, as well as by a number of noted professors.[44]

It is interesting to note that there is no mention of any "vice-president" in Lindsay and Holland's listing of officers of general administration.[45]

It is equally interesting that, in speaking of faculty governance, the authors baldly state, "The tendency today in academic circles is distinctly that of centralization."[46] They do not recommend extreme centralization of authority in the hands of administration, the authors hasten to add, for "the teaching faculty in each college or division should have some representation in the affairs of that institution."[47] Lindsay and Holland's solution? They suggest "discussion groups" which would elect one faculty representative from each college or division to meet with the college or division deans in a central body. That central body, of course, would include the bursar, registrar, statistician, and other administrators to "effectively break the balance between the deans and the faculty representatives in favor of the central administration." Any such central body would not participate in actual decision-making, but would nevertheless be significant, for "if faculty feelings and emotions have an outlet, they do not accumulate and gather the force necessary for a destructive explosion."[48]

If Lindsay and Holland's ideas were regarded as the latest word in administrative theory, it seems obvious that Ruthven's Michigan System was innovative, for it certainly surpassed Lindsay and Holland in sophistication and foresight, particularly in the introduction of vice presidents and in the democratic, meaningful participation of faculty in governance.

When the *Journal of Higher Education* was founded in January, 1930, the editors turned to Ruthven for their first article on college and university organization.[49] However, the probability that Ruthven introduced a new system of organization to American higher education has never been acknowledged. Frank E. Robbins, who was present at the creation of the Michigan System, felt that it was Ruthven's finest contribution to the university's history, but Robbins apparently never realized that Ruthven's form of administration was new to higher education.[50]

Ruthven seemed to realize it, though he made only one effort to note it publicly. In a rare press conference in 1944, called to announce administrative personnel changes, he spoke of the Michigan System when he said: "Michigan pioneered in developing this type of organization for universities, one which is being adopted every year by more and more of our educational institutions."[51] Later, reminiscing with retired regent Ralph Stone, he wrote: "I am sure that one of the improvements in administration which we put in early in my regime was the decentralization of responsibility for major fields of activities. This was new in the educational world."[52]

The Michigan System

When reminded of the Michigan System in a 1970 interview, he reaffirmed that Michigan had introduced this form of organization to higher education. "Come to think about it," the aged ex-president recalled, "it did arouse a good deal of interest around the country."[53]

NOTES

1. Alexander G. Ruthven, "The Organization of the University," *The Michigan Alumnus*, Vol. 36, No. 27 (1930), p. 523.
2. *Survey of Land-Grant Colleges and Universities*, Vol. 1, Bulletin 1930, No. 9 (U.S. Office of Education, Washington, D.C.: U.S. Government Printing Office, 1930), pp. 66–67.
3. Interview, Alexander G. Ruthven, January 27, 1970.
4. Howard H. Peckham, *The Making of the University of Michigan* (Ann Arbor: University of Michigan Press, 1967), pp. 69–70.
5. Interview, Alexander G. Ruthven, February 13, 1970.
6. Interview, Alexander G. Ruthven, January 23, 1970.
7. *The Michigan Alumnus*, Vol. 51, No. 10 (1944), p. 171.
8. Alexander G. Ruthven, "Administration at Michigan," *Journal of Higher Education*, Vol. 2, No. 1 (1931), p. 9.
9. *The President's Report for 1933–34*, Vol. 36, No. 29, p.3.
10. Interview, Alexander G. Ruthven, January 27, 1970.
11. Alexander G. Ruthven, *Naturalist in Two Worlds* (Ann Arbor: University of Michigan Press, 1963), p. 38.
12. Letter of William L. Clements to Ruthven, June 8, 1932, Ruthven Papers, box 5, MHC.
13. Alexander G. Ruthven, "Administration at Michigan," p. 9.
14. *The Michigan Alumnus*, Vol. 36, No. 22 (1930), p. 432.
15. *The President's Report for 1929–30*, pp. 8–9.
16. Alexander G. Ruthven, "Administration at Michigan," pp. 8–9.
17. Interview, Alexander G. Ruthven, January 23, 1970.
18. Ruthven to J. B. Edmondson, December 23, 1929, Ruthven Papers, box 1, MHC.
19. Ruthven to G. Carl Huber, June 27, 1930, *ibid.*
20. Ruthven to J. R. Effinger, May 23, 1930, *ibid.* The new curriculum: "No student shall be accepted as a candidate for a degree until he has received at least 60 hours credit, and unless the average of all his work is of C grade or better. . . . Each student, upon becoming a candidate for a degree, shall select a department or division of concentration." (*Proceedings of the Board of Regents*, May Meeting, 1931, p. 630.) This meant that the Literary College, on its own initiative, had decided to incorporate the major principles of C. C. Little's unsuccessful University College.
21. Ruthven to Henry M. Bates, October 18, 1930, Ruthven Papers, box 1, MHC.

22. H. C. Sadler to Ruthven, October 28, 1930, Ruthven Papers, box 4, MHC.

23. Ruthven to Sadler, November 6, 1930, *ibid.*

24. Bates, apparently, never did get used to it. He complained to Regent Murfin in a "Personal and Confidential" letter that "nothing like this has happened before," for he was "being treated very much like a subordinate foreman." (Bates to James O. Murfin, January 20, 1931, Murfin Papers, Vol. 6, MHC.) Bates' law school was conceded to be one of the best in the country, and Ruthven and the regents decided that they would be well advised not to force the reorganization of the law school but instead wait for Bates to retire. Ruthven to Murfin, November 30, 1935, Ruthven Papers, box 18, MHC.

25. Letter of Frank E. Robbins to Archie M. Palmer, Association of American Colleges, January 7, 1932, Ruthven Papers, box 7, MHC. Robbins, as Assistant to the President, answered inquiries about the university's organization.

26. Letter of Robbins to Tom D. Rowe, March 7, 1944, Ruthven Papers, box 47, MHC. Rowe was chairman of a committee to organize a faculty senate at the medical college of Virginia.

27. *Proceedings of the Board of Regents,* Special August Meeting, 1933, p. 193.

28. Letter of Robbins to Charles H. Tuttle, March 4, 1938, Ruthven Papers, box 25, MHC.

29. Memorandum of Alexander G. Ruthven, February 9, 1932, Ruthven Papers, box 7, MHC.

30. Ruthven Papers, box 6, July–November, 1931, MHC.

31. Alexander G. Ruthven, "A Decade of University History," *31st General Bulletin, Bureau of Alumni Relations,* Vol. 41, No. 68 (1940), p. 3.

32. Alexander G. Ruthven, "Administration at Michigan," p. 10.

33. Speech of Alexander G. Ruthven to the University Senate, November 30, 1931, Ruthven Papers, box 77, MHC.

34. Interview, Alexander G. Ruthven, January 27, 1970.

35. Speech of Alexander G. Ruthven to the University Senate, November 30, 1931, Ruthven Papers, box 77, MHC.

36. *American Universities and Colleges* (American Council on Education, Washington, D. C., 1928). Chicago's Vice President and Business Manager functioned similarly to Vice President Shirley W. Smith at Michigan, but the Vice President and Dean of the Faculties was an educational maverick. The president assigned to him various projects, but he had no set functions, and no real authority. Floyd W. Reeves, *et al., The Organization and Administration of the University,* The University of Chicago Survey, II (Chicago: University of Chicago Press, 1933), p. 57.

37. Quoted in *Bulletin of the American Association of University Professors,* Vol. 15, No. 6 (1929), p. 468.

38. See Rensis Likert, *New Patterns of Management* (New York: McGraw-Hill, 1961).

39. *American Universities and Colleges* (American Council on Education, Washington, D. C., 1932). Historically, Pennsylvania had called its chief executive Provost rather than President and, since 1926, had designated three "vice provosts": one responsible for faculty personnel and relations; one in charge of student government and welfare; and one in charge of public relations. Edward Potts Cheyney, *History of the University of Pennsylvania 1740–1940* (Philadelphia: University of Pennsylvania Press, 1940), pp. 415–16. In 1931 the Pennsylvania statutes

were revised to provide, in addition to a president, a provost and four vice presidents. Two of these vice presidents were in charge of the professional schools of law and medicine; a third was placed in charge of the undergraduate schools; and the fourth was responsible for the business departments of the University. (*Statutes of the Corporation*, University of Pennsylvania, June 1, 1931, pp. 13–17.) It would appear that the functions of the first three corresponded to those of the deans of Law, Medicine, and Literature, Science, and the Arts at Michigan. There is no evidence in the *Statutes* that there was faculty involvement in governance as there was at Michigan.

40. Arthur E. Morgan, "The Antioch Program," *Journal of Higher Education*, Vol. 1, No. 9 (1930), p. 501.

41. Edward C. Elliot, M. M. Chambers, and W. A. Ashbrook, *The Government of Higher Education* (New York: American Book Company, 1935), pp. 162–63.

42. E. E. Lindsay and E. O. Holland, *College and University Administration* (New York: The Macmillan Company, 1930).

43. Since 1959 Washington State University at Pullman, Washington.

44. Lindsay and Holland, *College and University Administration*, Introduction.

45. *Ibid.*, p. 25.

46. *Ibid.*, p. 462.

47. *Ibid.*, p. 466.

48. *Ibid.*, pp. 468–69.

49. Alexander G. Ruthven, "Administration at Michigan," January, 1931.

50. *Michigan: An Encyclopedic Survey, 1,* p. 98. Robbins wrote the section on Ruthven's presidency.

51. Alexander G. Ruthven, Statement to the Press, December 4, 1944, Ruthven Papers, box 50, MHC.

52. Ruthven to Stone, July 11, 1951, Stone Papers, box 1, MHC.

53. Interview, Alexander G. Ruthven, January 23, 1970.

6

The Depression and the Legislature

In October, 1929, the same month Ruthven became president, the stock market crashed. F. Clever Bald recounts:

> Because of its highly specialized industrial structure Michigan suffered sooner and more severely than most of the other states. Automobile production fell off from five million units in 1929 to two million in 1933. In 1930, 20 per cent of the state's nonagricultural workers were unemployed; in 1931, 29 per cent; in 1932, 43 per cent; and in 1933, nearly 50 per cent. More than half a million people were dependent on public funds for their daily bread.[1]

A tax on land, buildings, and personal property was the major source of revenue for the state government. When the Depression hit, people were unable to pay these taxes; delinquencies in the state averaged about one-third.[2] From 1929 to 1932 nearly two hundred Michigan banks failed. By early 1933 it was necessary for the governor to declare a bank holiday.

FOURTH ARM OF GOVERNMENT

With Depression gripping the state, an economic crisis at the university was inevitable. The unanswered question was whether readjustments caused by the state's own economic crisis would nullify the university's favored position as a fourth arm of government. It was a question crucial to the university's future.

In 1850, soon after the university's founding, the Michigan Constitutional Convention had granted the Board of Regents "general supervision of the University" and the "direction and control of all expenditures from the University interest fund." This provision, and litigation subsequent to it, provided the basis for the university's autonomy.[3]

In 1867 the legislature, responding to increasing university costs, passed a tax act which allocated to the university one-twentieth of a mill on the dollar on all taxable property of the state. This mill tax was extremely important to the university, for it meant that future budgets could be planned and growth predicted as the wealth of the state increased.

The famous case of *Sterling v. The Regents of the University of Michigan* further fixed the precedent that an elected, autonomous board of regents would control the university and that the legislature could not encroach.

Historians of the University generally agree that the guidance of an independent board and the guarantees of increasing income from the mill tax were the two factors which initially set Michigan apart from other state universities and permitted its position of preeminence.

Until the time of President Burton these cornerstones of a great university were accepted by the other branches of government. Burton, the ambitious builder, needed legislative approval of vast capital expenditures for new structures on the campus. He got it, but at a price. In 1921, the university appropriations act contained a clause giving the State Administrative Board the right to release (or hold) funds previously appropriated to the university, and in 1923 the legislature placed a limit on revenues from the mill tax of $3,000,000 per annum. In the general campus euphoria over Burton's driving leadership and the consequent building program, these unwelcome incursions seem to have been overlooked. Some have suggested that the regents were uneasy with these evidences of legislative meddling, but felt that Burton's powers of persuasion were sufficient to restore university autonomy and the unfettered mill tax after the building program was well underway.[4]

Burton, however, died prematurely in 1925, and the task of dealing with the legislature fell to Burton's successor, Clarence Cook Little. As has been noted, Little's outspoken advocacy of unpopular causes produced tension in Lansing as well as Ann Arbor. In 1927 Governor Fred Green—perhaps to squelch Little—vetoed portions of the university's appropriations bill; Little's relationship with the legislature was not good either.

The university's position vis-à-vis the legislature and the governor had clearly eroded. When Little resigned in 1929, Alexander G. Ruthven, Dean of Administration, was asked to present the university budget to a dubious legislature. Perhaps it was Ruthven's skill, perhaps it was Governor Green's fondness for him, or perhaps the legislature saw the merits of the university proposals; in any case, the university's two-year budget was approved in perfunctory fashion, and the timing could not have been more fortunate. The stock market crash came only a few months later.

Despite the reprieve, Ruthven knew that, with as many as one third of the state property owners unable to pay taxes, support for his institution might well be curtailed. From September, 1930, until May, 1931, Ruthven, the new president, wrangled with the new governor, Wilber M. Brucker, over the principle of the mill tax. Brucker's proposal to eliminate the mill tax, Ruthven told him, "will be the death knell of the institution as we have known it."[5] In May he told Brucker that the university was faced with the largest enrollment in its history, faculty salaries were low, and "Michigan has dropped from first place to far down the line."[6] Ruthven's reproach reaped rewards, for the legislature cut the university's request by only $140,000, a moral victory for the university. Regent William L. Clements wrote Ruthven: "Some one, and I believe it was you, is entitled to much credit in getting even as favorable action."[7] The victory was only temporary since state revenues were plummeting, and in 1932 a special session of the legislature reduced the university's income from the mill tax by 15 per cent, or about $738,000. As the regular 1933 legislative session approached, President Ruthven and the regents were faced with the likelihood of a discarded mill tax and the unwelcome possibility of appealing to the legislature for appropriations from the state general funds every two years. "I believe that we should cling to the principle of the mill tax at all cost," Ruthven wrote Clements.[8] In 1933 the mill tax was first repealed by the legislature, then retained as Governor William Comstock vetoed repeal.[9] Nevertheless, the university's appropriation was reduced to $3,200,000—approximately a 30 per cent decrease in income. When mill tax revenues on real property continued to shrink, the 1935 legislature abolished this form of income and substituted a sales tax. Ruthven had foreseen that this was inevitable, but he fought to retain some means by which the university could plan its financial future without relying for funds on the whims of each new legislative session. Ruthven appealed to Governor Frank D. Fitzgerald:

> We could seek to amend the sales tax law to provide a continuing appropriation of a *portion of the sales tax proceeds equal to a predetermined percentage of property valuations of the state.* This arrangement would

give the University the same revenues, both as to amount and stability . . . but they would have the advantage of not being actually derived from a tax on property. They would simply be *measured* by property valuation.[10]

Law professor E. Blythe Stason drafted such a bill. The bill became law, and the law resulted in slightly increased income for the university and, even more important, a yardstick against which future development could be planned. The new system of support remained in effect until 1947 when the legislature required the university budget to operate on an annual appropriation from the general fund. Peckham, the university historian, regarded this as a "great Ruthven victory," and he called him "a magnificent rear guard fighter" for his struggles with Depression legislatures.[11] Sagendorph recorded: "President Ruthven pulled a financial rabbit out of his hat."[12]

There was no question that Ruthven had the knack for working with the state legislature and with a procession of Republican and Democratic governors as well. A great deal of his success was due, no doubt, to the fact that Ruthven was basically apolitical. He scrupulously avoided making his personal preferences known in regental elections. With rare exceptions (e.g. World War II) he refrained from speaking out on national issues. Ruthven limited his national exposure to membership in such non-controversial organizations as the Conference of Thirteen Midwestern Universities, the Rhodes Scholarship selection committee, various adult education groups, and the governing board of the National Association of State Universities. He was president of the latter group from 1941 to 1942.

It was extremely important to him to "keep the University out of the newspapers." Ruthven realized that every controversial topic which was publicized inevitably made new enemies. The contrast in the public relations approaches of Ruthven and his tempestuous predecessor was striking. Little believed in birth control and promoted its merits to civic groups all over the state; Ruthven believed in birth control and made casual reference to it in one speech to the faculty nineteen years after succeeding Little.[13] Little told the Ann Arbor landladies that they were gouging students for their rooms and therefore he would build dormitories to supplant rooming houses; Ruthven waited until there were so many students that dormitories were an obvious necessity even to the landladies. Little utilized faculty expertise to urge new bills on state legislators; Ruthven told the legislators that faculty experts were at their service

101

whenever called.[14] Little held press conferences; Ruthven organized a university news service. Ruthven established cordial relationships with key newspaper editors of the state; and when there were controversies involving the president or the university, favorable reporting was assured.

In fact, Ruthven was so apolitical that even his good friends had no idea whether he was a Democrat or a Republican. His son did not believe he was either, and thought "he was very careful about this."[15] Mrs. Julie Furstenberg Owens, whose family was close to the Ruthvens, thought "he would hang all the Democrats together," but Bryant Ruthven recalls his father's admiration for Franklin D. Roosevelt—anathema to most conservative Republicans.[16] On rare occasions Ruthven could be ingenious in getting his political message across. "There is an old saying that Caesar's wife must be above suspicion," he wrote to State Senator George P. McCallum of Ann Arbor. "This observation is meant to illustrate my belief that a college president must also be above suspicion as far as political preferences are concerned. . . . At the same time there is no reason why Mrs. Ruthven cannot express . . . her opinion. You will hear from her shortly and may read a lot of things between the lines of her letter."[17]

In any case, Ruthven determined that he would give the state's public officials no cause to criticize university leadership because of any careless utterance on sensitive political matters. It may have been bland; it may have been leadership by default; it was hardly courageous; but it was effective, as he knew it would be.

Ruthven had several tricks up his sleeve when he went to the legislature seeking funds. Marvin Niehuss, who as Vice President in Charge of University Relations was deeply involved in appropriations struggles, recalls that Ruthven favored a direct personal approach with legislators, many of whom came from rural districts and liked "straight talk" rather than finesse.[18]

E. Blythe Stason, then a law professor and later provost and dean of the Law School, frequently worked with Ruthven in preparing budget data for the legislature. Stason remembers:

> I sat in with Mr. Ruthven in his negotiations with the House Ways and Means Committee and the Senate Finance Committee and he and I got rather close. He used to go to those meetings . . . in an old Ford or some beatnik contraption . . . and he'd swing around and put his feet up on the desk in the committee room and say "Well, fellows,

what are we going to do this year? It's your university as much as it is mine and more. . . . We've given you the facts as we've seen them and there is no padding and now do you have any questions you want to ask me?" And he'd sit there just like an old shoe, don't you know, but very, very effective. He gave the impression always of extraordinary candor and at the same time extremely good knowledge of what the University needed.[19]

Such feet-on-the-desk mannerisms, of course, were a bit out of character for Ruthven, who had an innate dignity but, at least in the early years of his presidency, brought himself to do whatever the occasion demanded.

He also believed that it was a tactical error to present any budget over two pages in length. "That way," he explained, "they can all understand it. If it were any longer they wouldn't read it anyway."[20]

Like Presidents Burton and Little before him, Ruthven invited the entire legislature to the campus for a day. He further "insisted that the Ways and Means Committee of the House and the Finance Committee of the Senate visit the University during the sessions as many times as I could get them."[21]

Typically, Ruthven used these campus visits to promote specific university interests. His reminiscences describe one such visit:

At a meeting of the legislature in Ann Arbor a new representative from northern Michigan was present who had been very vocal in criticism of the University. Early in the session he had read an item in a Detroit newspaper facetiously commenting on a study being made by one of the professors on "waltzing mice." He was so excited about this item that he had secured copies of the paper and given them to each of his colleagues. I ignored his attacks.

When the group was assembled in Ann Arbor I introduced my talk by pointing out that the University was a very complex institution. I hoped the members would clear with us whenever they had any doubts as to work that was being done on the campus. I pointed out as an example of something that might have puzzled them the report on the professor and his dancing mice. I then asked them abruptly if they had ever seen a child with epilepsy and briefly described some of the symptoms. The smiles about the room when I first mentioned the matter quickly disappeared. I told them that perhaps they had visualized a bespectacled old gentleman sitting in front of a cage of dancing mice accompanying the gyrations of his pets with a mouth organ. Actually, I explained, he thought that the peculiar trait of these animals was related to epilepsy and that if this could be established there might be good experimental material for studies leading to the treatment of the malady. I then went on to discuss the aims and objectives of the University.

At the end of a rather long session, as we were about to disband, the critical representative rose to his feet and said, "Gentlemen, I have been a fool. From now on anything the University asks I am going to vote for." I did not find out until a year or two later that his little granddaughter had the disease. I wrote him a letter of apology to which he replied that no apology was necessary, for he had needed just that lesson.[22]

Ruthven was a firm believer in presenting the legislature with an uninflated budget year after year. He was at times criticized for his honesty and unfavorable comparisons were made with his counterpart John Hannah at Michigan State, who was known for presenting exaggerated budget requests, but Ruthven and his associates were confident that, over the long haul, legislative respect for the integrity of their requests paid dividends for the university.[23]

Despite Ruthven's acknowledged skill with the legislature, the biennial and (later) annual battles for appropriations were something he endured rather than relished. Ruthven remained forever frustrated by continuing questions about the efficacy of enrolling out-of-state students, about continuing demands to produce cost per student data, and about the niggardly amounts some legislators favored for their state university. "We are all as God made us and some of us even worse" was one way Ruthven recollected legislators.[24]

DEPRESSION ON THE CAMPUS

For the first three years of the Depression, student enrollments remained constant, but in 1933–34 the number of students dropped to 10,573, almost 2,000 below the pre-Depression figure. Sagendorph tells the story dramatically: "More than a thousand students had packed up and gone during the early stages of the Depression. . . . A thousand more who should have left hung doggedly to their college careers, and more than one faced actual hunger."[25] Most students found that, since there were no jobs available in industry or agriculture, it was better to struggle through college. After the low enrollment year of 1933–34, attendance increased markedly, and by 1939–40 over 16,000 students were enrolled.

The Depression and the Legislature

Early in the Depression, income from the legislature decreased, contributions from past benefactors dried up and, after 1931, the legislature cancelled all outstanding building plans. Inevitably, the university was forced to economize. Ruthven told Glenn Frank, President of the University of Wisconsin: "We are undertaking to reduce expenditures by eliminating superfluous instructors and assistants and by limiting current expense and equipment. . . . I have been opposed to faculty salary decreases but much to my surprise the staff has informally asked that reductions be made."[26] Reductions were made. In 1932–33 all salaries were reduced on a graduated scale of 6 percent, 8 percent, and 10 percent. Those with the highest salaries (over $10,000) received the 10 percent cuts.[27] Ruthven's salary was reduced from $18,000 to $16,200.[28] The following year further graduated across-the-board pay decreases were made. The first $1500 was exempt, but 8 percent was cut from the next $2000, 12 percent from the next $2000, 15 percent from the next, and 20 percent from anything above $7500.[29]

The faculty responded philosophically, and Professor W. C. Hoad spoke for many others: "I think we are all coming to appreciate the extreme seriousness of the situation by which the University is faced; but, pay or no pay, come Hell or High water, we'll all stand by and see the job through."[30]

In fact, faculty status at the university was to be envied, for the academic routine was not appreciably disrupted and, with two exceptions, payrolls were met on time.[31] The Ruthven Papers indicate that literally hundreds of letters requesting faculty appointments were received during the Depression years and, although many applicants presented excellent credentials, the requests would be routinely met with the reply: "I regret to say that there is very little possibility of a suitable opening on the staff." Some faculty were released, and no replacements were appointed for those who died or retired. In 1933 alone, 60 teaching and 29 non-teaching positions were eliminated and 122 additional staff members had their time reduced. Of the 66 teaching positions eliminated, 45 were at the instructor level.[32]

President Ruthven did what he could to keep morale high. When members of the University Senate expressed concern that Ann Arbor banks would fail, Ruthven promptly announced to them that he would continue to deposit his check in one of the local banks.[33]

In 1930, when 162 faculty members were caught in a transitional

105

squeeze between the retirement plans of the Carnegie Foundation for the Advancement of Teaching and the Teachers' Insurance and Annuity Association, the budget was expanded to include pensions for retiring professors.[34]

Ruthven suggested a scheme to enroll Michigan's displaced instructors in the graduate school without payment of the usual fees. The idea, presumably, was that these men, who were unable to secure jobs, would at least have the opportunity for professional development without added financial burden.[35]

In November, 1934, Ruthven initiated a policy that permitted faculty who had served in administrative capacities for fifteen years or more to relinquish their administrative duties and assume "distinguished professorships." This was an educational innovation and Ruthven explained his reasoning to the Association of Governing Boards of State Universities and Allied Institutions. Administration was a burden, he said, and since scholarship was the first love of any academic-turned-administrator, a change back to faculty status was, therefore, a promotion. "Distinguished professorships" would recognize the academic skills of mature scholars and pave the way for younger men to fill the more physically demanding administrative positions.[36]

When many students were unable to pay tuition at the beginning of the academic year, they were allowed to enroll for classes anyway. Credit for the year's work, however, was not awarded until tuition had been paid.[37] The Federal Emergency Relief Agency (FERA) and the National Youth Administration (NYA), two federal agencies, contributed financial aid for which students agreed to work on various campus projects. By 1939–40, approximately half of the students held part-time jobs, and President Ruthven sent strong letters to his congressmen urging continuation of the NYA program.[38]

Scholarship and loan programs were strengthened. It was specified that an Earhart Foundation grant of $10,000 was to be used in part for scholarships for senior students, and the Brousseau Foundation gave $115,000, primarily as a student loan fund.[39] The Rackham Foundation contributed $100,000 for the same purpose.[40]

Welcome though these private benefactions were, President Ruthven realized early in the Depression that additional scholarship funds were needed if the university was to insure an equal opportunity for the young people in the state. Thus, in 1931, the regents established a number of Michigan Alumni Undergraduate Scholarships. These were tuition scholarships, and each alumni club in the state was to have the privilege of recommending one or more candidates (no more than three) every year.[41]

The regents also created a number of loan funds to supplement gift income, and by 1935–36 nearly 2600 students were receiving loans totaling more than $145,000.[42] The need for even more scholarship funds for deserving students was frequently mentioned in Depression-era *President's Reports*, but not until 1943 was a major new university scholarship program established.[43]

Just as "necessity is the mother of invention," adversity on the campus seemed to breed a surprising esprit de corps. Sagendorph recalls that Depression-era students found "ingenious solutions to the everyday problems of existence."[44] Football was undoubtedly one reason morale remained high, for the Michigan Wolverines, under Coach Harry Kipke, won Big Ten and national titles in 1932, 1933, and 1934. Although prohibition ended in 1933, any resultant revelry was tempered by Ruthven's caution to the students: "The University will not continue as a student a man or woman who brings disgrace upon it."[45]

Despite legislative curtailment of capital funds, contributions from a few wealthy donors resulted in increased campus building. When W.W. Cook died in 1930, his estate provided funds for the continued construction of the magnificent law school, completed in 1933. In 1935, as a result of President Ruthven's negotiations with the executors of the Rackham Fund, $6,500,000 was given to the graduate school for a building and for program endowment.[46] Also in 1935 plans were undertaken for Burton Tower and the Baird Carillon.

As job cutbacks encouraged students to prolong their educational experiences, graduate schools turned out a surplus of scholars with advanced degrees. It seemed an opportune time to raise standards for the faculty and in 1935 the "Standing Committee on Educational Policies" made such proposals. The committee suggested to Ruthven that "junior instructors" be called thereafter "teaching fellows," and recommended that the title of associate professor no longer be conferred as a reward for faithful service, but instead designate a person with all the attributes of a full professor. These individuals would remain as associate professors, the committee suggested, until an opening occurred in the professors' ranks.[47] Ruthven concurred, and the regents instituted the new standards.[48]

As conditions improved, Ruthven proudly told President Angell of Yale: "Michigan has not decreased salaries this year. On the contrary we have made increases totaling approximately three hundred and eight thousand dollars. Salary cuts were not restored by percentages, but increases were given where most merited."[49] Ruthven remembered Depression times as some of the better years of his regime since, despite forced economies, teaching and learning continued unabated and morale was higher than expected in hard times.[50] His papers reveal that he once confided to friends: "I am not at all discouraged. . . . I must even admit that the curtailment of our resources has permitted me to make certain changes in the organization which I believe will be of lasting benefit."[51]

NOTES

1. F. Clever Bald, *Michigan in Four Centuries* (New York: Harper and Brothers, 1954), p. 404.

2. *Ibid.*, p. 405.

3. For much of the discussion of legislative history which follows the author is indebted to David B. Laird, Jr., "The Regents of The University of Michigan, and the Legislature of the State 1920–1950," doctoral dissertation, University of Michigan, 1972, pp. 45–117, passim.

4. See Laird, pp. 77–80.

5. Alexander Ruthven to Wilber M. Brucker, April 17, 1931, Ruthven Papers, box 3, MHC.

6. Ruthven to Brucker, May 11, 1931, *ibid.*

7. William L. Clements to Ruthven, June 9, 1931, *ibid.*

8. Ruthven to Clements, January 12, 1933, Ruthven Papers, box 8, MHC.

9. Michigan governors were elected every two years. During the 1930's a pattern was established: When Franklin D. Roosevelt won in national elections, he swept Democratic governors into office in Michigan; in off-year elections the predominantly Republican state returned a Republican governor to the state house. Willis F. Dunbar, *Michigan: A History of the Wolverine State* (Grand Rapids: William B. Eerdmans Publishing Co., 1965), p. 654.

10. Ruthven to Frank D. Fitzgerald, December 10, 1934, Ruthven Papers, box 15, MHC.

11. Howard H. Peckham, *The Making of the University of Michigan* (Ann Arbor: University of Michigan Press, 1967), p. 173.

12. Kent Sagendorph, *Michigan: The Story of the University* (New York: E.P. Dutton and Co., 1948), p. 312.

13. Ruthven, Speech to "The Club," December 11, 1948, "Miscellaneous IV" folder, Ruthven Papers, box 77, MHC.

14. Ruthven to Ralph Stone, December 20, 1930, Ruthven Papers, box 4, MHC.

15. Interview, December 17, 1974.

16. Interviews, December 18, 1974 and December 17, 1974. For the record, Ruthven was listed in various "Who's Who" publications as a Republican.

17. Ruthven to George P. McCallum, October 4, 1938, Ruthven Papers, box 28, MHC.

18. Interview, April 30, 1970.

19. Interview, February 17, 1970.

20. Interview, January 20, 1970.

21. Alexander G. Ruthven, *Naturalist in Two Worlds* (Ann Arbor: University of Michigan Press, 1963), p. 82.

22. *Ibid.,* pp. 82–83.

23. *Ibid.,* pp. 83–84. For a comparison of the growth of Michigan colleges and universities, see Willis F. Dunbar, *The Michigan Record in Higher Education* (Detroit: Wayne State University Press, 1963).

24. *Ibid.,* p. 80.

25. Sagendorph, *Michigan: The Story of the University,* p. 315.

26. Ruthven to Glenn Frank, April 25, 1932, Ruthven Papers, box 6, MHC.

27. Ruthven to Walter A. Jessup, February 28, 1933, Ruthven Papers, box 9, MHC.

28. Fred I. Chase Commission of Inquiry, undated 1932, Ruthven Papers, box 8, MHC.

29. *The President's Report for 1933–1934,* Vol. 36, No. 29, p. 2

30. Letter of W. C. Hoad to Ruthven, March 30, 1933, Ruthven Papers, box 9, MHC.

31. Interview, Alexander G. Ruthven, February 3, 1970. Dr. Ruthven told the author that Mr. Christensen, the Controller, would drive to Lansing with a state police escort, gather up the "nickels and dimes" from the state treasury, and return to Ann Arbor where he would spend all night counting the money so that the next day's payroll could be met. This story is also mentioned in Ruthven's *Naturalist in Two Worlds,* pp. 63–64.

32. *The President's Report for 1933–1934,* Vol. 34, No. 29, pp. 1–2.

33. Interview, Alexander G. Ruthven, February 3, 1970.

34. The Carnegie Foundation had originally intended that its annuity plan would be sufficient for retiring professors. It was not, and so the plan under TIAA (originally associated with the Carnegie Foundation but independent since 1930) provided that both the faculty member and the institution pay premiums toward a retirement allowance.

35. O. J. Campbell to Ruthven, September 28, 1933, Ruthven Papers, box 12, MHC.

36. Alexander G. Ruthven, "Some Thoughts on Retiring Ages." *Proceedings of the Association of Governing Boards of State Universities and Allied Institutions,* November 15–17, 1934. While Ruthven's candor was usually unquestioned, the first two appointments to "distinguished professorships" removed from deanships Marcus L. Ward of the School of Dentistry and Herbert C. Sadler of the College of Engineering. The Ruthven Papers reveal that he was unhappy over the lack of progress in both of these units, and the deanships were filled by Russell Bunting and Henry C. Anderson, both known to be sympathetic to Ruthven's wishes.

37. *The Michigan Alumnus,* Vol. 39, No. 20 (1933), p. 327.

38. NYA folder, Ruthven Papers, box 30, MHC.
39. *The President's Report for 1930–1931*, Vol. 33, No. 14, p. 11.
40. *The President's Report for 1933–1934*, Vol. 36, No. 29, p. 11.
41. *Proceedings of the Board of Regents*, May Meeting, 1931, p. 629.
42. *The President's Report for 1935–1936*, Vol. 38, No. 36, p. 47.
43. "Scholarships for Tomorrow's Leaders," *The Michigan Alumnus*, Vol. 49, No. 8 (1943), pp. 139–140.
44. Sagendorph, *Michigan: The Story of the University*, p. 318.
45. *The Michigan Alumnus*, Vol. 39, No. 30 (1933), p. 516.
46. When asked about the origin of the Rackham gift Ruthven related the following story: Three men named Anderson, Couzens, and Rackham were members of a small law firm in Detroit. They were attorneys to Henry Ford and, since Ford had no money, he reimbursed the attorneys with stock in the Ford Motor Company. When the company boomed, the three attorneys suddenly were millionaires many times over. Rackham, however, was a shy, unambitious man who continued his frugal existence in a little house in Detroit.

Horace Rackham became acquainted with Dr. Francis W. Kelsey and secretly financed Kelsey's archeological work in Egypt for many years. Ruthven met Rackham only once—at a dinner at The Detroit Club—and had the impression that Rackham was more interested in Kelsey as a person than in either archeology or the University of Michigan.

When Horace Rackham died, he left several million dollars to his wife and had several million dollars in a trust fund. Bryson Horton, Mrs. Rackham's brother, was the administrator of the fund; he was assisted by a committee of Mrs. Rackham, a Detroit lawyer named Wilcox, and Judge Arthur Lacey, also of Detroit.

Horton, as a Michigan alumnus, discussed with Ruthven the disposal of the trust. Horton announced that he intended to give the trust funds to either the Rockefeller or Carnegie foundations and Ruthven concluded that the University would receive nothing. Horton visited both Rockefeller and Carnegie and was disappointed that neither had any suggestions which interested him. He and Ruthven talked again, and discussed a number of university projects, all in the one hundred to two hundred thousand dollar range. Then Ruthven had a sudden insight. He suggested to Horton that the trust be used to build a real graduate school, for the present graduate school—consisting of a dean, a secretary, and a floating office—was only a "paper" school. Horton liked the idea and, since he virtually dominated the trust committee, coerced the others into agreement. Plans proceeded rapidly, and it was agreed that the magnificent building would be named for Mr. Rackham. Ruthven was insistent on an endowment to accompany the building.

During all of the discussions Ruthven never met with Mrs. Rackham. He continued his conversations with Horton, for he was interested in having Mrs. Rackham's funds support a project in geriatrics. Horton thought that Mrs. Rackham, who was a Christian Scientist, would not be interested. Nevertheless, Ruthven invited Mrs. Rackham and her sister to the campus so that he might present his ideas. When the two women called on the president in his office, neither was moved by his presentation, and all Mrs. Rackham would say was, "I'm not interested."

Dr. Ruthven then suggested that the sisters stop by the Ruthven house to rest a bit before proceeding to Detroit. Mrs. Ruthven was not in when they arrived but was in the arbor picking grapes for jelly. When Mrs. Ruthven came into the house she was covered with grape juice, and the women were surprised to see each other. Mrs. Ruthven then told the sisters that she could make jam better than the cook and didn't mind washing clothes if she had to. Mrs. Rackham liked this common touch, and the ice was broken.

About three weeks later when the president went into his office his secretary, Miss Rouse, said, "I hope you have a strong heart today." In his mail there were envelopes containing $2,000,000 in securities, but no name or note was attached. Ruthven knew Mrs. Rackham was responsible, and phoned Horton to tell him that he proposed to write Mrs. Rackham "the nicest letter you ever saw." Horton was horrified and said that Ruthven must not write because Mrs. Rackham might change her mind. This gift became the Institute for Human Adjustment. (Interview, February 3, 1970. Also, with slight variations, in *Naturalist in Two Worlds,* pp. 139–40 and pp. 147–49.)

47. Ruthven to Professor H.A. Sanders, February 8, 1935, Ruthven Papers, box 16, MHC.

48. *Proceedings of the Board of Regents,* April meeting, 1935, pp. 563–65.

49. Telegram from Alexander G. Ruthven to James R. Angell, October 10, 1935, Ruthven Papers, box 17, MHC.

50. Interview, Alexander G. Ruthven, February 3, 1970.

51. Ruthven to Dr. Howard A. Kelly, October 7, 1933, Ruthven Papers, box 12, MHC.

7

Daily Routine

The thirties were good years for the Ruthvens. To be sure, some sacrifices had to be made. One was leaving the lovely home on Fair Oaks where the family had lived so comfortably for eight years. The huge white presidents' house at 815 South University was hardly a hovel, but despite its roominess and its luxuries, it was never truly "home" to the Ruthven family. It was a "goldfish bowl" and the Ruthvens felt it their obligation to "install three telephones in the house, and proceed to let parents, staff members, students, and alumni know that they were welcome to appeal for help at any hour of the day or night."[1]

"The furnishings for the house were our responsibility," Ruthven remembered, "and we decided that they should reflect the type of architecture and the Angell tradition. Being a family of collectors we had through the years assembled pictures and other art objects and interesting and rare books which we arranged to attract student attention. We also placed in the library copies of the publications of members of the faculty and a bronze bas-relief of President Angell. Our objective was to create an interesting home atmosphere for the family, the staff, the alumni, and particularly the students."[2]

Dr. H. Marvin Pollard of the Medical School confirmed Ruthven's availability. "Any time there was a faculty tragedy, day or night, Dr. Ruthven wanted to be called," Pollard said. "Many times I called him in the middle of the night."[3]

STUDENT TEAS

The Ruthvens especially enjoyed having students in their house for two reasons: Ruthven, who was paternalistic, liked to think that even students in a huge university had a home they could visit and, secondly, he felt that a university should accept the responsibility for the informal training of its students. For these reasons he and Mrs. Ruthven introduced weekly student teas. At first few students attended, but as the custom was established the Ruthven house overflowed. Eventually as many as 500 people would gather for a Ruthven tea; visiting alumni came, too. Ruthven enjoyed these gatherings and mingled easily with the students.[4] He was particularly proud that the student teas made campus adjustments easier for foreign students.[5] Furthermore, the teas had a practical value: informal tête-à-têtes with campus leaders provided insurance, Ruthven felt, against personal attack in student publications.[6]

Stories of Michigan's rich traditions never fail to mention the Ruthven student teas, and old-time faculty recall with favor the first family's willingness to open its home, not only to students, but also to faculty groups.[7] Visiting personalities were often Ruthven house guests: Eugene Ormandy, Charles A. Lindbergh, Marian Anderson, Ezio Pinza, Eleanor Roosevelt, Robert Frost, Robert M. Hutchins,

815 South University, The Presidents' House

Alexander G. Ruthven of Michigan

Arthur Vandenberg, Madam Chiang Kai-Shek, and Cornelia Otis Skinner were only a few of the campus guests entertained by the Ruthvens.[8] Nevertheless, it was a hectic life for Michigan's president and his family. Mrs. Ruthven supervised the maid, gardener, and cook (who were provided along with the house), entertained frequently, and managed the family budget. Genteel, and very much a lady, she cared little about the trappings of gentility: clothes, jewelry, or gourmet food. Like her husband, she was frugal to an extreme. She was a heavy smoker and suffered all her life from ulcers and migraine headaches, but never allowed her personal discomforts to limit her daily support for her husband.[9]

Although the Ruthven children had grown to maturity by the thirties, they were frequently with their parents. Kate, the oldest, after graduating from the university, married Laurence Stuart, a young zoology professor, and the Stuart family regularly joined the Ruthvens for Sunday dinner.[10] Peter also received his degree from Michigan and continued his studies in Islamic art. He was at home unless with the Michigan archeological expeditions at Karanis, Egypt. Bryant ("Bud"), the youngest, after completing University High School, studied at Albion College, and was the frequent recipient of affectionate letters full of fatherly advice.[11]

One concludes, in retrospect, that the Ruthvens were considerate, loving parents to their three children, but that relationships suffered in direct proportion to the increasing responsibilities of the parents. Ruthven was a wise, practical man on most issues, and child-rearing was no exception. He gave his views to the Parent-Education Institute in 1932:

> Too little control encourages the development of a self-centered, unhappy, and intemperate individualism which closes the mind to impressions and suggestions and thus retards the learning process. Excessive control conduces to timidity, dependence, and an apathetic social attitude which makes for ineffectualness, and robs learning of the important element of independent thinking. Somewhere between the extremes . . . there is a degree of parental direction which keeps a child from playing with sharp tools until old enough to appreciate the danger, and at the same time leaves him free to venture and to make those mistakes which are better than no mistakes in the process of learning.[12]

The philosophy is sound; unfortunately, one suspects that reality was somewhat less so, and that the Ruthven children would have profited from more time with their parents and, perhaps, more control.[13]

Dr. Ruthven worked hard. *The Michigan Daily* reported that he followed an "exhausting schedule" of university activities for six days a week, for he would rise at 6:30 a.m. and not retire until 11:30 p.m.[14] Typically, he would appear at his office at 9:00 a.m. and Ruth Rouse, his secretary, would take dictation until 10:00 a.m., when he would see his first appointment.[15] In the afternoons there were more appointments and, usually, committee meetings, for Ruthven continued to attend the meetings of divergent campus committees throughout his presidency. Those senior staffers with whom he felt comfortable—Bruce, Stason, and Yoakum—were sometimes invited to Ruthven's home for individual sessions. Part of each day was usually spent with Shirley W. Smith, vice president and secretary of the university, who managed business affairs, and with Frank E. Robbins, assistant to the president. Robbins, in fact, was a deft letter writer who answered the bulk of routine presidential correspondence. Whenever possible, Ruthven tried to save three half days each week for self-renewal. On these occasions he might read—he read voraciously all his life—or write or, best of all, steal away for a ride on horseback.[16] Dinners were frequently business occasions, and Bryant Ruthven recalls that many times an entire week would pass and the family would not have an evening meal together. In the evenings, the senior Ruthven would often work on his speeches, since he preferred to write his own. Ruthven had bouts with insomnia on occasion and passed the hours in reading.[17]

Obviously, it was impossible to feel entirely comfortable in what was, essentially, a public house and a public office. "I felt fine strolling along the sidewalk on South 'U'," Bryant Ruthven recalls, "but the moment I turned into the walk leading to the President's house I felt everybody's eyes on my back."[18] His father felt the same kind of pressure. Ruthven admonished the Lawyers' Club: "It does not seem quite fitting that, when the University girls call on me and sing songs as they do once or twice a year, they should be accompanied by hootings and catcalls from across the street."[19]

Ruthven found relief from these pressures by rediscovering horseback riding, the sport of his youth. During his years as a serious scientist, his interest in horses lay dormant, and he seldom found the opportunity to ride. However, Bryant, his younger son, was growing up to be a promising equestrian and both cherished the associations promoted by this common bond. Furthermore, horses pro-

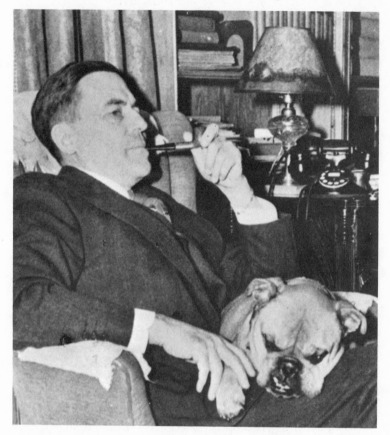

In the Study

vided a welcome and necessary escape from the rigors of the presidency. Sometimes, when faced with a weighty problem, Ruthven found that a brisk ride on horseback would clear his mind. It was for these reasons that, soon after becoming president, Ruthven and a riding companion, Dr. Albert C. "Octy" Furstenberg—later dean of the medical school—agreed to keep a stable outside of Ann Arbor near Dixboro. In addition to the stable the Ruthvens and Furstenbergs bought "Knollcrest," a house near Dixboro which they used for weekend retreats.

However, both Ruthvens were essentially private people and,

although the Dixboro arrangement provided some relief from the pressing public functions of his office, they yearned for a more permanent hideaway. His friend, Dr. Russell Bunting of the dental school, had a summer home on Crystal Lake near Frankfort and, while visiting Bunting, Ruthven surveyed the area. He especially liked Frankfort, a tiny resort community tight to the eastern shore of Lake Michigan about two hundred miles north and west of Ann Arbor.[20] Here, in 1931, he bought a wooded tract high on a bluff overlooking the lake and began to build his "summer cottage." The house was constructed of wood and cinder block in long, low ranch style, and one is reminded again that Ruthven spent his youth on the Iowa frontier. The spacious living room, with stone fireplace and exposed beams, looks out at the lake from tall picture windows. Two wings jut back from the lakeside; they enclose bedrooms for family and guests. A long farm lane leads to the house on the bluff, and in the open fields around the lane are the stables, riding ring, and jumps Ruthven built for his beloved horses.

Stanerigg Stables

117

Alexander G. Ruthven of Michigan

Soon after the Ruthven summer home was completed, the Furstenbergs bought land and built a cottage adjoining the Ruthven property on the bluff north of Frankfort. These closest of neighbors became the closest of friends. President Ruthven, head of a great university, was just plain "Buzz" to the Furstenberg kids. A typical summer evening would find both families in one living room or the other where the paterfamilias talked quietly, usually of university matters, while Mrs. Ruthven knit or read and Mrs. Furstenberg played cards with Peter, the elder of the Ruthven boys. These family friendships were cemented by a common love of horses, since everyone was expected to ride. Even Mrs. Ruthven learned, for it pleased her husband to have "Lizzie," as he affectionately called her, ride the quiet woodland trails with him. The children worried, for "Lizzie" was over fifty when she began riding and frail besides. She took at least two bad falls, but, undeterred, continued astride Wineglass, her favorite.

The horses were transported from the stable at Dixboro to Frankfort by various means. Sometimes a special Arms Yager railroad car—a relic of army cavalry days—was chartered. That wasn't entirely satisfactory because the horses balked at entering the car and, once in, they were bumped and bruised in transit. Sometimes the horses were carried by truck, but since there were usually a dozen or more in the stable it was necessary to take more than one trip. Twice Bryant Ruthven and Jimmy Dolan, the stable manager, rode their own horses all the way to Frankfort, the string in tow. However they came, the arrival of the horses was cause for rejoicing by the children of Frankfort, for the horses signalled the advent of summer and with it the annual rodeo.

The rodeos were staged, ostensibly, for the Ruthven and Furstenberg offspring and for the youth of Frankfort, who were invited to participate, too. Sometimes professional bucking stock were imported for the occasion, and the Frankfort high school band performed, though its summer repertoire was limited. The elders shared in the excitement, and rode in the "Grand Parade" which introduced the festivities. The pièce de résistance was provided by stable manager Jimmy Dolan, his wife Catherine, and Bryant Ruthven. The Dolans were former professionals and adept trick riders, while the youngest Ruthven liked to demonstrate his skill as a roper and steer rider. In later years, some rodeo circuit riders Jimmy Dolan knew were contracted to perform.

The early rodeos were staged to coincide with the arrival of the

Frankfort Summers

regents and their spouses, for during the thirties Ruthven invited the entire board to informal summer meetings at Frankfort. The local performances, although enthusiastic, occasionally failed to captivate the audience. Bryant still remembers "Mrs. Beal, in her lovely, imperious way, pointing her cane and ordering the clown, played by a local boy, to move on down the track so she could get a better view of the action." One another occasion, a "wild" steer volunteered by a local farmer ambled to the center of the arena and lay down, much to the consternation of Bryant, its rider, who was derisively dubbed "Sitting Bull" by Regent David Crowley.

When the rodeo was over, the regents might get in a round of golf at the nearby Crystal Downs Country Club, or help the host as he supervised the preparation of the martinis and steaks. The goodwill generated by this easy summer camaraderie must have seen the president and the regents through the stresses of many difficult meetings in the months that followed.

The Ruthvens' summer residence became a focal point for many colleagues and friends for, in addition to the Furstenbergs, the Bruces and the Buntings were at nearby Crystal Lake. "Aunt Maud" Hagle, Mrs. Ruthven's sister, built a small summer cottage nearby as did Mr. and Mrs. Donald Bacon of Ann Arbor, personal friends of Alexander and Florence Ruthven. After Bryant married his Albion classmate, Beatrice Nesbitt, in 1940, they, too, had a summer place on the bluff north of Frankfort.

Senior staff were invited to visit the Ruthven compound on occasion, and mixed business with pleasure. Dr. Ruthven continued university correspondence from Frankfort, although it was sometimes necessary for him to take the train to Ann Arbor when university business pressed. Still, for much of the time from mid-June to early September university cares were at a minimum.

Ruthven was at his bucolic best at Frankfort. He loved the peaceful upland pasture where his herd grazed, the wind rustling the oaks on his bluff, the waves pounding on his beach. There was joy in a leisurely ride with "Lizzie," and delight in watching "Bud" or "Octy" dash their mounts across the fields and through the woods. Surrounded by family and friends, with time for his horses, freed temporarily from the cares of office, he was at home in Frankfort.

On two occasions during the thirties Ruthven supplemented time spent at Frankfort with lengthy excursions from the campus.

In 1930, he and his son Bryant spent the summer near Salt Lake City collecting specimens. The trip was great therapy for the father, and it left indelible memories with the son, too:

> On our trip in 1930, I was old enough [twelve] to be a full-time collecting partner, shooting and collecting specimens, and 'pickling' at the end of the day. I was, however, not the most heroic half of the team. Our quarry was largely lizards and snakes—mostly rattlesnakes. The procedure was to locate a specimen, then shoot it. We used .22 caliber bird shot which was often not immediately fatal to a snake or large lizard, especially since, when shooting, we were to try not to damage the neck scales (which, as I recall, were important in the classification process). Then we would pick up the specimen with a pair of obstetrical forceps, put it in a cloth bag, and put that bag in the knapsack we each carried.
>
> "Be as careful as you can," Dad warned me at the beginning of the trip but, should I be bitten, I needn't worry, as he carried an antivenom kit. That was reassuring, but not completely. To this day I remember how Dad would pick up a squirming rattlesnake, bag it, put it in his knapsack, and stroll unconcernedly across the desert

searching for more specimens, with only a piece of canvas between his back and that writhing, rattling snake. I wouldn't get within twenty feet of him on those occasions. Most of that summer our base was at an isolated ranch in Skull Valley, Utah, where Dad and I shared a small cabin. It was a relationship we always fondly remembered and we talked about our experiences years later. On those occasions I would remind Dad how, after boarding the train at Wendover on our return trip, he was sorting through our equipment and suddenly began to chuckle. When I asked what was so funny, he showed me the anti-venom kit. It contained no needle.[21]

Then, in December, 1933, President and Mrs. Ruthven sailed for Karanis, Egypt, to see their son, Peter, and to inspect the university's archeological site there. The sojourn was most enjoyable for the Ruthvens, who were impressed with the cordial reception accorded them, not only by the site team from Michigan, but also by their Arab hosts. Much to his surprise, Ruthven was asked to have an audience with King Fuad, who had personal knowledge of the university's explorations in Egypt.[22]

These two off-campus field trips in the early thirties represented Ruthven's weaning from the university museum. At first, he deluded himself into believing that he could retain, concurrent with the presidency, all of his titles and responsibilities in the museums. However, before two years of presidential office were concluded, it became obvious that his new master, the university, demanded his total allegiance. The museums were suffering from neglect, and so he asked Frederick M. Gaige, his trusted protégé, to take the responsibility for the Museum of Zoology and, later, all university museums.[23] Gaige replied that he would take responsibility reluctantly, on condition that Ruthven retain the title of "Director." "I know of no one so qualified except yourself," Gaige explained; "the job has been a life one . . . and to terminate it would be quite unfair to yourself and [the] museums." "You must remember," Gaige added, "that regardless of the success you are achieving as president . . . there is a lot of the world that will think of you as a museum director first, then herpetologist, then president."[24]

There is no question that "Dick" Gaige's appeal was genuine, just as there is no question that Ruthven sincerely wanted to keep his ties to the museums. In 1931, he published 600 copies of A Naturalist in a University Museum for his scientist friends and colleagues. The small book was his testimonial to over a quarter of a century of museum life; he outlined precisely what a university museum can and should be. In another sense, the book closed a chapter on his life. It was impossible to be both university president and active scientist and, despite the entreaties of his scientific colleagues and his own infrequent efforts to "keep his hand in," the museums began to fade from his thoughts. In 1933 he offered a course, Zoogeography 242, with Laurence Stuart, his son-in-law.[25] That same year he wrote to a faculty colleague, "I do not think much of titles but I suppose you better refer to me as president of the University and director of University Museums. The second half of this title is the one that really appeals to me."[26] Ruthven continued to shepherd museum activities for a few more years, but it was a frustrating and fruitless endeavor. He could not keep up, his museum staff did not do things as he would have done them, and he was reduced to sending the loyal Gaige sharp reminders because "you do not answer your correspondence."[27] By 1936 it was obvious to everyone that the charade could not be continued, and Ruthven relinquished all direct responsibility for the museums. He was fleetingly tempted when, in 1937, he was approached about becoming Managing Director of the Philadelphia Zoological Garden, but he refused, saying he was certain "that the Board of Regents would not want to release me from my present duties."[28] Ruthven served as chairman of a doctoral committee in zoology in 1940; this is the last evidence of direct involvement in his chosen profession. He would always be haunted by thoughts that he had made a mistake in leaving it.

NOTES

1. Alexander G. Ruthven, *Naturalist in Two Worlds* (Ann Arbor: University of Michigan Press, 1963), p. 30.

2. *Ibid.,* p. 31. The only structural changes made by the Ruthvens during their twenty-two years at 814 S. University were a private study for the president and a glassed-in plant room for Mrs. Ruthven. ("The Presidents' House," J. Fraser Cocks, III, Michigan Historical Collections.)

3. Interview, H. Marvin Pollard, January 13, 1975.

4. Interview, Erich Walter, February 21, 1970.

5. *Naturalist in Two Worlds,* pp. 92–93. Michigan was one of the leading American universities in enrollment of foreign students, and in the mid-30s had more oriental and Latin-American students than any other university in the United States. *The President's Report for 1935–1936,* vol. 38, no. 36, pp. 54–58.

Daily Routine

6. Interview, Alexander G. Ruthven, February 6, 1970.
7. Interview, Hazel Losh, February 11, 1970.
8. Interview, Bryant Ruthven, December 17, 1974.
9. Interview, Bryant Ruthven, December 17, 1974 and Mrs. Julie Furstenberg Owens, December 18, 1974.
10. Letter, Enoch E. Peterson, December 9, 1974. They were married on either June 17, 1931 or June 18, 1931. "Kate" and her husband never agreed on the date! (Letter from Laurence C. Stuart, February 1, 1976.)
11. Alexander G. Ruthven to "Bud," October, 1937 to June 3, 1938, Ruthven Papers, box 20–20, MHC. E.g. "I have been noticing . . . that you are still wondering about what you are going to do and what you should be training yourself for. I have tried to persuade you that you should not worry your head about such a thing, but apparently without success. I am now giving you an order. Put the matter entirely out of your mind. There are 100,000 different things you could do and there is no reason at your time in life to begin to fuss. Just forget about the whole thing and get an all-around college course—and some fun out of it. Thus speaks a great educator!" (January 4, 1938).
12. "A Compilation of Addresses Presented at the Third Annual Parent-Education Institute at the University of Michigan," *Parent Education,* November 3, 4, and 5, 1932, speech file, MHC.
13. Bryant Ruthven told the author that neither of his parents were disciplinarians and that both avoided any family conflicts. (Interview, December 17, 1974.)
14. *The Michigan Daily,* May 21, 1951, p. 5.
15. Ruth Rouse was Ruthven's secretary during the twenty-two-year presidency. She was the epitome of efficiency, loyalty, and discretion although, in private, she willingly offered the president her opinions of university affairs.
16. This description of Ruthven's presidential routine is taken from notes on 3×5 cards in the Stason file, Ruthven Papers, box 32, MHC. These notes are undated and unsigned, but are undoubtedly Ruthven's work.
17. Interview, Bryant Ruthven, December 17, 1974.
18. *Ibid.*
19. Ruthven to Professor E. C. Goddard, May 2, 1934, Ruthven Papers, box 12, MHC.
20. The descriptions of Frankfort activities which follow are based on interviews with Bryant Ruthven (December 17, 1974) and Mrs. Julie Furstenberg Owens (December 18, 1974).
21. Bryant Ruthven, November 26, 1974.
22. Ruthven, *Naturalist in Two Worlds,* pp. 14–18. For further information about this trip see correspondence between Ruthven and Enoch E. Peterson, Ruthven Papers, box 10–18, MHC.
23. Ruthven to Frederick M. Gaige, July 11, 1931, Ruthven Papers, 5–11, MHC.
24. Gaige to Ruthven, July 14, 1931, Ruthven Papers, 5–11, MHC.
25. Ruthven to G.R. LaRue, July 11, 1933, Ruthven Papers, box 9, MHC.
26. Ruthven to A.F. Shull, June 1, 1933, Ruthven Papers, box 10, MHC.
27. Ruthven to Gaige, February 11, 1935, Ruthven Papers, box 15, MHC. Some faculty in the museum eventually felt betrayed because Ruthven left his work with them. (Interviews, Dr. Theodore H. Hubbell, January 13, 1975 and Dr. Edgar Kahn, December 8, 1974.) Gaige, despite Ruthven's admonitions about his

lax administrative habits, frequently passed friendly notes and little gifts to Ruthven. One Ruthven response was:
"Dear Dick:
I am late with my thanks for the stimulating birthday gift. Such things are good for the old man—and I do surely feel old at times. You really do too much for me, Dick. I do not want you to feel ever that I am not appreciative. This job has done something to me."
(April 13, 1939, Ruthven Papers, box 20, MHC)
28. See "Philadelphia Zoological Gardens," Ruthven Papers, box 25, MHC.

8

Character Education

Alexander Ruthven's personal attitudes and values and his sense of obligation *in loco parentis* formed the basis of an interesting program which he introduced to the Michigan campus during the Depression years. He called it "humanizing" the university or "character education"; the terms referred to the whole range of student activities now referred to as "student affairs."

Ruthven's attitudes and values were, not surprisingly, in keeping with his times and his midwestern heritage. His parents were humorless, Bible-toting Methodists, and he had a well-developed ethical system in keeping with the religious instruction he received as a boy. During his years as a student, the scientific search for truth became for him a religion unto itself. The blend that eventually emerged deviated little from the social standards established by church and society, although it spurned organized religion itself as intolerant, sterile, and stilted. Except for a few rare occasions he did not attend church. Religion for him was "not a matter of external observance of creeds and dogmas, but the unifying force in the life of the individual and the coordinating factor in group living. . . ."[1]

"Ethical and religious values are to be determined only with a full knowledge of the nature of the world and of man," Ruthven thought, and he defined a religious attitude as "the product of a confidence that there are rules of conduct which are right for us because [they are] established on known principles; a knowledge that we are as a world improving our organization by individual effort; and a faith that sometime our knowledge will be sufficient to reveal a coordinated universe of which we are a part."[2]

Ruthven's creed obviously shed the fundamentalism but not the ethical standards of his Methodist forebears who might well have been scandalized to know that he indulged in drinking, smoking, and dancing and did not regard these as moral issues.[3] His rejection of dogma, mysticism, and blind faith, his optimistic belief in the worth of the individual and humanity, and his endorsement of the methods of science showed his religious attitudes more nearly akin to Universalism than Methodism. Indeed, his son thought that his attitudes were more nearly Universalist than any other religion.[4] In any case, Ruthven had enough confidence in his beliefs to open them to public scrutiny through speeches, sermons, and articles.

It was these somewhat liberal attitudes, tempered by traditional ethical standards, that Ruthven sought to impose on the Michigan students of the thirties. He fully appreciated, as a parent and as a zoologist, that living organisms undergo gradual development and that the environment enveloping a plant or animal influences that development. Students were still developing, he felt, and could not yet be considered adult. To Ruthven, they were children or, at best, young adults. Moreover, they were, in a real sense to him, his children. He felt strongly that it was wrong for them to be cast, rudderless, into the impersonal milieu of a huge university. The Depression, with its destitute families at home and its inadequate housing and reduced faculties on the campus, heightened Ruthven's resolve.

He began to develop the theme of "character education." He told the National Association of State Universities meeting in 1933 that the nation's teachers and administrators had been stressing "aptitudes to the neglect of spiritual growth and unified development. It has not been fully recognized," Ruthven said, "that the final and net result of the educational process should be . . . a person trained to maintain his physical well-being and to grow continuously both mentally and spiritually." He went on to say that the college graduate was "handicapped by lack of experience . . . in the broad field of human relations." Doctors, he explained, had hospital practice and lawyers performed before a mock court, but the typical college graduate who would be required to pass judgment on his community's social problems would be "little more inclined than anyone else to act upon knowledge and reasoned judgements rather than upon his emotions in the field of human relations."[5] In his *President's Report for 1933–1934* he urged careful study of the possibilities of "orientation to life" and he quoted Emerson's thesis that "character is higher than intellect. . . ."[6]

On the campus Ruthven launched a broad "humanizing" program. He wrote to his riding companion H. B. Earhart that he was "trying to make every individual member of the staff feel the responsibility of furthering the interests of the institution. . . ."[7] He advised the veteran registrar, Ira M. Smith, to be more considerate with students who came to that office, for parents, students, and alumni had complained to him of mistreatment.[8] The qualifications for admission to the university were rewritten. "While definite evidence of intellectual capacity is indispensable," the new guidelines stated, "the University believes that . . . positive qualities of character and personality should operate as determining factors in admission." Ruthven further recommended that the registrar's office utilize personal interviews, aptitude tests, and psychological examinations in choosing an entering class.[9]

It was also agreed that "ability as a teacher includes not only proficiency in classroom instruction but also interest and success in student guidance. . . ."[10] Within the College of Literature, Science, and the Arts, Professors Russell Hussey, Erich Walter, and Lewis Vander Velde began to offer their services as academic counselors to students.[11] When the new dean of dentistry told Ruthven that he wished the dental school to stress a professional attitude, Ruthven reminded him: "I would like to see emphasized always in the professional schools the desirability of a broad cultural training underlying the professional work. . . . You are also interested in turning out doctors who have the training to be intelligent citizens."[12] He informed university benefactor Tracy W. McGregor: "Our student health service is by far the best in the country. . . . Among other things, we introduced a psychiatrist so quietly that the youngsters accepted him without question." He added that the faculty had recently done away with its disciplinary committee and had substituted instead a committee on student conduct which would "try to train students to be good rather than punish them for being bad."[13]

RELIGIOUS EDUCATION

In Ann Arbor, by 1930, it had become customary for the local churches to sponsor religious programs for students and to retain an assistant pastor to counsel university students of each denomination. Many churches had their own religious activity buildings on the campus periphery. The university-supported religious activities were under the aegis of the Student Christian Association, which dated from pre-Civil War days, but which had aroused little campus enthusiasm since about 1920.[14]

127

Ruthven determined to revitalize the university's religious program. C. Grey Austin, who has chronicled the university's religious history, says of Ruthven: "It was not his intention to take religious activities out of the hands of students, but rather to establish the principle that the state university, which could never afford to be sectarian, could not, on the other hand, afford to neglect religion."[15] Ruthven recognized that Depression economies and the legislature's reluctance to get involved in a church-state controversy would preclude any funds from the state treasury, so he began to search for private support.

He had once talked with Cecil B. deMille about the need for greater emphasis on religious instruction, and he tried an indirect approach to the mogul of the movies. He told deMille that some of his plans at Michigan were already in progress, but that "owing to the well-known shortage in financial assistance" it would not be possible to employ a religious counselor, as he had hoped.[16] When deMille apparently did not respond to this broad hint, Ruthven turned to H. B. Earhart. This liaison paid dividends, for in July, 1932, the Earhart Foundation voted $2,500 for a Director of Religion at Michigan.[17]

The regents added funds to the Earhart grant, and renamed the position Counselor in Religious Education. The individual was to: "improve facilities for spiritual development; advise students about religion and other personal matters; act as a contact person between the University and religious agencies and be an advisor to the University in religious affairs."[18]

During the academic year 1932–33 many names were proposed to Ruthven and a number of clergymen wrote to recommend their own services, for not only did the Depression render any academic position attractive, it was understood that the Counselor in Religious Education would be a major university appointment. Many applicants were considered for almost a year, and Dr. Edward W. Blakeman, Director of the campus Wesley Foundation, was appointed.[19] Blakeman proved to be an active member of the administration and his close relationship with Ruthven enabled him to influence the course of all religious affairs on the campus.

The Student Christian Association was changed to the Student Religious Association in 1937 in order to include a very active group of Jewish students under the leadership of Rabbi Bernard Heller.[20] That same year a degree program in Religion and Ethics, which included fifty-three courses, was instituted in the Literary College. This program was not aimed at preparing ministers, but intended to prepare students "for intelligent spiritual and moral leadership in the modern world."[21]

RESIDENCE HALLS

President Little had advocated residence halls for women, but the wrath of the Ann Arbor landladies had forced him to abandon those plans. Ruthven, too, favored on-campus residential living, but resolved to move cautiously.[22] Even though the accommodations in Martha Cook, Mosher–Jordan, and Betsy Barbour residence halls were comfortable, their space was not adequate and there was a constant waiting list of Michigan women.[23] The shortage of men's housing was even more acute, for with the exception of the Lawyer's Club and Fletcher Hall, which housed only 124 men, there were no on-campus residences for a male student population of 7000. Assistant Dean of Students Fred B. Wahr and Dean of Students Joseph Bursley stressed to President Ruthven that more dormitories must be built promptly.[24] In 1936–37 Allen–Rumsey House, accommodating 120 men, was erected, and in 1938–39 a series of dormitories housing approximately 1500 students was constructed with federal funds from the Federal Emergency Administration of Public Works (PWA). Additional residence units were planned, and Ruthven and his student service deans turned their attention to the organization of these new dormitories.

A chance conversation with a group of visiting students from Oxford and Cambridge suggested the foundation for what became known as the Michigan House Plan.[25] The plan provided that dormitories be separated into "houses," each house to have its own student government, and its own shared dining facilities. High house morale was to be promoted through athletic, scholastic, and social competition.[26] Furthermore, a faculty resident advisor and a staff of graduate students were appointed for each house; their responsibilities were to set the academic tone and discipline. Each house also had a woman house director to oversee social life. A Board of Governors of residence halls was appointed and Professor Karl Litzenberger became Director of Residence Halls.[27] Houses were relatively small, for each unit accommodated only slightly more than 100 men. Lounges and recreation rooms added to the comfortable atmosphere. As a result of Ruthven's negotiations with the vice president of the J. L. Hudson Company, over 500 prints were obtained for house walls.[28] *The Michigan Alumnus* proclaimed the houses "comfortable as a club."[29]

FRATERNITIES

President Ruthven was not a fraternity man, but the Michigan campus had a long-standing fraternity tradition. The president's position was stated very simply: fraternities should "live up to their own ideals."[30] One reason he was so anxious to develop the dormitory system, Ruthven wrote an alumnus, was that fraternities "all too often have demonstrated . . . antisocial tendencies."[31]

When fraternities were lax in upholding their social codes, Ruthven did not hesitate to chastise them. In 1935, he called the fraternity officers and their alumni advisors together and told them that they must produce an immediate change in their social conduct or he would not hesitate to request that their national organizations withdraw charters. He did not, he told them, possess a reputation for attempting to "run a bluff. . . ."[32] *The Michigan Alumnus* reported: "Within a week society meetings had resulted in new house rules or a determination of strict adherence to hitherto unenforced regulations."[33]

Ruthven continued his attempt to tie fraternities more closely with university affairs. He insisted that fraternities be solvent in order to open their doors and thought it "very much to be desired" that fraternity business affairs be managed by the university.[34] However, in 1938 he told Joe Bursley, the Dean of Students, that a university-appointed Fraternity Relations Counselor would not be effective: "While I am willing to admit that some of the house presidents might cooperate with him, it is my opinion that the rank and file of fraternity members would immediately take the same attitude toward him as they do toward the staff of your office. . . ."[35] Peaceful coexistence was the only policy to take with fraternities, Ruthven concluded eventually. He knew that the fraternity experience was cherished by many loyal alumni and he understood that fraternities were an important and beneficial socializing influence on his huge campus, but he was troubled by doubts that fraternities were basically "undemocratic" and "intolerant."

FOOTBALL

Ruthven also learned to live with Big Ten football, but not willingly. He had played football at Morningside College, but football then was on a club basis, managed by the students strictly for fun. Michigan's football, by contrast, was big business. Newspaper reporters covered every aspect of Saturday's game and the stars on the football team became the mightiest heroes on campus. Michigan had the second largest college football stadium in the country, and crowds from all over the midwest filled it.[36] The alumni rose and fell with every electrifying victory and every heartwrenching defeat. Clearly, Ruthven felt, such "public spectacles" had no place in an institution of higher learning.

Ruthven attacked football in a manner befitting his deposed predecessor, C.C. Little. Speaking to the National Association of State Universities, he railed against "college administrators too much concerned with advertising and money values . . . professional coaches . . . the wasted time of the student . . . and the methods of securing athletes. . . ." He predicted that there would be a decline in football interest and suggested that intercollegiate athletics be reduced to "voluntary student activities within the physical education program."[37]

To Ruthven's surprise, his recommendations fell on deaf ears; he was told he "might as well have kicked the crucifix."[38] Regent Murfin, a football fan, was incensed. "This comes to me like a bolt from the sky," he wrote Ralph Aigler, Chairman of the Board in Control of Athletics. "If this is the forerunner of a suggestion from him to change the general scheme of things in connection with athletics . . . he is going to meet with some very lively opposition."[39]

Ruthven continued to retain a forlorn, and perhaps naive hope that intercollegiate athletics would return to the simple games of youth which he recalled from his undergraduate days. He suggested to Regent Ralph Stone that "we should 'halt the construction' of our physical education plant. . . . In the not too distant future I may need your help in developing the idea with the Board that we cannot go on as we have been."[40] The board, however, turned a deaf ear to the president's pleas.

When Coach Harry Kipke, whose teams had fallen on lean years, was forced to resign in 1937, it seemed that the resulting controversy was of major import to every citizen of the state. Ruthven told Regent David H. Crowley: "I have been so offended at the talk of those groups that I . . . have refused to attend games in recent years, hoping in a small way to indicate that I do not feel that intercollegiate athletics are of paramount importance in an educational institution."[41] It was like trying to stop an eclipse of the sun, for the new Michigan teams under Coach "Fritz" Crisler began to win again and were mentioned as likely participants in the Rose Bowl. "I will oppose such a game to the last ditch," Ruthven vowed, but few others would stand beside him and he could not combat the excessive pressure to send the team to California, particularly from the West Coast alumni. Even after Michigan defeated Southern California 48–0 in the 1948 Rose Bowl, he called the Rose Bowl arrangement a "mistake."[42]

When *The Michigan Alumnus* attempted to capitalize on the smashing victory by advertising cocktail glasses depicting the Rose Bowl champions, Ruthven termed the ads "offensive." "I shall talk with the Secretary of the [Alumni] Association," he vowed. "I shall make it clear that . . . it was very poor taste to print such an advertisement."[43]

After the reaction to his tirade at the National Association of State Universities, Ruthven refrained from public exposition of his antipathy to intercollegiate athletics in its present state, perhaps content in the knowledge that Michigan's athletic program, under the gentlemanly Directors of Athletics Fielding Yost and "Fritz" Crisler, was more honorable than most. He never again made athletics an issue with either students or staff, and in later years his opinions on the subject were not common knowledge.[44]

MINORITY GROUPS

Ruthven was, perhaps, well ahead of his time in his views of intercollegiate athletics. With regard to minority groups he was less progressive, but, once again, more tolerant than some of his contemporaries. He spoke out strongly against bigotry and intolerance in a powerful baccalaureate address to the class of 1932.[45] The record found in the Ruthven Papers indicates that his views were not always shared by the majority, for before World War II prejudice against Jews and, especially, blacks was often open. For example, an alumnus sent Ruthven a newspaper clipping of a track meet [his son was third behind two blacks] and spoke of his "extreme repugnance" to see blacks competing with whites.[46] Ruthven replied that he did not find such competition objectionable because, "after all, there will have to be a certain amount of association between the races when the boys are through college." Then, as was his usual practice when he disagreed with an alumnus or donor, he invited the irate parent to call on him the next time he was in Ann Arbor.[47]

On another occasion, the Board in Control of Athletics decided that a talented black football player, Willis Ward, should not, for his own safety, be allowed to play against Georgia Tech.[48] Ward was held out of the game "out of deference to the southerners," and Georgia Tech, as a goodwill gesture, told its own star to remain on the sidelines.[49] Ruthven felt that the Board in Control of Athletics should have foreseen the difficulty and was in error in scheduling the game, but—and this was another usual practice—he did not want to second-guess the board's decision.[50] The Ward incident became a cause célèbre on campus and in the press, and Ruthven told Shirley Smith, "My life is being made miserable by arguments with the colored brethren. . . . I wish now that I had taken the Ward matter into my own hands."[51]

In 1931, Ruthven addressed a primarily black audience on the subject of "Pride and Prejudice." Thinking persons should gain patience and hope, he told his audience, "from the obvious fact that in a reasonably short time there will be but one race in the United States. . . . The fact is one of biological inevitables." The vision of the biologist was tempered by the caution of the public figure, for he continued: "Racial changes are slow, can seldom be hurried . . . and may be promoted . . . not by exhibits of pride, by opposition, and by wrangling . . . but by modesty, by faithful performance of duties, and by frank recognition of the characteristics of mankind."[52] Ruthven's preaching to his "colored" friends would today be readily dismissed as a servile "Booker T. Washington" approach to racial inequities, but forty years ago his words were those which one would expect from an enlightened leader in higher education.

Of course, during most of Ruthven's regime there were fewer than one hundred blacks enrolled at the university.[53] This was before the days of affirmative action, Black Action Movements, and similar attempts to correlate the numbers of black students at the university with their numbers in the population at large. Black students posed very little challenge to a university president in the days when Ruthven was president.

Jews may have presented the president with more of a challenge. The legislature constantly asked why the university enrolled so many out-of-state students; the basis for this challenge may have been prejudice, for many out-of-staters were Jewish students from New York. Ruthven was firm in his defense of a diverse student body, and he was adamant when the governor of Michigan queried him about discrimination against Jews: "You may on every convenient occasion deny this vigorously."[54] He acknowledged, however, that in the medical school first preference was given to Michigan residents, that only a restricted number of out-of-state students were admitted, and that an attempt was made to achieve a distribution of these students from all over the United States. This, of course, could be interpreted as a subtle form of discrimination which placed Jewish students from New York at a distinct disadvantage.

It is impossible to estimate the permanent effect of Ruthven's efforts at "character education." Predictably, the requirement that faculty members concern themselves with student guidance drew some caustic comment from them "to the effect that promotion should not be a reward for minding other people's business."[55] Members of the faculty then have only hazy recollections now of those efforts. Understandably, on a campus with a faculty of almost 1000 few remember more than superficial personal contact with Ruthven.[56] Perhaps students saw more of their president. Ruthven recalled that he told his secretary to follow this simple rule when arranging office appointments: "Students get in first, faculty members second, and deans when they can."[57]

Those who recall the Ruthven years agree that most of the students found him genial, fair, and available. Sometimes at dusk Ruthven liked to dress in an old rain hat and tramp the campus with his bulldog, Eleanor, at his heels. He would stop at campus residence halls to chat amiably with the students, some of whom never realized the identity of their visitor until he left.[58] He was always willing to advise a student with troubles. Among themselves, the students knew Ruthven as "Butch."

Yet, a 1934 report of "Student Understanding and Attitude" showed that only 16 of 103 students felt they were an integral part of the university and just as important as faculty or administration.

Character Education

To the question of, "Do you have a feeling of resentment or rebellion toward University supervision, control, and direction of your conduct other than while in class?" 43 replied yes; 57 no.[59]
In retrospect, about the only conclusion that can be drawn from the president's attempt to introduce "character education" at Michigan is that the idea was noble in concept, but it had little chance of achieving the pervasive campus impact the idealistic president wanted. The ancient Greeks found that humanitarian impulses flourished only during prosperity and peace; similarly Ruthven's plan to humanize Michigan foundered in the face of Depression exigencies. More than anything, perhaps, the unmanageable numbers of students and faculty made "character education" difficult.

NOTES

1. Alexander G. Ruthven, "The Common Sense of Religion," C.B.S. radio broadcast, April 2, 1939, miscellaneous Ruthven materials, MHC.
2. Alexander G. Ruthven, "Ethical and Religious Values in Education," *Religious Education,* Vol. 27, No. 4; April, 1932.
3. An exception may have been drinking, however, for his attitudes were ambivalent on this subject. Prohibition was in effect when he became president, and he soon had a cause célèbre on his hands. In February, 1931, local police raided five fraternity houses and discovered bootleg liquor in the rooms. Seventy-nine students were arrested, and Dean of Students Bursley, with the backing of a University Senate committee, closed down the five houses. *The Michigan Daily* vehemently opposed the severity of the discipline in an editorial sarcastically entitled, "This Liquor-Ridden Campus!" (February 17, 1931, p. 4.)
Ruthven received many letters from alumni, most applauding the firm action in stamping out "lawlessness." A number of writers noted that practically all college men drink and protested that the action seemed harsh, but one combative ancient voiced prevailing sentiment when he declared: "Were I in Ann Arbor, I should very gladly join a mob to take those young fellows out and publicly whip them at a post." (I.W. Smith to Ruthven, February 13, 1931, Ruthven Papers, box 3, MHC.)
Ruthven's reponse, as always, was measured. He replied courteously to those who agreed with the university's position; he told those who disagreed that they "did not have all the facts," and offered to discuss the matter in person. Thereafter, when anyone asked, the president's posture was that there was no liquor problem at the university.
4. Interview, Bryant Ruthven, December 17, 1975.
5. Alexander G. Ruthven, "Religious Instruction at the University of Michigan," *The Educational Record,* Vol. 15, No. 1 (1934), p. 42.

6. Ruthven, *The President's Report for 1933–1934*, Vol. 36, No. 29, p. 18.

7. Ruthven to H.B. Earhart, September 23, 1932, Ruthven Papers, box 8, MHC.

8. Ruthven to Ira M. Smith, November 21, 1934, Ruthven Papers, box 16, MHC.

9. *The President's Report for 1934–1935*, Vol. 37, No. 23, p. 3.

10. *Ibid.*, p. 565.

11. "Counselors Befriend Troubled Students," *The Michigan Alumnus*, Vol. 44, No. 12 (1938). This service was begun informally about 1931.

12. Ruthven to Russell Bunting, October 5, 1936, Ruthven Papers, box 20, MHC.

13. Ruthven to Tracy W. McGregor, July 11, 1934, Ruthven Papers, box 15, MHC. This may have proved to be a special challenge to the law students, for President Ruthven received a number of complaints about their moral behavior. One "distracted parent" asked him if he was "aware that at [a] dance held in [the] Lawyer's Club . . . some of the students . . . took young women to their rooms, filled them with liquor, and debauched them?" ("Distracted parent" to Ruthven, November 13, 1933, Ruthven Papers, box 11, MHC.) Ruthven suggested to Dean Bates that an independent investigation by the law school Board of Governors was required. Ruthven to Henry M. Bates, November 15, 1933, box 11, MHC.

14. *The University of Michigan: An Encyclopedic Survey*, ed. by Wilfred B. Shaw, Vol. 4 (Ann Arbor: University of Michigan Press, 1958), pp. 1892–93.

15. C. Grey Austin, "A Century of Religion at the University of Michigan" (University of Michigan, 1957), p. 39.

16. Ruthven to Cecil B. deMille, May 10, 1932, Ruthven Papers, box 5, MHC.

17. Margaret Earhart Smith to Ruthven, July 20, 1932, Ruthven Papers, box 10, MHC.

18. *Proceedings of the Board of Regents*, December meeting, 1933, pp. 269–70.

19. Erich Walter remembered that when Blakeman was appointed many faculty resented the significance attached to the position. Interview, Erich Walter, February 24, 1970.

20. On questions of religion Ruthven turned to a Catholic Priest, a Protestant Minister, and Rabbi Heller. (Ruthven, *Naturalist in Two Worlds*, p. 114.) Ruthven found Heller particularly helpful and told him: "Whatever philosophy I have can be said to be the result of cross fertilization between science and Jewish ethics." (Ruthven to Bernard Heller, December 8, 1937, Ruthven Papers, box 24, MHC.) Heller wrote: " 'Rabbi' in Talmudic literature means 'my teacher'. . . . On the basis of the instruction and inspiration which I received from your writing and discourse, I feel it is I who ought to call you 'Rabbi' instead of the reverse." Heller to Ruthven, February 8, 1939, Ruthven Papers, box 27, MHC.

21. C. Grey Austin, "A Century of Religion," p. 41.

22. "Platform statement," *The Ann Arbor Daily News*, October 5, 1929.

23. Ruthven Papers, MHC, *passim*.

24. *The Michigan Alumnus*, Vol. 42, No. 19 (1936), p. 357.

25. Interview, Alexander G. Ruthven, January 30, 1970.

26. *The Michigan Alumnus*, Vol. 44, No. 26 (1938), p. 534.

27. *The Michigan Alumnus*, Vol. 45, No. 25 (1939), p. 497.

Character Education

28. Ruthven to James B. Webber, Jr., January 4, 1947, Ruthven Papers, box 55, MHC. The idea came from the daughter of Dean of Students Erich Walter. She was an Oberlin student, and told her father that Oberlin had a picture-lending library. Walter told Ruthven of this, and he persuaded the J. L. Hudson Company to donate the prints. Interview, Walter, February 24, 1970.

29. *The Michigan Alumnus,* Vol. 46, No. 7 (1939), p. 141.

30. Harris P. Ralston to Ruthven, June 20, 1935, Ruthven Papers, box 16, MHC.

31. Ruthven to George Levey, October 13, 1939, Ruthven Papers, box 31, MHC.

32. *The Michigan Alumnus,* Vol. 41, No. 13 (1935), p. 213.

33. *Ibid.*

34. Ruthven to Dr. Wilfrid Haughey, October 4, 1934, Ruthven Papers, box 15, MHC.

35. Ruthven to Joe Bursley, May 28, 1938, Ruthven Papers, box 23, MHC.

36. When Michigan Stadium was constructed in 1927, Stanford's stadium was larger. Additional seats have given the stadium a capacity of over 100,000 spectators, and it is now the largest college stadium in the United States.

37. Alexander G. Ruthven, "Predicts Decline in Athletic Interest," *The Michigan Alumnus,* Vol. 37, No. 9 (1930).

38. Ruthven, *Naturalist in Two Worlds,* p. 54.

39. James O. Murfin to Ralph Aigler, November 21, 1931, Murfin Papers, box 6, MHC.

40. Ruthven to Ralph Stone, February 4, 1930, Ruthven Papers, box 2, MHC.

41. Ruthven to David A. Crowley, December 13, 1937, Ruthven Papers, box 23, MHC: Apparently President Ruthven felt exactly the same way about beauty contests, popular on college campuses during his presidency. When it was decided that a Michigan coed should not participate in a Big Ten beauty contest, a University of Michigan student wrote: "Dear President Ruthven, alias the prize heel of the Big Ten: In case you don't know it 'grandpa' this is 1937, not the Middle Ages. . . . To prevent the participation of Michigan's fairest coed in the annual Big Ten Beauty Contest was narrow-minded and unfair. . . ." (1937, Ruthven Papers, MHC.)

42. Letters of Ruthven to Edward H. Lauer, November 4, 1940, Ruthven Papers, box 35, MHC, and Ruthven to John B. Fuller, December 23, 1948, Ruthven Papers, box 59, MHC. Lauer was Dean of the College of Arts and Sciences at the University of Washington; Fuller was a professor at Ohio State.

43. Ruthven to Louis T. Orr, Sr., April 5, 1948, Ruthven Papers, box 57, MHC.

44. Interviews with Hazel Losh, February 11, 1970, and Walter B. Rea, February 20, 1970.

45. Alexander G. Ruthven, "The Anatomy of Tolerance," *The Michigan Alumnus,* Vol. 38, No. 34 (1932), pp. 558–688.

46. Woolsey H. Hunt to Ruthven, March 4, 1935, Ruthven Papers, box 15, MHC.

47. Ruthven to Hunt, March 13, 1935, *ibid.*

48. "Board in Control of Athletics" folder, Ruthven Papers, box 14, MHC.

49. *The Michigan Alumnus,* Vol. 41, No. 3 (1934), p. 54.
50. Ruthven to H. Richard Frank, October 31, 1934, Ruthven Papers, box 14, MHC.
51. Ruthven to Shirley Smith, October 12, 1934, Ruthven Papers, box 16, MHC.
52. Alexander G. Ruthven, "Pride and Prejudice," sermon at Second Baptist Church, Ann Arbor, October 18, 1931, Ruthven Papers, box 78, MHC.
53. Frank E. Robbins to Ruthven, Ruthven Papers, box 16, MHC.
54. Ruthven to Frank D. Fitzgerald, March 6, 1935, Ruthven Papers, box 15, MHC.
55. University Council meeting, May 13, 1935, in *L. S. and A. Faculty Minutes, 1934–35 and 1936–37,* p. 203.
56. Interviews with Hazel Losh, February, 1970, and Robert Cooley Angell, February 4, 1970.
57. Ruthven, *Naturalist in Two Worlds,* p. 78.
58. Interview, Walter B. Rea, February 12, 1970.
59. Report published by Student–Faculty Committee of the Michigan Union, July, 1934, Ruthven Papers, box 14, MHC. The report cited polled only male students, and there was no attempt at random sampling.

9

Student Unrest

There was another, less laudatory, aspect to President Ruthven's concept of character education. He, like most college administrators until recent years, was remarkably thin-skinned when it came to student activists. With them, paternalism could become punitive rather than benign. They were, he felt, an irritant to be excised.

Ruthven's treatment of students was generally praiseworthy. In disciplinary cases where feelings ran high, Ruthven customarily invited the involved student to his office so that they could discuss the matter in person. Probably because of the definiteness of the written word and the possibility of misunderstanding, Ruthven preferred not to commit himself in print when controversial matters could be discussed face to face. This is not to say that he was either devious or afraid of conflict. Ruthven, for instance, did not hesitate to tell a mother that her son was "decidedly lazy."[1] Neither did he hesitate to threaten the dismissal of the son of a friend and wealthy benefactor of the university for, as he told the father, he had been unable to develop in the son "a spirit of loyalty and cooperation which is fundamental in social organization."[2] Throughout the Ruthven Papers, one is struck by the consistency with which Ruthven dealt with pressures from influential people trying to gain favors for students. He would refer the request to the appropriate person or committee and, if the response was negative, he would stand steadfastly behind the decision. When two governors of Michigan, a regent, and several state legislators urged him not to allow the suspension of a student who was academically deficient, he answered coldly, "We do our best to run the University for those students who can make good use of the facilities provided."[3] In the two notable exceptions in which he overruled a committee decision, Ruthven's conclusion was that the student involved deserved clemency.[4]

Ruthven's troubles with student activists began during the Depression, when a small but vigorous number of students began to focus on social and political concerns. The Michigan Socialist Club first drew the attention of *The Michigan Alumnus* in the fall of 1931. Editor Tapping observed that the Club's newspaper "shows a daring and a crusading spirit of admirable proportions."[5] The program of the Socialist Club called for the overthrow of campus paternalism, elimination of racial discrimination, free tuition for needy students, and abolition of ROTC.[6] In 1933, the National Student League (NSL) achieved campus recognition.[7] The League Against War and Militarism, the Student League for Industrial Democracy, and other leftist groups competed for memberships as objectives changed and new alliances were born.[8] These organizations were passionate advocates of anti-war activities and the labor movement. Ruthven thought the groups "amusing" and observed to a curious alumnus, "the members have a good time wrangling with each other."[9]

This cavalier attitude of the administrators toward the nascent leftist organizations was shattered by the publicity ensuing from the participation of thirty-five Michigan students in a May Day, 1934, Communist demonstration in Detroit. The students involved rented a truck, draped it in a University of Michigan banner and, led by a member of the NSL, drove around downtown Detroit shouting their solidarity with workers and singing the "Internationale." When police requested the students to leave their truck, two students who responded too slowly were hit with blackjacks.[10] "Trouble Seekers Usually Find It," wrote the *Daily* and the *Detroit Free Press* editorial was equally unsympathetic: "They Got What Was Coming."[11]

Public reaction was again mixed. The NSL mounted a letter-writing campaign to protest "police brutality," and also to condemn Ruthven for the quote attributed to him: "When university students create a disturbance, they must take the consequences." Ruthven ignored these protests, but he personally revised the report of the University Committee on Discipline.[12] The committee found the students "guilty of bad taste, poor judgement, and a regrettable immaturity of attitude," and concluded that any such future action "will be cause for dismissal." Ruthven modified the latter phrase to read "severe disciplinary action."[13]

Nevertheless, the implication was clear: neither the president nor the disciplinary machinery would tolerate any extreme of social or political deviation on the part of the students. This was spelled out in official statements. The regents voted that a student who did not observe the usual rules of conduct of the university and the community or acted "in such a manner as to make it apparent that he . . . is not a desirable member of the University . . . shall be liable to disciplinary action."[14] The following year, Ruthven buttressed the regents' statement: "Attendance at the University of Michigan is a privilege and not a right," he said. "The University reserves the right, and the student concedes to the University the right, to require the withdrawal of any student at any time for any reason deemed sufficient to it."[15]

This statement was actually ex post facto, since earlier in 1935 events involving student activists had so irritated Ruthven that he had taken the unprecedented step of summarily dismissing four of them from the university. Trouble had started in March when British communist John Strachey was denied permission to speak in Hill Auditorium. Strachey's lecture, which was to be sponsored by the NSL, had previously been approved by Vice President Shirley Smith, who was informed that the subject would be international peace.[16] However, Smith changed his mind when the lecture was announced as "The Coming Struggle For Power," and the request was referred to the University Committee on Lecture Policy, which denied permission to speak, saying: "The Committee is not convinced of the responsibility of this organization [NSL] to sponsor public lectures in University buildings. . . ."[17] A group of faculty, students, and townspeople was then created to sponsor the lecture under different auspices.[18] This proposal was also denied by the Lecture Policy committee, despite a petition by fifty faculty concerned with "free speech."[19] Strachey came to Ann Arbor on March 14 as scheduled, but his talk to 1000 people was held off campus in Granger's ballroom.[20] Ruthven, who supported the decision of the Lecture Policy committee, received eighty-seven student signatures on petitions protesting the refusal to allow Strachey to speak on campus.[21]

Shortly after this brouhaha a peaceful anti-war strike occurred which attracted between 1000 and 1200 students.[22] The strikers deserted classes and hanged William Randolph Hearst in effigy as part of their program. Some of those present took the "Oxford Oath" pledging that they would not participate in war.[23] President Ruthven pooh-poohed the significance of the students' involvement and depreciated their numbers. He insisted that only "about three hundred" had listened to a "professional agitator," that most attended the meeting out of curiosity, and that only a few took the

Oxford Oath.[24] He did, however, release a statement to the news-papers saying that "perversive activities" would not be tolerated, and he added, "No meetings will be permitted on the campus or in University buildings without permission being first obtained from University authorities. Before granting such permission, the officers of the University will ascertain that such meetings are not subversive in nature, that they will not interfere with the work of the University, and that they will not damage the reputation of the University. . . ."[25]

Ruthven's statement, he explained to University of California at Berkeley President Robert Sproul, "had nothing to do with [the] thinking or speaking which had been going on. . . . I am referring to 'perversive' and not 'subversive' activities of students."[26] He admitted privately that he was entirely in sympathy with the aims, at least, of the anti-war demonstrators.[27] Letters began to stream into the president's office; most concurred with the resolutions of the Manistee Fraternal Order of Eagles and the De Molai Knights Templars of Grand Rapids that student pacifists were a threat to American patriotism and deserved punishment.[28]

At the time of the Strachey incident the president had discussed the matter of student activists with the Conference of Deans and had said then that he felt the university could refuse re-registration on other than academic grounds.[29] At the June meeting of the regents the board agreed that "it lay in the President's hands to refuse re-registration to any student who has shown himself to be, in the considered opinion of the president, undesirable as a member of the student body."[30] This appeared to be the only public attention the regents gave to the issue; neither do their private papers indicate that they were involved in discussions regarding leftist students.

Ruthven then conferred with the discipline committee and in-formed Deans Kraus and Sadler, "I have decided that certain leftist students should be asked not to return to the University. . . ."[31] His letters to the deans cited four active members of the National Student League who had been referred to him as "undesirable" by the secretary of the Lecture Policy committee. The Discipline Committee and the Conference of Deans, with whom Ruthven had conferred, were unanimous in agreeing that the four students should not be allowed to re-enroll at Michigan.[32] Ruthven later admitted to the university counsel that he intended: "to establish the precedent . . . that . . . attendance at the University is to be considered a privilege and not a right, especially for out-of-state students. The four boys, is it necessary to say, were from New York and New Jersey and they all belong to one particular persuasion."[33] He then informed each of the four offenders that "the authorities" had decided that he should not re-enter the university. "It has proved to be impossible," the president wrote, "to persuade you to refrain from interfering with the work of the University and with the work of other students."[34]

The summer *Daily* reacted in boldface headlines: "Good Riddance of Bad Rubbish." The *Daily* called the four students "troublemakers" and praised the "courage" and "indisputable rightness" of the university officials.[35] The *Student News*, organ of the Michigan National Student League, ran a cartoon comparing Ruthven to Hitler.[36] Three of the four dismissed students reacted in righteous indignation and one, Daniel Cohen, brought suit in a Federal Court in Detroit. Cohen complained that he was a student in good standing and expelled with no stated reason and without the customary hearing by the disciplinary committee provided for in the regents' regulations.[37] Feldman and Fisch, two other dismissed students, were equally combative, and applied for re-admission with the understanding that "agreement to adhere and abide by the rules . . . shall not be construed as a relinquishment . . . of any constitutional or statutory rights guaranteeing free speech, free assemblage, free press and freedom of worship. . . ."[38] All three were denied re-admission.[39] Ovsiew, the fourth student, was contrite and pleaded for reinstatement, saying: "If given another chance, I will refrain from all political activity and social agitation so long as I am a member of the University."[40] Ruthven was pleased with Ovsiew's response and agreed to "sponsor" his case before the "proper administrative authorities." Ovsiew was readmitted.[41]

Where previous controversies had prompted a stream of letters, the dam now burst and a veritable flood of responses poured in. The university's decision to dismiss the four students was opposed by more than a two to one margin. Libertarian organizations, labor unions, and National Student Leagues at other universities were particulary vehement. A *New Republic* editorial stated that "the reputation of the University among those whose opinions are worthy of consideration has been badly injured. . . ."[42] Ruthven's standard response was, "You have been badly misinformed. . . . There has been no desire on the part of the University to curtail freedom of speech but we must insist upon honesty and noninterference with the regular activities of the institution." The president never deviated from this posture, and judiciously refrained from calling the students "communists"—as many did—or "subversives." Even thirty years later he recalled that the dismissals were based upon breaking university rules and dishonesty.[43]

Neither the University Senate nor the University Council had any comment to offer on the dismissals.[44] In fact, faculty reaction appeared mild. Political scientist James K. Pollock told Ruthven that he had done a "magnificent job" in "literally saving the University."[45]

Once the precedent was established two more National Student League leaders found guilty in October of distributing handbills on campus without university authorization were suspended by the Discipline Committee. The committee ruled that the two students were guilty of "misguided enthusiasms and bad taste rather than malicious intent" and could be re-admitted after written apologies to their respective deans.[46]

The purge appeared to break the spirit of the student leftists, since campus turmoil abated. An "avowed communist," Scott Nearing, and socialist Norman Thomas spoke without incident in campus auditoriums during 1936.[47] In 1937 a chapter of the National American Student Union was recognized and, soon after, a Young Communist League succeeded the National Student League. Student activists were concerned with the Spanish Civil War, and the growing militarism of Hitler and Mussolini. In the Spring of 1937, 1500 students assembled in a peaceful anti-war demonstration. Classes were dismissed at eleven o'clock so that students could march and listen to speeches. The ROTC band led the marchers![48] *The Michigan Daily* and the Student Religious Association sponsored a "Peace Poll," and of the 1821 respondents, only 202 said that they would support the United States in "any war."[49] A later poll by the Bureau of Student Opinion revealed that most students would not support a European war even if it appeared that Germany was defeating France and England.[50]

Unexpectedly, in the Spring of 1940, there was another student crisis. The student paper reported no spectacular incidents comparable to those preceding the 1935 dismissals, but President Ruthven and his advisors must have grown increasingly alarmed as the American Student Union, an activist group of the student left, gained a growing following in campus politics. Its candidate for the Student Senate, Harvey Goodman, polled 162 votes, sufficient for election.[51] Another member of the American Student Union, Hugo Reichard, was elected vice president of the Student Senate.[52]

In his commencement address of 1940, Ruthven issued the following warning: "Michigan welcomes any students who are convinced that democracy is the ideal form of government for a civilized people. . . . [The university] will deal firmly, without fear or favor, with subversive, or so-called 'fifth column' activities."[53] On June 18 the president sent this blunt letter to twelve Michigan students: "It is the decision of the authorities of the University of Michigan that you cannot be readmitted to the University." Five other students were told by Ruthven that they could not enroll in the fall "except with my approval"; they were to request an interview with the president if they wished reinstatement. None of the seventeen students was told why he was not to return; none had had a previous warning; and none was offered a hearing. Although two did not respond, the students and parents who did respond were shocked and alarmed, and they requested that the reasons for the action be enumerated. Those who requested a hearing were told that the president or one of the student service deans would be pleased to meet with them.[54]

Two of the seventeen students were black and many of the group were members of the American Student Union. Only one of the seventeen was in academic difficulty. The Ruthven Papers do not shed much light on the reasons for dismissal. Perhaps the best clue is found in undated papers in the handwriting of Assistant Dean of Students Walter B. Rea. The names of each of the seventeen offenders were listed with some of their activities following. "Active in the promotion of the rights of colored people," "active in ASU," "displayed radical attitude," "distributed handbills in dorms," and "attended CIO meetings," were apparently some of the more damning charges made against the students.[55] Perhaps the most straightforward explanation was provided by Alice C. Lloyd: "She organized the distribution of pamphlets at the dormitory," the Dean of Women told the mother of a dismissed girl. "In addition, she and several other students used one of the University buildings on a Sunday afternoon, when the building was supposed to be closed, for a meeting."[56] Ruthven, however, claimed that the university had

145

"made no inquiry as to the membership of these individuals in any organization, nor as to their political beliefs."[57] Moreover, he claimed that "we did not know that they belonged to the American Student Union or any other organization."[58]

During the summer, as requests for an interpretation of the university's action mounted, no explanations were proffered. Ruthven's usual response to questions was that the dismissed individuals "were interfering seriously with the work of other students." He would say no more and remained "as silent as the pillars of Angell Hall," according to *The Michigan Daily*.[59] Ruthven stated privately to Professor John P. Dawson that one reason he would not make specific statements was "because this would mean the revealing of sources of information which, for the present at least, cannot be disclosed."[60] The papers on the case, though, indicate that the president was in contact with the Federal Bureau of Investigation at this time.[61] Ruthven retired to his summer home in Frankfort, Michigan, and kept in contact with Assistant Dean Rea, who was conferring with many of the seventeen students and their parents, as well as fielding questions from the press.

As in the previously described disciplinary case, the university was careful to point out that the students were "asked not to return" rather than "expelled." This distinction allowed them to enroll in other universities. Ruthven also insisted that to give the students an open hearing before the usual university disciplinary bodies would be "unkind," for they would then almost certainly be expelled and their futures would be jeopardized.[62] Most of those who were refused admission eventually were admitted elsewhere.

On and particularly off the campus the pot began to boil. The dismissals were front page news in Ann Arbor and in Detroit.[63] The local editor regarded the university position approvingly: "Emissaries of organized revolution from the East or elsewhere carrying out dictates from abroad cannot be permitted to use the University as a tool."[64] A *Free Press* editorial called the action a "purge . . . and a highly timely one." It also spoke of the "ingratitude" of the easterners.[65] The summer *Daily* did not mention the case of the dismissed students until June 29, when a letter by Bill Gram, '42, appeared in support of the university's action and attacking "radical" students.[66] The Michigan Committee for Academic Freedom claimed that Gram "later admitted that the letter was neither of his own composition nor sent in of his own volition."[67] The summer *Daily* offered no editorial comment on the dismissals, and apparently the student government did not react either.[68]

The Nation called the university decision a "cold, calculated effort to silence a sizable group by the decapitation of a few." The author, S. R. Kaye, charged that four of the dismissed students, all freshmen, had helped to organize a CIO union among the 3000 non-academic employees at the university and had been barred for that reason. Kaye further charged that Ruthven, who "yearns to achieve the reputation of a liberal educator," had been unduly influenced by "a group of reactionary aides."[69] Hundreds of letters, petitions, telegrams, and resolutions from all over the United States again flooded Ruthven's office. Opposition to the action again outnumbered the support. Many of the writers either asked or demanded that the president state the university's reasons for dismissal and grant the students an open hearing.

"It seems to me that the situation is reaching a point where some sort of definitive statement from you would serve to clear the air," Provost E. Blythe Stason wrote to Ruthven.[70] Ruthven agreed, and in October, as the fall semester convened, a public statement was issued. Calling the dismissals "the unanimous decision of the administrative officers in charge of student affairs," it refuted the charges that the dismissals were politically inspired. "All who asked for conferences have been heard by proper University authorities. . . . These students were not good University citizens, and as guests of the state they had abused the hospitality extended them."[71]

When this pronouncement did little to explain matters, Ruthven told the fall meeting of the University Council and University Senate of the ways in which the dismissed students had disrupted the university:

1. Misrepresentation of residence as a result of which the State of Michigan was cheated out of non-resident tuition.
2. Falsification of applications for facilities and opportunities to hold meetings.
3. Attempts to interfere seriously with the operation of residence halls.
4. Interference with the work of freshmen to such an extent that some of them had to leave the University.
5. Jamming locks on University buildings to permit the holding of unauthorized meetings.
6. Attempts to incite racial antagonisms in Ann Arbor to the distress

147

of students who are working with the University authorities to eliminate intolerance.

7. Flagrant dishonesty in conferences with University officials.

These students, Ruthven told the faculty, "interpret their civil rights to include license to do anything they want to do on the plea that they are 'liberals.' This is a perverted concept of civil liberties and not 'liberalism' in the best sense of the term."[72]

Following Ruthven's explanations, the Senate and the Council did not speak directly to the matter of the dismissed students, but the Council did receive without comment "a communication . . . from certain members of the faculty who expressed concern over the recent dismissal of certain students."[73] This, and a later call from Professor Preston W. Slosson for "a general code governing student activities" appear to be the only faculty response to the matter.[74] Nothing in the minutes of the American Association of University Professors (AAUP) indicates that group's concern.[75] At the September regents' meeting, a delegation appeared to demand a hearing for the dismissed students. The regents expressed the "informal and apparently unanimous" view that "a hearing should not be held because the President had acted in accord with the Regents' views . . . and the case was to be regarded as closed when the President acted."[76] This was the board's only formal consideration of the matter.

The fall semester proceeded. Tom Harmon led the all-conquering football team, many of the dismissed students had enrolled elsewhere, and those students who did return were apparently bound by a pledge to Ruthven to refrain from political activities.[77]

The uneasy quiet was broken by the Michigan Committee for Academic Freedom. This group determined that the dismissed students must receive a trial and, after the Masonic Temple, the Methodist Church, the high school, the County Building, and the Armory had refused assembly permission, it was finally agreed that the Committee would sponsor a public meeting and mock trial at Island Park in Ann Arbor on November ninth. *The Ann Arbor News* reported: "After hearing 'evidence' presented by two 'ousted' students and by students still at the University, the 'jury' returned a verdict accusing the University of disciplining its students 'for exercising their civil rights and democratic liberties.'"[78] Among the speakers at the meeting were Rev. Owen Knox, president of the Michigan Committee for Academic Freedom, and Professor E. A. Ross, chairman of the American Civil Liberties Union.[79]

There was no official response to the Island Park meeting, but when the *Daily* editorial staff published a letter from the Chairman of the American Student Union containing excerpts from *The Nation* article of September 14, two editors were suspended for one week by the Board in Control of Student Publications and ordered to publicly apologize.[80] On December 7, the Discipline Committee of the University Committee on Student Conduct suspended the American Student Union indefinitely.[81] As the European war gained momentum and American involvement appeared imminent, student activism took a back seat to military preparedness.

THE MICHIGAN DAILY

Disciplinary measures against leftist students caused sporadic outbursts of passion, but President Ruthven's most persistent problem with students was undoubtedly the student newspaper. Very soon after he became president, Ruthven told the *Daily* editor that "certain articles" had caused the public to send him "a storm of letters." He did not want the editor to resign, Ruthven assured him, but he was concerned that "we all do what we can to keep the University from being misrepresented to the public."[82]

In the spring of 1931 the chairman of the Board in Control of Student Publications told the president that he supported the present policy of allowing articles to go "uncensored," for a "sound student criticism" would be beneficial.[83] Ruthven appeared to share this opinion, for he told a parent who wanted careful boundaries to the *Daily's* prose: "It is educationally a dangerous practice to curb too much the thinking and talking of students. . . . The proportion of students who say things carelessly is very small—I sometimes think too small."[84] Still, when piqued, the president struck at the source of his irritation. "I cannot refrain from expressing my disappointment in this morning's *Daily,*" he once told its editor. "It deliberately, and apparently maliciously, misinterpreted the aims, motives, and actions of the administration."[85] That fall a trio of crusading seniors introduced a series of articles attacking the national American Legion convention for public drunkenness, exposing the exorbitant rates of Ann Arbor taxi drivers, and charging that a Buildings and Grounds foreman required his men to buy homes in a subdivision which he owned.[86]

Vice President Shirley Smith, a lifetime antagonist of the *Daily*, temporarily cancelled the 917 faculty subscriptions for which the University paid the *Daily* $3600. The Managing Editor, Richard L. Tobin, was temporarily suspended.[87] The Board in Control of Student Publications decried Smith's high-handed action, saying, "If we are not really the Board in Control, we might as well all resign."[88]

Ruthven was in a delicate position with regard to the student paper throughout his presidency. He expressed the classic administrator's dilemma in letters to ex-regent Edmund Shields and future regent Frederick C. Matthaei. "I am really ashamed of myself that after ten years I am no nearer the solution of the problem than I was at the beginning . . . ," he wrote Shields. "All we can do is offer advice and counsel. If we undertake to supervise the paper more closely . . . there is not only an uproar in the student body but also considerable criticism . . . from newspaper men."[89] "On the other hand," he told Matthaei, "whenever the boys and girls step on someone's toes, there are violent protests out of all proportion to the importance of the paper as a news agency."[90]

Ruthven attempted to resolve this dilemma by influencing the agencies which supervised the student press. In 1931, the regents approved an "experimental" plan "whereby the *Summer Michigan Daily* shall be edited and managed in a manner satisfactory to the Dean of the Summer Session."[91] The following year the regents agreed to continue this plan.[92]

The Board in Control of Student Publications, as its name implied, was the supervising agency for the student paper. The Board in Control was composed of three faculty members—one of whom was the chairman—three students, and the Dean of Students, ex officio. The faculty members were appointed by the president; the students were elected in a campus-wide ballot. The Board in Control appointed each Managing Editor from a list of nominees supplied by the *Daily's* outgoing editors. When Ruthven first inquired about the extent of the board's control, he was told by its chairman: "It has not been our notion that we were in any way to censor the publication. . . . We wish it distinctly understood . . . that we cannot guarantee to prevent the publication of items which may offend certain individuals."[93]

In 1932, Ruthven named Professor Louis A. Strauss Chairman of the Board in Control. Ruthven told him: "Somehow we must make clear the obligations and responsibilities of the *Daily* staff. . . . . There is such a thing, of course, as freedom of the press but this has nothing to do with the type of relationship which should exist between the paper and the institution which owns it. It is an anomalous situation to have the official paper of an institution devoting space to attacks on the institution. . . ."[94] The following year *The Michigan Alumnus* published a lengthy article by Professor Strauss explaining the changes which the Board in Control had initiated under his leadership. The new policy was hard line. "The editors of the *Daily* and other publications understand that they are answerable to the Board for what appears in their columns. They realize that they stand in danger of losing their positions if their work is displeasing to . . . the Board which appoints them." Strauss further said that the *Daily* was regarded by many as the official journal of the university since its ownership was vested in the Board of Regents, and thus the relation of the editors to the university was "virtually the same as that of the editors of a privately owned newspaper to its proprietor." If the student editors did not agree to university policy, Strauss implied, "they may resign or be discharged. No question of censorship is involved, for there is no imposition of external authority. It is, so to speak, a family affair." To be sure that there was no question as to who the head of the family would be, Strauss called for the addition to the Board in Control of two alumni advisors appointed by the president.[95] Two newspapermen, Lee White and Stuart Perry, were named to the Board, in an ex officio capacity, shortly thereafter.[96]

Strauss's statement seemed to leave little doubt as to the nature of *The Michigan Daily.* President Ruthven, however, continued to exert pressure. "To me it is very distressing that an official University publication cannot be kept closer to the University and serve the institution," he told Strauss. He added that the university needed "the facts which an organization paper should furnish, but in my opinion we do not need a newspaper in the usual meaning of the term."[97]

The Board in Control must have exerted a positive influence, for in 1937 the Associated Collegiate Press named the *Daily* a "pacemaker" for the third consecutive year. It was one of seven selected from 355 college papers submitted.[98]

Also in 1937, Ruthven reported to Strauss that it was the feeling of the Board of Regents that the *Daily* should change the heading on the editorial page to read that the paper is published "by the students of the University of Michigan" instead of "by the Board in Control of Student Publications." He also suggested that each student writer affix his school or college, his class, and his name to any editorial.[99] By the following fall this became *Daily* policy. And, as Peckham happily reported, "the editorials now carried no more weight than letters to the editor."[100]

President Ruthven still was not appeased. Corresponding with Stuart H. Perry, editor of *The Adrian Telegram* and alumnus advisor to the Board in Control, Ruthven proposed "a director of student publications."[101] What he had in mind, the president later explained, was a coach for the *Daily* similar to a coach for the football team.[102]

Apparently the students retaliated as best they could. When the president forcefully told the New York City alumni that university administrators should encourage students to question the status quo, the *Daily* began to publish this excerpt from his speech under its masthead: "It is important for society to avoid the neglect of adults, but positively dangerous for it to thwart the ambition of youth to reform the world. Only the schools which act on this belief are educational institutions in the best meaning of the term."[103] In 1939, Vice President Shirley Smith complained to the president that an "oligarchy" of student editors had been protesting the journalistic restrictions to the Board in Control and to the regents.[104]

In October, 1940, the University Council received the report of Professor Axel Marin, who had headed a special committee appointed by Ruthven to study the educational value of student publications. The Marin committee endorsed the 1933 Strauss report, and further recommended the strengthening of the Board in Control of Student Publications by the addition of two University Senate members appointed by the president. Marin's committee also recommended that the two alumni advisors become full voting members of the Board in Control. At the same time, the *Daily* editors, who had cooperated with Marin's committee, enumerated a comprehensive set of publishing regulations which became part of the Marin committee report. The University Council endorsed the Marin committee report in its entirety.[105]

The following May, at the request of thirty members of the

University Senate, a special meeting of that body deliberated a petition of the thirty which called for an investigation as to how the University Council's endorsement of the Marin committee report would affect educational policy. The request of the thirty petitioners was not approved by the Senate.[106]

At the May meeting of the regents, the president announced he had received "a petition of several thousand names opposing the action of the Regents in increasing the number of faculty representatives on the Board in Control of Student Publications."[107] At least seven former editors of the *Daily* wrote Ruthven protesting the "packing" of the Board in Control.[108] Ruthven and the Board of Regents held firm, and the revised Board in Control was legalized in the revised *By-Laws*.[109]

The University Senate then reversed itself and, with an eye to asking the Board of Regents to reconsider its action, asked to review the University Council's endorsement of the Marin committee report. The Senate reminded the regents that it had the right to review actions by the University Council.[110] The Board of Regents responded by telling the Senate that the additional appointments to the Board in Control could be postponed no longer; however, any future Senate advice regarding student publications would receive "careful consideration."[111] There the matter rested.

The students again retaliated as best they could. The *Daily,* on January 19, 1943, carried a front-page picture of a student pasting copy paper over the word "Student" on the facade of the building previously named "Student Publications University of Michigan." The student paper lodged a vehement protest against the Board in Control, and an accompanying page one article asked for the resignation of the Board's chairman, Professor G. E. Densmore. The Managing Editor charged that Densmore had little respect among the students, knew little about the *Daily's* operations, and "appears to act on the assumption that any protest . . . necessarily means a flaw in the *Daily.*" The battle between the *Daily's* editors and the Board in Control raged throughout the pages of the paper during much of January. "Board Cripples Michigan Daily," charged eight retiring editors and five incoming editors in another front-page editorial. The student editors were unusually indignant because the Board refused to approve the appointment of "one of the most deserving applicants on the staff."[112] The editors followed this with another sally: "If the present trend of Board policies continues you will soon be reading a *Daily* which says only what it is told to say, and it will not be able to do that very well."[113] The *Daily* garnered considerable campus reinforcement for its defiant stand, but the Board's membership remained unaltered.

One more attempt was made to subjugate *The Michigan Daily*. The regents acted upon President Ruthven's long-standing idea that the *Daily* have a "coach." This person, the regents explained, was not to be responsible for the content of student publications; rather, he was to guide the fledgling journalists in their tryouts for *Daily* positions so that they might have "a deepened sense of responsibility and more discerning judgement."[114] Despite the objections of at least one staff member to the plan, Ruthven went ahead and appointed Donald Hamilton Haines to the position.[115]

This action ended Ruthven's prolonged struggle with the student paper. After the war, he noted, a "different crowd . . . much more concerned about world affairs than about things nearer home" took over the student publications.[116] The president never considered himself the winner of this struggle; he admitted that the "annoying" problem of the *Daily* was never resolved and probably never would be.[117] One of his closest advisors, Erich Walter, concurred with his chief's conclusion; Walter remembers that the *Daily* was a "hair shirt" which Ruthven never wore comfortably.[118]

His relationship with student leftists and *Daily* editors demonstrated that Ruthven's policy of tolerance had its limits. One wonders why the president was unable to exercise more patience with the challenges of these few students. Students of that era claimed few "rights," while the faculty and the public generally approved of Ruthven's actions. Despite these considerations, however, the feeling persists that to arbitrarily dismiss students without regard for established disciplinary procedures, without stated cause, and without hearing was, to borrow a word used by one of the dismissed students thirty years afterward, "disgraceful."[119] It was equally disappointing to see Ruthven's continual clandestine attempts to suppress *The Michigan Daily*, particularly so since Ruthven was a frequent and forceful speaker on the topics of tolerance and the necessity for free exchange of ideas in a university community. Ruthven realized that the student newspaper was a "hair shirt" but, unfortunately, there were times when he scratched harder than the itch justified.

He probably reacted as he did for two reasons. Ruthven's advisors looked askance at student dissenters; their counsel favored strong presidential prosecution. Ruthven also abhorred public conflict. He may very well have believed that a temporary outcry was preferable to continuing public embarrassments from student leftists or muckraking *Daily* editors. "Keep the university out of the papers" was a central theme to the Ruthven administration. Viewed today, the actions seem arbitrary and unduly harsh. During Ruthven's presidency, however, it was generally accepted that university attendance—even at a public university—was a privilege rather than a right and that students ought not challenge administrative authority.

NOTES

1. Alexander G. Ruthven to Mrs. A. W. Decker, March 29, 1930, Ruthven Papers, box 1, MHC.

2. Ruthven to James Inglis, May 14, 1932, Ruthven Papers, box 6, MHC.

3. Ruthven to Hon. John K. Strack, October 2, 1933, Ruthven Papers, box 13, MHC.

4. In one case, Ruthven recommended greater leniency for a violator of student automobile regulations, for Ruthven had talked with him, liked his attitude, and thought "he has had a lesson." Ruthven to Dean Joseph Bursley, February 16, 1931, Ruthven Papers, box 3, MHC. On another occasion Ruthven arbitrarily reinstated a student who had been dismissed from the School of Nursing for drinking intoxicating liquors. This decision resulted in a furor during which the president of the student nurses' governing body disagreed with Ruthven's action; the Director of the School of Nursing resigned in protest; and the President of the Michigan State Nurses Association supported her resignation as a protest against Ruthven's decision. Karen Dahlberg to Ruthven, October 3, 1939, Ruthven Papers, box 31, MHC, and Mabel McNeel to Ruthven, November 9, 1939, *ibid.*

5. *The Michigan Alumnus,* Vol. 38, No. 5 (1931), p. 93.

6. *The Michigan Alumnus,* No. 29 (1932), p. 575, and Vol. 39, No. 4 (1932), p. 63. ROTC was voluntary and enrolled approximately 500 students.

7. The NSL had a University of Michigan membership of approximately sixty at its peak. *Ann Arbor Daily News,* April 11, 1935, p. 1.

8. Peckham, *Making of Michigan* (Ann Arbor: University of Michigan, 1967), p. 189.

9. Ruthven to Charles Englehard, March 5, 1934, Ruthven Papers, box 11, MHC.

10. *The Michigan Daily,* May 2, 1934, p. 1.

11. *The Michigan Daily,* May 3, 1934, p. 4; *The Detroit Free Press,* May 3, 1934, p. 6.

12. This disciplinary committee became a subcommittee of the University Committee on Student Conduct.

13. "May Day Celebration" folder, Ruthven Papers, box 12, MHC.

14. *Proceedings of the Board of Regents,* September meeting, 1934, p. 429.

15. *The President's Report for 1934–1935,* pp. 2–3.

16. Shirley Smith to Ascher Opler, February 16, 1935, in "Gag Rule at Michigan," National Student League handbill, Ruthven Papers, box 79, MHC.

17. *The Michigan Daily,* March 9, 1935, p. 1.

18. *The Michigan Daily,* March 10, 1935, p. 1. This group included John L. Brumm, chairman of the journalism department; Robert Cooley Angell, later chairman of the sociology department; and Neil Staebler, a future Democratic gubernatorial candidate.

19. *The Michigan Daily,* March 13, 1935, p. 1.

20. Peckham, *Making of Michigan,* p. 191.

21. "National Student League" folder, Ruthven Papers, box 79, MHC.

22. *Ann Arbor Daily News,* April 4, 1935, p. 1.

23. *Ann Arbor Daily News,* April 5, 1935, p. 1. On the same day, 1200 people listened to Professor Robert Morss Lovett of the University of Chicago speak to a Hill Auditorium peace rally which was sanctioned by the Lecture Policy committee and enjoyed the blessing of the president. Peckham, *Making of Michigan,* p. 191.

24. Ruthven to Governor Frank D. Fitzgerald, Ruthven Papers, box 15, MHC, and Ruthven to J. H. Schouten, April 19, 1935, "National Student League" folder, Ruthven Papers, box 79, MHC.

25. April 15, 1935, "National Student League" folder, Ruthven Papers, box 79, MHC.

26. Ruthven to Robert Sproul, May 5, 1935, Ruthven Papers, box 16, MHC.

27. Ruthven to Milton J. Shear, April 29, 1935, "National Student League" folder, Ruthven Papers, box 79, MHC.

28. "National Student League" folder, *ibid.*

29. "Minutes of the Conference of the President and Deans," March 13, 1935, miscellaneous manuscript material, MHC. Dean Bates concurred with Ruthven, saying that the courts recognized the university's power "where a reasonable ground was present."

30. *Proceedings of the Board of Regents,* June meeting, 1935, p. 627.

31. Ruthven to Kraus and Ruthven to H.O. Sadler, June 21, 1935, "Cohen, Feldman, Fisch, and Osview [*sic*]" folder, Ruthven Papers, box 79, MHC. The "Rules Concerning Student Affairs, Conduct, and Discipline," revised November 23, 1936, appear ambiguous, yet the president's jurisdiction in disciplinary cases seemed unlimited. "The President shall exercise such powers of discipline as are inherent in a chief executive and as are necessary in connection with the proper performance of his duties. . . ." (The reference cited was the *By-Laws,* Chapter II, Section 2(b), which actually read: "The President of the University shall exercise such general powers as are inherent in a chief executive, for the protection of the interests, and the wise government of the University, the improvement of its standards and functions, and the maintenance of health, diligence, and order among the students. . . .") The 1923 By-Laws were operative until 1936, when E. Blythe Stason began supervising a major revision.

Student Unrest

32. Ruthven to George J. Burke, September 21, 1935, "Cohen, *et al.*" folder, Ruthven Papers, box 79, MHC.

33. Ruthven to Burke, October 19, 1935, *ibid.* This comment raises questions about the sincerity of Ruthven's public statements on tolerance.

34. Ruthven to Burke, July 9, 1935, *ibid.* The terms "dismissed" and "expelled" were avoided by the university so that the four students would be eligible to enroll elsewhere. Burke to Nicholas V. Olds, October 28, 1935, *ibid.* Burke was the university's attorney; Olds represented the four students.

35. *Summer Michigan Daily,* August 1, 1935, p. 1. It is impossible to know whether the *Daily* represented student opinion for, although printed by the students, it was admittedly a "house organ" responsible only to the dean of the summer session. A handbill distributed by "A Hundred Michigan Men" warned seven of the leftist students by name that they should refrain from their "subversive" activities or "meet with our *active* disapproval." "Cohen, *et al.*" folder, Ruthven Papers, box 79, MHC.

36. September 27, 1935, Vol. 2, No. 1, p. 1, "Cohen, *et al.*" folder, Ruthven Papers, box 79, MHC.

37. *Trenton Evening Times,* November 8, 1935, "Cohen, *et al.*" folder, Ruthven Papers, box 79, MHC. The attorney for the dismissed student based his case on the *By-Laws,* 1923, Ch. VI, C, Sec. 3: "A student may be suspended, dismissed, or expelled by a two-thirds vote of a Disciplinary Committee appointed by the Faculty of the School or College in which he is registered, after a full and impartial hearing before said Committee, and with the approval of the proper Dean." (Olds to Ruthven, October 18, 1935, "Cohen, *et al.*" folder, Ruthven Papers, box 79, MHC.) It is interesting to note that this section was removed from the *By-Laws* when they were revised in 1936. Cohen's case in Michigan was doomed from the start. Harry Toy, the Michigan Attorney General, assured university counsel George Burke that he was very glad that the university had taken its stand, and would defend it "all the way." Burke to Ruthven, September 26, 1935, "Cohen, *et al.*" folder, Ruthven Papers, box 79, MHC.

38. Joseph Feldman to Ruthven, September 27, 1935, "Cohen, *et al.*" folder, Ruthven Papers, box 79, MHC. Fisch and Cohen wrote identical letters.

39. Ruthven to Feldman, Cohen and Fisch, October 4, 1935, *ibid.*

40. Leon Ovsiew to Ruthven, August 14, 1935, *ibid.*

41. Ruthven to Ovsiew, August 17, 1935, *ibid.*

42. *The New Republic,* Vol. 84, No. 1080, August 14, 1935, p. 3.

43. Ruthven, *Naturalist in Two Worlds,* pp. 94–95.

44. *University of Michigan Council and Senate Records, 1934–1936.*

45. James K. Pollock to Ruthven, August 3, 1935, Ruthven Papers, box 19, MHC.

46. "Cohen, *et al.*" folder, Ruthven Papers, box 79, MHC.

47. Peckham, *Making of Michigan,* p. 193.

48. *The Michigan Alumnus,* Vol. 43, No. 20 (1937), p. 391.

49. *The Michigan Alumnus,* Vol. 44, No. 20 (1937), p. 124. Of the students polled, 360 said they would support their country in "no war"; 1259 agreed they would "defend continental United States."

50. *The Michigan Alumnus,* Vol. 46, No. 7 (1939), p. 150.

51. *The Michigan Daily,* April 28, 1940, p. 1.

52. *The Michigan Daily,* May 3, 1940, p. 1.

53. Ruthven, "Never to Grow Old," *Michigan Alumnus Quarterly Review,* Vol. 66, No. 24 (1940), p. 316.

54. "Correspondence with Dismissed Students and with Office of the Dean of Students" folder, Ruthven Papers, box 79, MHC. The decisions on three of the twelve dismissed students were eventually rescinded, and they were allowed to re-enroll that fall.

55. *Ibid.*

56. Alice C. Lloyd to Sarah Rosenbaum, July 5, 1940, *ibid.* The uncle of the student in question, Hilda Rosenbaum, was Yale law school professor Eugene V. Rostow. Rostow told Ruthven that his action "deprives these boys and girls of the essence of fair play." Rostow to Ruthven, August 28, 1940, *ibid.*

57. Ruthven to Honorable John D. Dingell, United States House of Representatives, August 9, 1940, "Favorable Comments A–L" folder, Ruthven Papers, box 79, MHC.

58. Ruthven to M.J. Robinson, November 27, 1940, "Favorable Comments M–Z" folder, Ruthven Papers, box 79, MHC.

59. *The Michigan Daily,* October 3, 1940, p. 4.

60. Ruthven to John P. Dawson, August 8, 1940, Ruthven Papers, box 34, MHC. In an earlier letter Dawson, a member of the Senate Advisory Committee on University Affairs (SACUA), made reference to the president obtaining, prior to the dismissal of the twelve students, faculty support in SACUA for dismissing "communist" students, "who conspired to commit sabotage." Dawson to Ruthven, July 16, 1940, *ibid.*

61. John S. Bugas to Ruthven, February 12, 1941, "Miscellaneous Correspondence, Statements, and Printed and Mimeographed Material" folder, Ruthven Papers, box 79, MHC. Bugas was the FBI agent in charge of the case.

62. Ruthven to Walter Agard, October 3, 1940, "Unfavorable Comments A–L" folder, Ruthven Papers, box 79, MHC. Agard was a professor at the University of Wisconsin.

63. *Ann Arbor News,* June 27, 1940, p. 1, and the *Detroit Free Press,* June 27, 1940, p. 1.

64. *Ann Arbor News,* July 4, 1940, p. 4.

65. *Detroit Free Press,* June 28, 1940, p. 6.

66. *Summer Michigan Daily,* June 29, 1940, p. 2.

67. "Without Fear or Favor," pamphlet published by the Michigan Committee for Academic Freedom, September, 1940, "Miscellaneous Correspondence, etc." folder, Ruthven Papers, box 79, MHC. Gram was the son of Lewis M. Gram, Director of Plant Extension.

68. "Minutes of the Student Senate," miscellaneous manuscript material, MHC. These files are fragmentary, but include most meetings in 1940–41.

69. "Ann Arbor Hysteria," *The Nation,* Vol. 151, No. 11 (1940), p. 215.

70. E. Blythe Stason to Ruthven, September 6, 1940, Ruthven Papers, box 36, MHC.

71. "Correspondence with Dismissed Students, etc." folder, Ruthven Papers, box 79, MHC. All of the 1940 offenders who were not permitted to re-register and all of the students dismissed in 1935 were not Michigan residents.

72. "Statement to the University Senate and University Council," undated (fall), 1940, Ruthven Papers, box 84, MHC.

73. *University of Michigan Council and Senate Records, 1936–1941,* October 14, 1940 meeting, p. 56.

74. "The Report of the Senate Advisory Committee on University Affairs," February 1941, in *L.S. & A. Faculty Minutes, 1939–1941,* p. 708.

75. Papers of the Michigan Chapter of AAUP, 1935–59, MHC.

76. *Proceedings of the Board of Regents,* September meeting, 1940, p. 377.

77. "Correspondence with Dismissed Students, etc." folder, Ruthven Papers, box 79, MHC.

78. *Ann Arbor News,* November 11, 1940, p. 5.

79. *The Michigan Daily,* November 10, 1940, p. 1.

80. *The Michigan Daily,* November 26, 1940, p. 4, and December 5, 1940, p. 4. The offending article pointed out Regent Harry Kipke's ties with the controversial Harry Bennett of Ford Motor Company and also remarked on the preponderance of corporation executives on the Board. The disciplinary case was initiated by the Student Judiciary Board and unanimously supported by the faculty Discipline Committee. Ruthven to Roland Goodman, January 29, 1941, "Discipline of *Michigan Daily,* American Student Union" folder, Ruthven Papers, box 79, MHC. One of those suspended from the *Daily* was Managing Editor Hervie Haufler, who upon his reinstatement suspended two other editors for a "libelous article." *Ibid.*

81. *The Michigan Daily,* December 7, 1940, p. 1.

82. Ruthven to George Tilley, December 4, 1929, Ruthven Papers, box 1, MHC.

83. Robert Cooley Angell to Ruthven, March 20, 1931, Ruthven Papers, box 3, MHC.

84. Ruthven to H. C. Jones, March 31, 1931, *ibid.*

85. Ruthven to Henry Merry, February 17, 1931, Ruthven Papers, box 4, MHC. The *Daily* article condemned administrative disciplinary measures against five fraternities and accused the administration of attempting to please the state legislature at the expense of the apprehended students.

86. *The Michigan Daily,* September 30, 1931, p. 4, and October 1, 1931, p. 1.

87. Peckham, *Making of Michigan,* p. 185. Tobin later had a distinguished career with *Saturday Review.*

88. Angell to Ruthven, October 5, 1931, Ruthven Papers, box 6, MHC.

89. Ruthven to Edmund Shields, February 3, 1940, Ruthven Papers, box 32, MHC.

90. Ruthven to Frederick C. Matthaei, February 16, 1944, Ruthven Papers, box 46, MHC.

91. *Proceedings of the Board of Regents,* December meeting, 1931, pp. 836–37.

92. *Proceedings of the Board of Regents,* December meeting, 1932, p. 87.

93. Angell to Ruthven, October 5, 1931, Ruthven Papers, box 6, MHC.

94. Ruthven to Louis A. Strauss, June 13, 1932, Ruthven Papers, box 7, MHC.

95. "Publication Policies Are Stated," *The Michigan Alumnus,* Vol. 39, No. 29 (1933).

96. *University of Michigan Council and Senate Records, 1932–1934,* p. 93.

97. Ruthven to Strauss, April 4, 1935, Ruthven Papers, box 16, MHC.

98. *The Michigan Alumnus,* Vol. 43, No. 20 (1937), p. 391.

99. Ruthven to Strauss, February 2, 1937, Ruthven Papers, box 21, MHC.

100. Peckham, *Making of Michigan,* p. 194.

101. Ruthven to Stuart H. Perry, July 10, 1937, Ruthven Papers, box 25, MHC. Ruthven went on to suggest to Perry: "I wish the suggestion could come from the board to me rather than to the board from me."

102. Ruthven to Frederick B. Richardson, October 9, 1944, Ruthven Papers, box 50, MHC.

103. Ruthven, "The Red Schoolhouse," *The Michigan Alumnus Quarterly Review,* Spring, 1938. In the fall of 1938 Ruthven asked the Managing Editor of the *Daily* to cease quoting this speech. Robert Mitchell to Ruthven, September 20, 1938, Ruthven Papers, box 28, MHC.

104. Smith to Ruthven, April 19, 1939, Ruthven Papers, box 29, MHC.

105. *University of Michigan Council and Senate Records, 1936–1941,* pp. 57–58.

106. *Ibid.,* pp. 112–18.

107. *Proceedings of the Board of Regents,* May meeting, 1941, p. 601.

108. Burton R. Benjamin to Ruthven, May 5, 1941, Ruthven Papers, box 35, MHC.

109. *Proceedings of the Board of Regents,* June meeting, 1941, p. 666.

110. *University of Michigan Council and Senate Records, 1936–1941,* p. 120.

111. *Proceedings of the Board of Regents,* June meeting, 1941, p. 666.

112. *The Michigan Daily,* January 17, 1943.

113. *The Michigan Daily,* January 19, 1943, p. 2.

114. *Proceedings of the Board of Regents,* October meeting, 1944, pp. 703–4.

115. Interview, Erich Walter, February 24, 1970. Walter disapproved.

116. Ruthven to Junius B. Wood, March 7, 1947, Ruthven Papers, box 56, MHC.

117. Interview, Alexander G. Ruthven, February 3, 1970.

118. Interview, Erich Walter, February 24, 1970.

119. A check of alumni files shows addresses for eleven of the eighteen survivors of the 1935 and 1940 purges. I sent letters to these eleven people asking them to give their account of the incidents leading to their dismissal and the effect of the dismissal on their subsequent lives. Three responded. One is a housewife who said she voted for Barry Goldwater in the 1964 presidential election; another is a physician active in positions of civic leadership; and the third is a full professor at Case Western Reserve University.

10

Academic Freedom and the Faculty

Academic freedom was a luxury not afforded students during the years when Dr. Ruthven was president of Michigan, but the precepts of academic freedom for faculty had clearly emerged by then. When the national American Association of University Professors (AAUP) was founded in 1915, the University of Michigan had already experienced one shattering example of what could be called an abuse of academic freedom, and it would soon experience another.

The university's first president, Henry Philip Tappan, a brilliant scholar and educator who possessed vision and vigor in equal parts, was unceremoniously removed from the presidency by the Board of Regents. There was little question of Tappan's leadership or abilities, but the regents were offended at Tappan's "eastern" behavior—his thoughts and actions were too progressive for the midwest of that time.[1]

During World War I, anti-German sentiment in the state and in Ann Arbor, a city with many German families, reached such a crescendo that the regents in 1917 summarily dismissed a member of the German department. The following year the regents granted a leave of absence to another member of the German department "indefinitely"; when he attempted to reclaim his position his request was refused.[2]

However, when Ruthven assumed the Michigan presidency, the academic freedom of the faculty was not a primary concern. President Little had encouraged freewheeling expression, and President Ruthven, a respected colleague, was expected by the faculty to at least defend freedom of expression even if he did not promote it. Ruthven's early efforts to include faculty in democratic governance strengthened this belief, and so did his written and oral pronouncements.

John L. Lovett was general manager of the Michigan Manufacturer's Association and self-appointed watchdog of the Michigan fac-

161

ulty. When he complained to Ruthven that university professors were preparing a state tax bill without prior clearance from Alfred P. Sloan, President of General Motors, Ruthven said in reply:

> It will doubtless always be true that university professors will make statements which do not meet with general approval. . . . I insist that the university can be a service institution and that information can be given to any citizen if it is requested. . . . I insist, further, that any man on the faculty has entire freedom to express his opinion if the opinion is the result of careful investigation and study. Even carefully considered opinions will from time to time be irritating. This cannot be helped and should, in the long run, prove of benefit. A properly constituted university faculty is composed of men who are going down the road of social progress at least a mile ahead of the institutions of society. These men are, or should be, trail blazers and it is not always going to be easy to follow them.[3]

When the chairman of the Associated Technical Societies of Detroit asked Ruthven to explain the university's attitude "regarding the political persuasions of its teachers," Ruthven responded:

> The University does not pay any attention to the political affiliations of its teachers. . . . The only thing that is insisted upon is that the men shall teach their subjects and not use the class rooms as political forums. So meticulous is the faculty on this score that I honestly think some times they are too conservative. . . . The popular conception is that universities are centers of radicalism. As a matter of fact, they are centers of ultra-conservatism.[4]

Those faculty members who attempted to break away from the "centers of ultra-conservatism" sometimes found that their iconoclasm had been reported to Ruthven. English professors were especially vulnerable, particularly if their required reading lists challenged convention. A minister once denounced the "unmitigated filth" of John Dos Passos' *U.S.A.*, and a parent claimed that the university was "being used as a tool of undemocratic and subversive propaganda" because his daughter was assigned the *New Republic*. The same magazine aroused the concern of congressman George A. Dondero. Ruthven's typical response to these protestations was to give the complaint to the departmental chairman and suggest that he respond. His own attitude was spelled out succinctly. "It seems to us here at the University," he wrote Dondero, "that it is only fair to the students to present both sides of every question. . . . We have little sympathy with the attitude that our young people should have their minds developed by propaganda. . . . This is the method of totalitarianism."[6]

"COMMUNISTS"

The Depression years brought disillusionment with democracy for many people, and some sought answers in other ideologies. Sagendorph devoted a whole chapter to the incursion of radical thought, not only among the students, but also within the faculty at the university during this time.[7] "Among the younger instructors," he noted, "there were many with radical views."[8] When rumors raced about the state that socialists or communists dominated the university, Ruthven was sure to hear from those citizens who felt particularly threatened by the galloping gossip.

Faculty watchdog John L. Lovett wrote again requesting verbatim reports of class discussions on a New Deal course offered in the School of Business Administration. Ruthven's orders to his secretary were:

> Please tell Jamison [the instructor of the course] that I do not believe a stenographic report of the New Deal lectures should be supplied to anyone. . . . If, as I think most probable, the material is wanted as a basis for criticizing the faculty then Lovett should come out and listen to the talks.[9]

Probably the most dramatic encounter during the Depression involved Wesley Maurer, a young instructor. Maurer had already achieved a reputation as an outspoken advocate of liberal ideas when he was asked to debate Malcolm W. Bingay, an editor of the *Detroit Free Press,* on the topic "Freedom of the Press." On February 24, 1935, Maurer confronted Bingay in a crowded Detroit church. According to Maurer, Bingay treated their topic in a "Fourth of July" manner, whereas his own forthright rebuttal challenged many of the current assumptions of the establishment, particularly those of bankers and newspapermen. Bingay was incensed and charged that Maurer had, in effect, called him a "murderer, liar, cheat, and a thief"! Maurer then joined the verbal donnybrook by saying, "Mr. Bingay, being an authoritarian, can't stand criticism."[10] Bingay carried his counter-attack to his "Good Morning" column, where he associated Maurer's "fuzzy opinions" with communism. "What are the taxpayers paying for?" he queried.[11] Bingay returned to Maurer in a later column, calling him "the parlor pink of the University of Michigan School of Journalism."[12]

The resulting furor did not escape Ruthven.[13] Fortunately for the young instructor, over twenty people who had attended the church debate wrote either Ruthven, John Brumm, chairman of the journalism department, or Maurer, denouncing Bingay's behavior in the church and in his column. There were a few who demanded Maurer's resignation, but, as Ruthven noted on his tally sheet of responses, they had not attended the debate but had instead taken their cue from Bingay's column. Unfortunately for Maurer, Regent Murfin wanted him fired.[14] Ruthven read Maurer's manuscript carefully, and then he forwarded it to Dean Kraus and some of the law school faculty for their scrutiny.[15] Ruthven's opinion was probably most candidly expressed in a letter which was dictated but not sent to Dean Kraus:

> I hold firmly to the opinion that a member of the staff has a right to express his own opinions and I shall defend that right.
>
> I wish to record with you, however, my opinion, which is the opinion of the Board of Regents . . . that Mr. Maurer's talk was ill-timed, in poor taste, and delivered under unfortunate circumstances.[16]

Ruthven called Maurer to his office, told him that he had been foolish to tangle with a journalist who would undoubtedly have the last word, and urged him to "keep his mouth shut" until the criticism abated.[17] To pacify the troubled regents he sent them copies of Maurer's manuscript and his own tally sheet which showed that most of his correspondents favored Maurer's side of the argument. Then, to reinforce the relationship—already worn thin by previous abrasions—between the journalism department and the newspaper editors of the state, Ruthven called them together—but did not include Maurer—so that they could discuss their differences.[18]

Among those citizens threatened by the "communists" were some of the regents. On October 31, 1936, the *Detroit Free Press* reported the results of a faculty political poll which was conducted by *The Michigan Daily*. The paper reported presidential preferences as follows: Alfred Landon, 276 votes; Franklin D. Roosevelt, 271 votes; Norman Thomas, 33 votes; and Earl Browder, 10 votes.[19] Regent Murfin did not care that the Communist Party was legal, or that the communist candidate, Browder, received only ten votes. "If we do have communists on the faculty I think they should be eliminated," Murfin publicly threatened.[20] Murfin immediately wrote the rest of the regents that "we should seek to ascertain who are these gentlemen; and when we shall have learned that, drop them from the payroll."[21] The Murfin Papers indicate that regents Richard R. Smith, Franklin Cook, and Charles F. Hemans fully supported Murfin's stand and urged him to pursue the matter further. At least a dozen citizens wrote to encourage Murfin's efforts.[22]

Ruthven attempted to hold the regents in check. The *Daily* poll was "slip-shod," he told them. A probe would result in unfavorable publicity for the university and, besides, "surely 10 Communist votes out of [1,000 faculty] are insignificant."[23] Ruthven must have felt relief when the senior regent, Junius Beal, conducted his own investigation and was unable to find any trace of a communist sympathizer on the faculty. Beal called the alarm a "hoax manufactured."[24] At the same time, Murfin's friend, Regent Ralph Stone, pointed out to him that, after all, "the laws permit putting the Communist Party ticket on the ballot."[25] Regent Mrs. Cram voiced her suspicion of the poll: "I haven't a particle of trust in the honesty of the University of Michigan *Daily*."[26] Murfin was eventually forced to conclude: "The response . . . to my recent letter concerning the possible presence of Communism on the campus was not such to justify further proceedings on my part."[27]

The Depression-era "Red scare" prompted the 1935 state legislature to pass the Baldwin-Dunckel Bill which required an oath of allegiance from all government employees, including university professors. Assistant dean W. R. Humphreys of the Literary College returned his signed oath with a note expressing his distaste, and the president retorted: "I find myself in complete agreement with your point of view." Ruthven did not object to the oath itself, he told the dean, but he was appalled by the "wave of hysteria" which produced such oaths.[28] The faculty grumbled about the oath, but none refused to sign. Ruthven told the secretary of the Flint American Legion that the academicians felt that the legislators were discriminating against them. "They cannot understand why teachers should be compelled to take the oath when business men, musicians, and others are not."[29]

Agitation for removal of campus "reds" and "pinks" faded as World War II consumed the energies of all citizens. Immediately following the actual war, however, the United States and the Soviet

Union fought the "cold war," and "witch hunting" became a national obsession. Fearful legislators and concerned citizens cast suspicious glances at the University of Michigan. Ruthven's friendly antagonist, Allen B. Crow, President of the Economic Club of Detroit, sent him a constant barrage of clippings and circulars warning about communist-oriented student organizations.[30]

Michigan Governor Kim Sigler had gained statewide prominence as a crusading prosecutor. Sigler recognized the political dividends which could accrue from a vigorous persecution of "communists," so very soon after taking office he began to direct his attention to "reds" on the state's campuses.[31] Faced with increasing pressure from the governor and the legislature, Ruthven tried to walk the tightrope. He had been troubled for some time by a student leftist group called Michigan Youth for Democratic Action (MYDA), an offshoot of the national American Youth for Democracy (AYD). University administrators were further alarmed when, in March, 1947, J. Edgar Hoover, Director of the FBI, testified before the House Committee on Un-American Activities that AYD was a communist front.[32] Vice president Marvin Niehuss promptly asked the Department of Justice to substantiate Hoover's statement.[33] Conversations with justice department officials ensued, and Ruthven became convinced that AYD was subversive and was controlling the actions of MYDA. Most of the members of the latter group, Ruthven thought, had unwittingly joined a "cell" which followed the party line prescribed by AYD.[34] On April 22, 1947, Ruthven informed the president of MYDA that, since the organization was an affiliate of AYD, he was declaring that MYDA would no longer be recognized as a university organization.[35] The letters and petitions which flowed in response to the MYDA ban followed the familiar pattern. Hundreds of student signatures protested the president's action; many alumni and state citizens applauded; faculty response was limited to a perfunctory protest by five professors associated with the State Committee for Academic Freedom.[36] A request by MYDA for reinstatement was denied.[37]

The ban on MYDA appeared inconsistent with the president's usual pronouncements during the post-war "red" anxiety. Except for that one time, he belittled communist influences and staunchly defended faculty members under suspicion.

The state commander of the American Legion wrote Ruthven that his organization was in full support of the governor's investigations, and he asked the president a series of questions about communist infiltration of the campus. Ruthven sent a long, polite reply denying that communist organizations existed on the campus. He wrote the Legion commander: "Personally, I have no sympathy with the communist ideology, but . . . I cannot act on the assumption that everyone who espouses this ideology is committed to the overthrow of our government by force. I feel that our greatest responsibility is to make our democratic form of government so effective that no type of foreign *ism* will . . . thrive here."[38]

S. W. Sedgwick, a member of the Alumni Advisory Council, told Ruthven that he was alarmed at the amount of dangerous, un-American activity in the institutions of higher learning.[39] "Our views are wide apart," Ruthven replied; "I believe I know what is going on in the colleges and I cannot see that they present any threat of communism."[40]

Ruthven reiterated his views on a radio panel which included Governor Sigler, President John A. Hannah of Michigan State College, and President David D. Henry of Wayne State University. The Michigan president stated forcefully that he did not fear communist organizations on campus, provided they abided by university rules, for discussion of controversial ideologies would only serve to strengthen democracy.[41]

That Fall, speaking to the University of Michigan Press Club, Ruthven expanded on this theme:

It is certainly no secret to members of this audience that there are large and important state universities . . . in this country in which instructors are afraid to express their convictions . . . and in which administrators are in the position of having to get the approval of certain pressure groups before they announce policies. . . . Communism is not the only threat to liberal education. Pressure groups have perverted instruction in the past and can do so again.[42]

At the beginning of the McCarthy era, the president's stand won the plaudits of at least two distinguished faculty.[43]

In 1949, the university received a request from John S. Wood, Chairman of the Un-American Activities Committee of the United States House of Representatives. Wood demanded a list of textbooks and supplementary reading materials currently in use.[44] After communicating with George F. Zook of the American Council on Education, Ruthven sent this curt response: "[The] University of Michigan cannot supply [the] list of books you request. In our opinion, your request is not within the rights of the Committee on Un-American Activities."[45]

One of the last men Ruthven was called to defend was a new appointment in the School of Education. An alarmed citizen wrote:

I am told that Algo D. Henderson has joined the faculty at the University of Michigan. . . . Mr. Henderson's name appears in the House Un-American Activities proceedings. Evidently at one time he was on the Committee of Education of the Council of American–Soviet Friendship which the Department of Justice has declared a subversive organization.[46]

Ruthven did not share the alarm and replied: "I understand that . . . before appointing Mr. Henderson we consulted with a number of persons. . . . We came to the conclusion that we were making no mistake in this appointment. . . ."[47]

THE AAUP AND TENURE

That traditional guardian of academic freedom, the American Association of University Professors, was a large organization at Michigan but hardly active. "This chapter has had a case of lethargy running for years," reported Professor Carl E. W. L. Dahlstrom to the national president of AAUP.[48] That year there was a local membership of approximately 150, of whom only 30 were active.[49] By 1948–1949 total membership had increased to 358, but the attendance at meetings averaged only about 35.[50]

The attendance must have increased when Ruthven gave one of his frequent talks before the local chapter, particularly when the subject was tenure. In 1935, he told the Michigan AAUP that, while the principle of tenure must remain inviolate, many faculty took advantage of that principle. If "drones and superfluous men on the staff" are to be tolerated, the president said, those able professors who tolerate them must realize "that they are contributing to charity." Ruthven went on to suggest a code of ethics for the profession.[51] "Your speech was quite devastating in its effects upon our old Bourbons," political scientist James K. Pollock told Ruthven. "You punched them in the nose and they had to take it because they knew it was true."[52]

The records of the AAUP indicate that one of the main concerns of the chapter during the Ruthven regime was faculty tenure. When

Ruthven became the chief executive, the Michigan tenure regulation read: "Unless otherwise provided by the Board of Regents, it is understood that Professors and Associate Professors are appointed on indeterminate tenure."[53] In 1930 the regents expanded this to read: "Assistant professors shall be appointed for terms of one, two, or three years, as in each case specifically designated in the terms of appointment. Whenever the term of appointment to an assistant professorship is not specified, it shall be for one year only."[54]

Despite the fact that it was outlined in the *By-Laws,* tenure was a foreign concept to some of the regents. "I am well aware of the fact that the amalgamated order of collegiate professors has always claimed some union rule to the effect that after he passed the rank of instructor he was engaged in perpetuity," Regent Murfin caustically observed. Murfin went on to say, "I have always insisted and still insist that the tenure of our teaching staff is from year to year . . . as a matter of law it is not necessary for us in order to drop a professor to prefer formal charges and have a hearing to justify our action."[55]

There is no record that either AAUP or the faculty governing bodies addressed themselves to the question of tenure until 1939 when the AAUP established a Resolutions Committee "to report on a plan for Faculty Committee Hearings in Cases of Dismissal and Demotion. . . ."[56] This report was discussed in the Senate Advisory Committee on University Affairs (SACUA) and then presented to the University Senate.[57] The Senate adopted the SACUA report, which contained the following provisions:

1. Whenever it is proposed to dismiss or demote any member of the University faculty who is on indeterminate tenure [i.e. associate professor or full professor]. . . the grounds for such dismissal or demotion shall be stated in writing to the individual in question, and he or she shall have an opportunity . . . to appear in person for a hearing before an appropriate committee. . . .

2. In schools or colleges in which an executive committee has been appointed, the hearing . . . shall be held before such executive committee or before a special committee appointed for the purpose by the executive committee. [If] no executive committee has been appointed, the hearing shall be held before a special committee appointed by the governing faculty. . . . In all cases [SACUA] may be requested by the person whose dismissal or demotion is in question to review the procedure followed and to receive any evidence that the committee deems relevant.[58]

The report went on to say that full reports of all hearings would be sent to the individual involved, to the president, and to the dean. This report was approved by the regents.[59]

In 1942, the regents revised the tenure regulations so that assistant professors and instructors who had been on the staff for six years or more were granted the same procedural safeguards as those faculty on tenure.[60]

Two years later the regents changed the regulations to read that instructors and assistant professors must serve eight years before falling under the procedural protections. The regents further agreed that any faculty member threatened with dismissal or demotion could appeal to SACUA if he was aggrieved by the initial hearing. SACUA's report of its hearing would be "deemed advisory" and dismissal or demotion would not be final until the complete record of the case had been transmitted, along with the president's written recommendation, to the regents. No specific justifications for initiating dismissal or demotion procedures were cited by the regents; rather, the ambiguous phrase "causes accepted by University usage, properly connected with the improvement and efficiency of the faculty" was instituted.[61] The *By-Laws* of 1945 incorporated these 1940–1944 tenure decisions.[62]

THE CUNCANNON CASE

The first actual case to test the evolving tenure regulations was that of Dr. Paul M. Cuncannon, an assistant professor of political science.[63] Cuncannon had been on the Michigan faculty since 1923, but in April, 1942, the executive committee of the political science department voted unanimously that he be given a one-year terminal appointment. The department cited as reasons Cuncannon's declining effectiveness as a teacher, lack of cooperation in administrative duties, absence of work with graduate students, and paucity of publications (Cuncannon had published only two brief articles since 1929). The departmental decision to terminate Cuncannon's services after one year was supported, again unanimously, by the executive committee of the College of Literature, Science, and the Arts. Cuncannon, as an assistant professor, did not have tenure, and at the time the department decided that his contract would not be renewed the *By-Laws* which provided for a hearing and for appeal procedures were not yet operative. Cuncannon did avail himself of the opportunity to present his views to his department in a brief hearing, although no records of the hearing were kept. When the regents changed the *By-Laws* Cuncannon was invited to present his case at a hearing before the executive committee of Literature, Science, and the Arts. He appeared and agreed that, rather than submit to a formal hearing, he would answer the charges against him in writing and abide by the executive committee's decision. In answer to Cuncannon's rebuttal—a lengthy, rambling epistle—both of the executive committees concerned agreed that they would not reverse their original decision. Cuncannon then appealed to Ruthven, who referred the appeal to the Senate Advisory Committee on University Affairs. SACUA heard the case fully, found that "all the required procedures were conformed with," and refused to overrule the previous decisions. The SACUA decision, too, was unanimous.[64]

At this point, after the three appropriate faculty committees had delivered their unanimous verdicts, there was a very unusual turn of events. Regent Herbert, the chairman, spoke for the Regents' Committee on Educational Policies and delivered this surprising opinion: "This committee [deems] the record to date as being insufficient to base a considered opinion as to the procedures and merits of the matter involved."[65] Regent Herbert and his committee arranged for their own "entirely informal" hearing.[66] Regents Herbert, Connable, and Kipke, President Ruthven, Provost Stason, Deans Kraus and Woodburne, Professor Brown, acting chairman of the political science department, Professor Cuncannon, and a variety of witnesses met in an all-day session to consider the Cuncannon case. The transcript of the meeting is interesting in that Regent Herbert, who did the lion's share of the questioning, appears as an apologist—and practically the only one—for Cuncannon. Ruthven did not speak during the entire proceedings. The proceedings were at times heated, and it was particularly evident that the members of the political science department who testified were unhappy with Regent Herbert's attempt to reopen Cuncannon's case.

After the testimony before Herbert's Educational Policies Committee, that committee reported to the regents that "the charges against the individual concerned had not been sustained." The Educational Policies Committee then recommended that Cuncannon be appointed for two more years, and receive any blanket salary increases to which he was entitled.[67] The committee further recommended that the final year of Cuncannon's two-year appointment be

a "leave of absence, with pay . . . to pursue his work on publications . . . and establish other connections." As will be seen in
Chapter XI, these recommendations came at a time when Ruthven's
influence with the regents was at its nadir. Ruthven apparently
made no effort to intercede in what he viewed as a quarrel between
the faculty and the regents. The recommendations of Herbert's
committee were approved by the regents.[68]

Predictably, the regents' action infuriated the faculty bodies
which had been involved in the Cuncannon case. The executive
committees of the political science department and the College of
Literature, Science, and the Arts, as well as the Senate Advisory
Committee on University Affairs, sent communications to the regents. A motion to "table" the faculty communications (i.e., to
ignore them) was defeated and the regents, by split vote, agreed to
hear the disgruntled members of the faculty committee at the next
meeting.[69] At the August meeting Dean Kraus presented the following requests of the executive committee of Literature, Science,
and the Arts: 1. The Board should "delete the severe and unjust
criticism of the good faith and procedure of the faculty committees
which have reviewed the evidence in this case"; 2. "The action of the
Board of Regents in giving Dr. Cuncannon a two-year terminal
appointment [should] be modified to the extent that Dr. Cuncannon
be not a member of the staff of the Department of Political Science
and that his salary be not a part of the budget of the Department,
effective as of July 1, 1943."[70]

Faced with an insurrection from the most powerful dean of the
most powerful faculty on campus, the board's only retreat was to say
that they had not intended to question the "good faith" of the
faculty committees. The regents, however, flatly refused the request
to immediately sever Cuncannon's connection with the political science department.[71] The regents' directives were followed, for the
university's *General Register* listed Cuncannon with the political science faculty—on leave—during 1944–1945.[72]

WENGER-DAHLSTROM

Christian N. Wenger joined the department of English, College
of Engineering, in 1919, and his friend, Carl E. W. L. Dahlstrom,
joined the same department in 1920.[73] Each was a stalwart member
of the struggling Michigan AAUP and, by 1942, each had attained
the rank of associate professor. For many years, both Wenger and

Dahlstrom had been in conflict with their departmental chairman and departmental policy.[74]

In the academic year 1942–1943 Wenger and Dahlstrom were each assigned two sections of a required course called "English I." On November 19, 1924, departmental chairman Carl Brandt met Professor Wenger in a hall corridor and, during a stormy argument, accused him of refusing to conform to the uniform departmental plan for teaching "English I." Brandt, after consulting with the dean of the College of Engineering and Dr. Yoakum, Vice President in Charge of Educational Investigations, then sent letters to Wenger and Dahlstrom outlining in detail the departmental requirements and requesting that the professors conform to these requirements by November 30. The professors flatly refused. Brandt then took the matter to the executive committee of the College of Engineering, which ruled that the professors must follow the uniform program. Dean Crawford informed Ruthven of the committee's decision, and Crawford told Wenger and Dahlstrom that, unless they agreed to the departmental plan, they were not to meet their classes after December 29. Wenger and Dahlstrom appealed to the Senate Advisory Committee on University Affairs and met their classes on December 30 as usual. Crawford and Brandt entered the classrooms and dismissed the students. Naturally, the students were curious and, by January 6, *The Michigan Daily* began to give the story front-page coverage. Wenger and Dahlstrom, however, would not present their arguments to the students, and the *Daily* refrained from editorial comment until January 19, when the student editors asked that the facts be made public. They condemned the manner in which the classes of the two professors were dismissed; it was, they wrote, as if the professors were "juvenile delinquents."[75] The same day that Crawford and Brandt dismissed the classes, Ruthven wrote Wenger and Dahlstrom that they were no longer to meet their "English I" sections "until the matter can be thoroughly canvassed."

The Senate Advisory Committee on University Affairs, meanwhile, called witnesses and considered Wenger and Dahlstrom's appeal in three January, 1943, meetings. SACUA decided that, since the controversy did not present any question of demotion or dismissal, tenure was not at issue and the governing faculty of the College of Engineering should resolve the dispute.

The engineering executive committee, in assigning teaching loads for the spring semester, then reduced the class time of Wenger and Dahlstrom by half. The executive committee ruled further that each

173

professor's salary would be adjusted accordingly. These rulings involved tenure regulations, and so Wenger and Dahlstrom appealed again to SACUA, which recommended that the salaries should not be reduced until the matter was resolved.

On January 23, 1943, Crawford wrote Ruthven that the recalcitrant professors should be dismissed.[76] Provost E. Blythe Stason carefully explained to Crawford that he must follow the tenure procedures as prescribed in the By-Laws. At this point the engineering executive committee appointed a special fact-finding committee to determine whether the uniform program in the basic English courses had been properly established, and whether Wenger and Dahlstrom had followed the uniform program. The deliberations of the fact-finding committee consumed the better part of a year. During these deliberations, the engineering governing faculty agreed that a policy requiring uniformity in basic courses had been followed for many years and voted unanimously to retain such a policy.

In February, 1944, the executive committee of the College of Engineering set forth the "Grounds on Which the Executive Committee, College of Engineering, Proposes to Ask for Dismissal of Associate Professors Christian N. Wenger and Carl E. W. L. Dahlstrom." Each of the charges was detailed in a five-page document presented to the two professors.

Wenger and Dahlstrom, acting in accordance with regulations found in the Regents' Proceedings, requested a formal hearing before the executive committee of the engineering college. The hearing was held in April, 1944, and a transcript of the proceedings was made.

Following this hearing the executive committee, again voting unanimously, formally requested Ruthven and the Board of Regents to dimiss Wenger and Dahlstrom. Ruthven, carefully following the recently established procedures, informed Wenger and Dahlstrom that they were entitled to appeal to SACUA if they wished. They did, and in the summer of 1944 SACUA heard the arguments in five lengthy sessions, but upheld the engineering executive committee.

Wenger and Dahlstrom then appealed to the regents, who upheld the work of the faculty committees and agreed that if the professors refused to resign, as requested, it would be the duty of "the proper administrative authorities to sever the connection of either or both. . . ."[77]

The embattled professors had one last recourse: AAUP. The national office of AAUP sent two fact finders to Ann Arbor and the

Associate Secretary filed a sixteen-page report with Ruthven.[78] The AAUP report was highly critical of Brandt and Crawford's dismissal of Wenger and Dahlstrom's classes in November, 1942. The report also criticized the hearing conducted by the engineering executive committee in April, 1944. The AAUP contended that this committee prejudged Wenger and Dahlstrom and did not hear them objectively. The AAUP findings detailed further but less important criticisms. They also requested that Ruthven give the report wide circulation. However, AAUP did not pursue the matter further, and Wenger and Dahlstrom were dismissed at the end of academic year 1944–45, more than two years after the controversy began.

The Cuncannon and Wenger-Dahlstrom cases demonstrate Ruthven's preference that faculty matters be resolved through well-established procedures. His silence during the Cuncannon case doubtless meant that he regarded his position as extremely awkward and embarrassing. His sympathy was totally with the faculty committees, and he preferred that they, rather than he, put Regent Herbert in his place. When Regent Herbert succeeded, Ruthven must have reasoned that his own standing with the regents at that time was so tenuous that the Cuncannon matter should be dropped. The Wenger-Dahlstrom case was a clear demonstration that, given time, faculty procedures would work; Ruthven felt no need to intervene.

The faculty, in turn, reciprocated the president's confidence. They approved of Ruthven and the manner in which he handled delicate faculty issues. He was, after all, an honest scholar, one of their own. He moved deliberately, even slowly, and he was content to wait for the collective judgment of the faculty rather than impose his personal judgment as he did with student activists. There was very little of the suspicion with which faculties frequently regard their president. Indeed, SACUA minutes, AAUP records, papers of faculty members, and minutes of the University Council and University Senate reveal almost no evidence of faculty carping at either Ruthven or his policies. Evidence indicates that Ruthven was regarded with respect and even genuine affection by his faculty.

CAMPUS SPEAKERS

During the tense days prior to World War I the regents agreed to deemphasize politics on campus. "The use of Hill Auditorium for free discussion of all topics," they decided, "is not now necessary nor expedient."[79] And by the time Ruthven became president, the regents had formulated some rather elaborate statements concerning campus speakers. The 1923 *By-Laws*, for instance, stated: "Lecturers may not be invited by students nor by student associations to lecture in University buildings, without the approval of the appropriate authority, obtained in advance."[80] The *By-Laws* went on to call for a "guaranty that during . . . meetings or lectures there shall be no advocacy of the subversion of the government. . . ." No addresses would be allowed, the *By-Laws* warned, "which advocate or justify conduct which violates the fundamentals of our accepted code of morals." Furthermore, "speeches in support of particular candidates of any political party or faction shall not be permitted." However, the regents did encourage "the timely and rational discussion of topics whereby the ethical and intellectual development of the student body and the general welfare of the public may be promoted and a due respect inculcated in the people for society at large and for the constituted government of the state and nation."[81]

In 1935 the regents approved a Committee on University Lectures with jurisdiction for all public lectures. The committee was authorized to make its own rules and procedures for registering campus speakers.

The 1940 *By-Laws* reiterated these procedures, and added that only student organizations recognized by the Dean of Students office would be permitted to sponsor lectures.[82] The *By-Laws*, as amended in 1945, carried the 1940 statements with only minor wording revisions.[83]

On December 15, 1947, Gerhart Eisler and Carl Marzani, both free on bail from congressional contempt citations for refusing to say whether they were communists, were denied permission to speak in the Michigan League. Eisler was generally believed to be a high official of the American Communist Party. The event was to be sponsored by the Michigan Youth for Democratic Action, but Ruthven released the following statement:

> Michigan Youth for Democratic Action's request for space to hold a public meeting for an address by Gerhart Eisler has been disallowed for two reasons: 1. MYDA's recognition as a student organization was cancelled last April. . . ; and 2. Mr. Eisler will not be permitted to speak on the University of Michigan campus at this time under any auspices.[84]

The speech was then scheduled for an Ann Arbor public park, but cancelled by Mayor William E. Brown, Jr.[85] The decisions not to allow the speakers a place to speak met with general favor. *The Ann Arbor Daily News* editorial headline was, "University Within Rights in Banning Eisler and Marzani."[86] Later, when Eisler and Marzani visited Ann Arbor anyway, a large crowd of hostile students pelted the private home where they stayed with snowballs and began the threatening chant, "We want Eisler."[87]

Provost James P. Adams was concerned and predicted that the university must decide whether it would permit "certain persons of Communist persuasion to speak on the campus. The University should have a formal policy," he cautioned Ruthven.[88] Ruthven apparently did not respond in writing; there was also no written response to Erich Walter when Walter, then Dean of Students, said that the *By-Laws* governing campus speakers did not provide sufficient guidelines for deciding which organizations should receive campus recognition.[89]

Ruthven must have been mulling over the matter, for it was of paramount concern to campus groups and to the regents as well. In 1948, at the March meeting, the regents received a resolution from the Student Affairs Committee asking them to "clarify and possibly liberalize" the ban on political speakers.[90] The regents agreed to ponder the question and one regent, at least, thought he had the answer. "Limited amounts of time and space are available at the University for extra curricular activities," Regent Eckert reasoned, and, thus, "a limited amount of time and space may be devoted to political discussions." Eckert hastened to add, "No person, not an employee of the University or a student, may carry on a political discussion on University property, without the invitation of the President or his authorized representative."[91]

In April, 1948, the Board of Regents reaffirmed existing *By-Laws* affecting political speakers, but agreed that political speeches would be acceptable provided meetings were open solely to members of the sponsoring group.[92] President Ruthven was absent from this meeting and confided to Professor Carl Brandt, chairman of the Committee on University Lectures: "I hope the decision of the Board will not cause your committee too much inconvenience. I would have liked to have seen them worded somewhat differently."[93]

When Professor Preston W. Slosson wrote to suggest that the regents further relax their political regulations, Ruthven replied: "I believe it is rather generally known that I do not approve of the present regulations. I realize that the Regents were sincere . . . but the regulations adopted are not . . . appropriate for a great democratic institution."[94]

The Young Democrats of the University of Michigan sent a letter to the regents "requesting that this group and other interested organizations be allowed to meet with the Regents to discuss these issues." The board's opinion was that "further discussion would lead to no useful purpose," and the request was denied.[95] The students were not deterred, and the regents agreed to allow the officers of the Student Legislature, led by Blair Moody, Jr., to offer their recommendations to the regents in a presentation not to exceed thirty minutes.[96]

Meanwhile the faculty also prepared to contest the regents. The University Senate established an ad hoc Special Committee on Public Discussions of Political Issues which also requested that a Senate delegation meet with the regents. The Michigan chapter of AAUP passed a resolution supporting the concern of the Senate.[97]

The Board of Regents met with both student and faculty representatives in January, 1949, and later a regental committee was appointed to study the regulations relating to political speeches.[98] The committee reported in February, and the board agreed to delete entirely the current *By-Law* paragraph banning political speakers.[99] Instead the board substituted this ambiguous statement: "These regulations [concerning political speakers] shall be administered by the Committee on University Lectures, with the understanding that they are designed to serve the educational interests of the academic community rather than the political interests of any party or candidate."[100]

This official policy modification led to frequent disputes concerning who could and who could not be a campus speaker. It was soon obvious that the question of a communist speaker would again be raised as the first test of the new policy. In 1950, the Committee on University Lectures refused permission for Dr. Herbert J. Phillips, an avowed communist who had been fired by the University of Washington, to debate with Dr. John Phillip Wernette, director of the university's Bureau of Business Research, on the topic "Capitalism vs. Communism."[101] The lecture committee cited the *By-Laws* statement that no "advocacy of the subversion of the government" would be permitted. The lecture committee ruled that "any Communist who seeks to promote the interests of the Communist Party is advocating the subversion of the government...."[102] The decision was interpreted as meaning that no member of the Communist Party could speak in any university building.[103]

Ruthven was off campus when the decision to deny Phillips permission to speak was reached, but his letters indicate that he supported that decision. "You may be sure that at all times the University authorities have in mind the protection and the promotion of the American way of life," was his typical response to those citizens who applauded the university's stand. To an alumnus who condemned the university's position, Ruthven wrote: "We can see no good reason why Mr. Phillips should come to the campus. . . . His only purpose was to publicize himself."[104]

The Michigan Daily, however, reacted with indignation. "The unfortunate decision of the University Lecture Committee... can do nothing but lower the University in the esteem of the academic world," the editors remarked. They charged that the lecture committee was motivated by "irrational panic."[105] The student legislature also disapproved the lecture committee's stand and voted overwhelmingly to ask the Board of Regents to place four students on the committee.[106]

The following year the controversial communist was J. Edward Bromberg. Bromberg was not asked to lecture, but was appearing on the university stage in "The Royal Family." Ruthven received over fifty letters and telegrams protesting Bromberg's appearance on campus, and the public relations department was forced to issue a strong statement asserting that the university was steadfastly anti-communist.[107]

Thus, as Ruthven's presidency drew to its close, he continued to steer the university on its precarious course between the scylla of societal solicitude and the charybdis of communistic caprice. His successor was not as fortunate.[108]

NOTES

1. The best work concerning Tappan is Charles M. Perry, *Henry Philip Tappan: Philosopher and University President* (Ann Arbor: University of Michigan Press, 1933). See also the Tappan Papers, 3 vols., MHC; Papers of Alexander Winchell,

Vol. 3, MHC; *Autobiography of Andrew Dickson White,* Vol. 1 (New York: The Century Co., 1905), Ch. 16, pp. 266–83; Paul E. Ligenfelter, "The Firing of Henry Philip Tappan, University Builder," MHC; and the usual university histories.

2. Shirley W. Smith, *Harry Burns Hutchins,* pp. 198–200; and papers of Harry Burns Hutchins, boxes 35–45, MHC; and the usual university histories.

3. Alexander G. Ruthven to John L. Lovett, October 20, 1932, Ruthven Papers, box 9, MHC.

4. Ruthven to C. W. Ditchy, February 9, 1933, Ruthven Papers, box 8, MHC.

5. Rev. A. C. Hueter to Ruthven, April 18, 1939, Ruthven Papers, box 27, MHC; William C. Dudgeon to Ruthven, February 22, 1941, Ruthven Papers, box 34, MHC; Ruthven to Hon. George A. Dondero, November 11, 1947, Ruthven Papers, box 58, MHC.

6. Ruthven to Dondero, November 11, 1947, Ruthven Papers, box 58, MHC.

7. Sagendorph, "Crisis Marks The Centennial" in *Michigan: The Story of the University,* ch. 18.

8. *Ibid.,* p. 332.

9. Ruthven notes, Ruthven Papers, box 15, MHC.

10. Interview, Wesley Maurer, February 20, 1970.

11. *Detroit Free Press,* February 26, 1935, p. 6.

12. *Ibid.,* February 27, 1935, p. 6.

13. "Maurer" folder, Ruthven Papers, box 15, MHC.

14. James O. Murfin to Ralph Stone, March 7, 1935, Murfin Papers, box 8, MHC, and Murfin to Ruthven, March 7, 1935, Ruthven Papers, box 15, MHC.

15. Interview, Wesley Maurer, February 20, 1970.

16. "Maurer" folder, Ruthven Papers, box 15, MHC.

17. Interview, Maurer, February 20, 1970.

18. This story had a happy ending. Ruthven eventually appointed Maurer as head of the journalism department, and Bingay—a longtime critic of the university—finally succumbed to Ruthven's personal charm. Ruthven–Bingay correspondence, Ruthven Papers, box 41, MHC.

19. *The Detroit Free Press,* October 31, 1936, p. 21.

20. *Ann Arbor Daily News,* October 31, 1936, p. 1.

21. Murfin to David Crowley, November 2, 1936, Murfin Papers, box 8, MHC.

22. Murfin Papers, November, 1936, box 8, MHC.

23. Ruthven to the regents, November 5, 1936, Ruthven Papers, box 21, MHC.

24. Junius Beal to Ruthven, November 6, 1936, Ruthven Papers, box 20, MHC.

25. Stone to Murfin, November 4, 1936, Murfin Papers, box 8, MHC.

26. Esther Marsh Cram to Murfin, November 5, 1936, *ibid.*

27. Murfin to Ruthven, November 10, 1936, Ruthven Papers, box 21, MHC.

28. Ruthven to W. R. Humphreys, October 9, 1935, Ruthven Papers, box 18, MHC.

29. Ruthven to Hugh Webney, October 2, 1936, Ruthven Papers, box 22, MHC.

30. Ruthven Papers, box 57, MHC.

31. *The Detroit Free Press,* February 17, 1947, p. 1.

Academic Freedom and the Faculty

tven
Papers, box 79, MHC.

33. Marvin Niehuss to Wendell Berge, Assistant Attorney-General, U. S. Department of Justice, April 16, 1947, *ibid.*

34. Ruthven to Rex Humphey, April 24, 1947, *ibid.,* and Ruthven to Junius B. Wood, April 28, 1947, *ibid.*

35. News release, April 22, 1947, *ibid.*

36. *Ibid.*

37. *Ibid.*

38. Ruthven to Earl F. Ganschow, February 13, 1947, Ruthven Papers, box 54, MHC.

39. S. W. Sedgwick to Ruthven, May 25, 1948, Ruthven Papers, box 58, MHC.

40. Ruthven to Sedgwick, June 19, 1948, *ibid.*

41. "In Our Opinion," WJR radio broadcast, March 14, 1948, text in "miscellaneous IV" folder, Ruthven Papers, box 77, MHC.

42. Ruthven, "Some Facts and Fears," speech to University of Michigan Press Club, September 30, 1948, *ibid.*

43. Rensis Likert to Ruthven, October 5, 1948, Ruthven Papers, box 59, MHC, and Theodore M. Newcomb to Ruthven, October 7, 1948, Ruthven Papers, box 60, MHC.

44. John S. Wood to Ruthven, June 1, 1949, Ruthven Papers, box 60, MHC.

45. Ruthven to Wood, June 13, 1949, *ibid.*

46. W. T. Donkin to Ruthven, July 31, 1950, Ruthven Papers, box 63, MHC.

47. Ruthven to Donkin, August 16, 1950, *ibid.*

48. Carl E. W. L. Dahlstrom to Anton Carlson, February 20, 1936, Papers of the Michigan Chapter of AAUP, 1935–1959, MHC.

49. Dahlstrom to Carlson, February 25, 1936, *ibid.*

50. "Report of the Secretary for 1948–49," *ibid.*

51. Ruthven, "A Code For Professors," *Bulletin of the American Association of University Professors,* Vol. 21, No. 6 (1935), pp. 482–86. The *AAUP Bulletin* also printed a Ruthven speech, "Leadership or Regimentation in Higher Education," in which he warned against state legislatures and "partisan political influences" as the "most imminent danger" to state universities. Vol. 23, No. 8 (1937), pp. 674–81.

52. James K. Pollock to Ruthven, February 9, 1935, Ruthven Papers, box 16, MHC.

53. *By-Laws,* 1923, ch. 5, sec. 6(a).

54. *Proceedings of the Board of Regents,* April meeting, 1930, p. 239.

55. Murfin to Ruthven, June 14, 1932, Ruthven Papers, box 6, MHC.

56. Letter of D. C. Long to "Harold" (probably Professor Harold Dorr), July 23, 1945, papers of the Michigan chapter of AAUP, 1935–59, MHC.

57. SACUA was a nine-member body elected by the University Senate. Its charge was to "consult and advise the President upon matters of University interest." (Frank E. Robbins to Jesse E. Adams, February 13, 1942, Ruthven Papers, box 38, MHC.) In actual practice, SACUA concerned itself largely with faculty interests such as tenure and salaries.

58. *University of Michigan Council and Senate Records, 1936–1941,* pp. 111–12.

59. *Proceedings of the Board of Regents,* second July meeting, 1941, pp. 688–89.

181

60. *Proceedings of the Board of Regents,* December meeting, 1942, pp. 170–71. The Papers of the Michigan Chapter of the AAUP, 1935–1959, show that the chapter had been advocating this safeguard since 1939.

61. *Proceedings of the Board of Regents,* January meeting, 1944, pp. 523–24.

62. Sec. 5.09 and 5.091. Although the record is nowhere explicit, one can infer that the usual "bargaining" between faculty interests and regents' interests produced the finalized tenure regulations. For example, when AAUP and the University Senate agreed that junior professors should be safeguarded by procedural guarantees, the regents first capitulated, then decided that eight years rather than six years of probationary status was required. Originally, the regents agreed to hearings by executive committees. The president appointed executive committees from lists submitted by the school or college, and thus could exercise some control. The AAUP records show that that body pressed for a hearing committee chosen entirely by the faculty, and the regents eventually agreed that SACUA, elected by the faculty members of the University Senate, might act as an appeal board.

63. The following description of Cuncannon's case is taken from testimony presented before the Regents' Committee on Educational Policies, April 23, 1943, Ruthven Papers, box 81, MHC, p. 123.

64. Minutes of a special meeting of SACUA, March 22, 1943, SACUA files.

65. Testimony before Regents' Committee on Educational Policies, April 23, 1943, Ruthven Papers, box 81, MHC, p. 4. What influenced Herbert to intervene in the Cuncannon case is difficult to determine. It has been established that Herbert's daughter was a student of Cuncannon; this was apparently the only connection between Cuncannon and Regent Herbert.

66. *Ibid.*

67. *Proceedings of the Board of Regents,* June meeting, 1943, p. 319. Cuncannon's salary in 1929 was $3,000; at the time of his "case," 1943, his salary was $2,800. Testimony before the Regents' Committee on Educational Policies, April 23, 1943, Ruthven Papers, box 81, MHC, p. 118.

68. *Ibid.*

69. *Proceedings of the Board of Regents,* July meeting, 1943, p. 363.

70. *Proceedings of the Board of Regents,* August meeting, 1943, p. 369.

71. *Ibid.*

72. *General Register,* p. 218. Two of Cuncannon's former colleagues recall that, after leaving Michigan, Cuncannon joined the faculty of a Chester, Pennsylvania "teachers college." He is not listed in the *Directory of the American Political Science Association* for either 1945 or 1953, and he is not listed in any of the standard directories.

73. Since October, 1969, this department has been part of the Department of Humanities, College of Engineering.

74. "Documents Considered By The Executive Committee, College of Engineering in Connection With the Case of Associate Professors C. N. Wenger and Carl E. W. L. Dahlstrom," Ruthven Papers, box 81, MHC, pp. 43–50. Unless other sources are cited, the text which follows is taken from the voluminous transcripts of the Wenger-Dahlstrom hearings before the executive committee of the College of Engineering, the Senate Advisory Committee on University Affairs, and a brief submitted by Wenger and Dahlstrom. All are found in the Ruthven Papers, box 81, MHC.

Academic Freedom and the Faculty

75. *The Michigan Daily,* January 19, 1943, p. 2.

76. Crawford to Ruthven, January 23, 1943, Ruthven Papers, box 41, MHC.

77. *Proceedings of the Board of Regents,* January meeting, 1945, p. 826.

78. Report of Robert P. Ludlum for the American Association of University Professors, November 14, 1946, Ruthven Papers, box 81, MHC.

79. Smith, *Harry Burns Hutchins,* pp. 152–53.

80. *By-Laws,* 1923, ch. 6, sec. 7.

81. *By-Laws,* 1923, ch. 36, sec. 2(a) and 2(b); also ch. 3a, sec. 6(c).

82. *By-Laws,* 1940, ch. 8, sec. 8.08.

83. *Ibid.*

84. Press release, December 13, 1947, "Eisler-Marzani" folder, Ruthven Papers, box 79, MHC.

85. *The Ann Arbor Daily News,* December 15, 1947, p. 3.

86. *Ibid.,* p. 4.

87. *Ibid.,* December 16, 1947, p. 3.

88. James P. Adams to Ruthven, December 26, 1947, Ruthven Papers, box 57, MHC.

89. Erich Walter to Ruthven, January 19, 1948, Ruthven Papers, box 58, MHC.

90. *Proceedings of the Board of Regents,* March meeting, 1948, p. 1205.

91. Otto E. Eckert to Ruthven, March 19, 1948, Ruthven Papers, box 57, MHC.

92. *Proceedings of the Board of Regents,* April meeting, 1948, p. 1210.

93. Ruthven to Brandt, April 19, 1948, Ruthven Papers, box 57, MHC.

94. Ruthven to Slosson, November 15, 1948, Ruthven Papers, box 62, MHC.

95. *Proceedings of the Board of Regents,* May meeting, 1948, p. 1264.

96. *Proceedings of the Board of Regents,* annual June meeting, 1948, pp. 1357–1358. Moody, Sr. was appointed U. S. Senator from Michigan in 1951.

97. Minutes of the University of Michigan chapter, AAUP, December 14, 1948, Papers of the AAUP, 1935–1959, MHC.

98. *Proceedings of the Board of Regents,* January meeting, 1949, p. 214.

99. *By-Laws,* 1945, sec. 8.08 (1).

100. *Proceedings of the Board of Regents,* February meeting, 1949, p. 239.

101. Wernette had been President of the University of New Mexico, but was fired by the regents of that institution in an unsavory political dispute. Wernette wrote Ruthven, inquiring about a position at Michigan, and was appointed as a professor soon after. Ruthven Papers, box 60, MHC.

102. "Report of the Committee on University Lectures," April 7, 1950, Ruthven Papers, box 62, MHC.

103. *The Michigan Daily,* April 18, 1950, p. 1.

104. Ruthven to Richard Nahabedian, June 5, 1950, Ruthven Papers, box 62, MHC. Phillips later appeared in Ann Arbor and debated history professor Preston W. Slosson off campus before a crowd of 2,000 people. *The Michigan Daily,* April 28, 1950, p. 1.

105. *Ibid.,* April 18, 1950, p. 1.

106. *Ibid.,* April 20, 1950, p. 1.

107. Ruthven Papers, box 63, MHC. One of the more vivid letters declared: "I would like to be among those in the first row . . . so that I could heave a few eggs at

your friend Bromberg." Spencer Carter to Ruthven, May 28, 1951, Ruthven Papers, box 63, MHC.

108. Very soon after Dr. Harlan Hatcher became president he was faced with an academic freedom case which resulted in an official national AAUP censure of the university. *Bulletin of the American Association of University Professors,* vol. 44, no. 1 (1958), pp. 53–101. See also a 1970 senior honors thesis by Marsha Novick in the Department of History, University of Michigan, and *The Ann Arbor News,* May 8, 1954 to May 25, 1954.

Nadir: The War Years

The first half of Ruthven's twenty-two-year regime was a triumph. He was vigorously and confidently in control of his institution. His quiet leadership was moving the university forward.

"Dear Prexy," the chairman of the journalism department wrote in 1939, "I felt very strongly that you had completed a great year and that the public had rallied to you, not only with approval, but with deep affection. You must have felt a sort of strident loyalty in the very air you breathed... more power to you!" Jack Brumm concluded. [1]

"Do not be impressed by proceedings of the Board of Regents," Ruthven told Dr. Karl Litzenberger when the director of the residence halls had asked to raise the rents; "the boat is where the captain says it is... the only approval you need is mine." [2] These sentiments flowed freely at a testimonial dinner given in Ruthven's honor in October, 1939. Seventy floats and skits, with over 1000 students participating, paraded before 2500 guests in the "Pageant of the Decade." Yost Field House was the only place large enough to accommodate the celebrants. It was the largest, most enthusiastic dinner ever held in Ann Arbor, and Ruthven was its focus. These were to be the best moments of his presidency.

After negotiating the Depression years so successfully, Ruthven had every reason to anticipate golden years of fulfillment for himself and the university. He had earned the respect of his campus and, indeed, the state. He had a capable and seasoned administrative team in harness and pulling together. His initiative had resulted in an acclaimed "platform statement," an innovative "Michigan System" of university organization, a scheme which replaced the mill tax, and a program for residential living. For the first half of his presidency, Ruthven was a leader of unquestionable skill. At age fifty-seven he complained to C. C. ("Pete") Little: "The only way to keep from being discouraged is to realize that new ideas are usually accepted by the young, and one must be contented to let the graybeards die off in their ignorance and conservatism."[3]

Ruthven felt young and vigorous. His children had left the home and gone their separate ways, while he and his wife devoted their time unreservedly to the duties of his office. It was tiring, to be sure, but there was pride in a job well done and, always, rejuvenation during the summer at Frankfort.

Horses, so long a part of his life, now became an avocation as he began to breed Morgans. Stable Manager Jimmy Dolan brought the first one back from Vermont in the mid-1930s, and Ruthven fell in love with this sturdy, barrel-bodied breed. He bought a farm near Fuller Road on the north side of the Huron River about two miles from the campus and called it Stanerigg after his ancestral home in Scotland. The barn became his stable for the dozen or so Morgans; his daughter Kate and her husband Laurence Stuart lived in the house. He had the only Morgans in Michigan and, since the breed

Pageant of the Decade (1939)

was almost extinct when he began raising them, he soon became known nationally as an authority on the Morgan horse. One other hobby flourished, but only briefly. This was breeding pedigreed boxer dogs. Ruthven had a favorite English bulldog, Eleanor, whose successor Alexis ("Lexy")—a boxer—gave birth to several litters of pups. As he did with his Morgans, Ruthven began to collect a small library devoted to boxer dogs. As Ruthven faced the decade of the forties the future looked bright.

THE "MINORITY GROUP" OF REGENTS

Ruthven's relationship with his first Board of Regents was unusually harmonious. Even Junius Beal, who had opposed Ruthven's ascension to the presidency, grew to be one of his strongest backers. When inevitable disagreements of policy would arise, the regents and the president would frankly—never acrimoniously—discuss their differences and, usually, find an agreeable solution. When Regents Stone and Murfin voiced their concern about the lack of direction of certain schools and colleges, for example, Ruthven replied with his candid and thorough evaluation, not only of the educational units, but of their leadership as well. He concluded: "I hope you will never hesitate for a moment to bring criticism to my attention. I will probably err from time to time but I have set for myself the objective of making Michigan take her place among the great universities. . . ."[4] The regents were satisfied.

But criticism was rare. The Ruthven Papers and the papers of the regents indicate that there was general accord on policy, mutual respect for personalities and opinions, and an absence of internecine politics.[5] Harmony appeared to prevail even after the composition of Ruthven's original board was altered. After the death of the respected veteran, Dr. Walter H. Sawyer, in 1931, Dr. Richard R. Smith, a Grand Rapids surgeon, was appointed as his successor. The solid phalanx of Republican regents was broken in 1932 when the Roosevelt landslide brought the unexpected election of Democrats Franklin Cook, a retired Hillsdale banker, and Charles F. Hemans, a Lansing attorney. Democratic representation was further bolstered when Governor Comstock appointed Edmund C. Shields, also a Lansing attorney, to replace L. L. Hubbard, who had resigned after twenty-two years as a regent. Shields was well known to the other regents, and Regent R. Perry Shorts, a Republican, told him:

Alexander G. Ruthven of Michigan

"You are the best democrat [*sic*] and also the best citizen I know of for the job. The Board will welcome you with open arms."[6] Shields was readily accepted by both Ruthven and the regents, and it became apparent that both Smith and Cook were quiet men who, judging by their dearth of correspondence with President Ruthven, preferred to leave the bulk of university decision-making to the faculty and the president. When Regent Murfin returned to the board in 1934, Ruthven remained blessed with regents who were, generally, able, interested in the university, and cooperative with its president.[7]

The one exception was Regent Hemans. The Democrats customarily were the minority party in Michigan, and Hemans personally held a long record of championing unsuccessful political activities. He had himself been an unsuccessful candidate for both circuit judge and for Congress.[8] Hemans must have subscribed to the political adage, "to the victors belong the spoils," for as regent he began to request that Ruthven deliver favors.

During the Depression Hemans casually suggested that his mother would like a job at the university. The president dutifully reported that he had checked with Librarian Bishop and Dean of Women Lloyd and no positions were vacant.[9] Hemans did not consider his request improper and was upset to think that Ruthven seemed reluctant to cooperate. He wrote Ruthven:

> It seemed to me of so little consequence that it could be cared for without the slightest effort on your part. . . . This came naturally to me . . . because for about fifteen years I have made similar requests of many state officials for many other people and without hesitation or remarks these people were secured a position.[10]

Ruthven explained to Hemans that he could not "hire and fire at will," and suggested that perhaps the question of employment for Hemans' mother should be raised with the board.[11] Hemans retreated from this kind of showdown and Ruthven glossed over the incident.

On another occasion Hemans told Ruthven that a state civil service bill, advanced by political scientist James K. Pollock, was causing "a very, very decided ill feeling towards the University," particularly among the Democrats who then controlled the legislature. "If Mr. Pollock continues to shoot off on its principles," Hemans warned, "the natural sequence is going to be that the University is going to suffer on his account." The regent suggested that Ruthven "curb" Professor Pollock.[12] Ruthven had no such intention. He pointed out to Hemans that Pollock had been asked by two governors to prepare a civil service bill, and his work was "nonpartisan." Ruthven concluded:

> I cannot possibly serve notice on the members of the faculty that they must not express any opinion contrary to that held by the ruling party in the State. I do not believe you would want me to do this even to save the appropriations of the University. If our funds are cut . . . I will be perfectly willing to go to the people of the State and lay the facts before them.[13]

Hemans' political maneuvering eventually won him a jail sentence, but not until he had served seven years as a regent.[14]

In the elections of 1937 Democrats Shields—who had been defeated in the 1935 election by David H. Crowley—and John D. Lynch of Detroit replaced Murfin and Dr. Smith. Lynch was interested in forcing a program of reform on the "old conservative Republicans" who had been running the university, and he began by attempting to liberalize athletic scholarships to ensure winning football.[15] Lynch, like Hemans, began to request favors from the president.[16]

Lynch and Hemans, occasionally aided by Shields, began to consider the possibility of changing some of the board's standard practices. Honorary degrees, for example, were customarily given to those recommended by the faculties and approved by the regents. In 1938, the board asked the president to appoint a regental committee to consider the question of honorary degree recipients. Regents Lynch, Shields, Crowley, and Beal were appointed.[17] The following year the board approved two honorary degrees without consulting the faculty.[18] President Ruthven told the board that the change in traditional procedure had proved an embarrassment to all concerned, and he urged a return to the old method of selection.[19]

Also in 1939 Ruthven received from Regent Shields a letter which raised some questions about university policy. "It seems to me," wrote Shields, "instead of the insurance being dished out by one man from the University [Vice President Shirley W. Smith] there are several of the regents who have friends that we would like to accommodate." The regent also called for a review of the Board in Control of Physical Education.[20] Ruthven responded in separate letters in which he masterfully answered each question. The university administration was convinced that its present method of handling insurance was the most economical, he said, but the regents could change this if they wished. The president also retorted that it would not be wise for the board to "take over the policies governing athletics," for athletics are controlled by the faculty—a requisite for membership in the Big Ten conference.[21] Apparently the Board of Regents had its way on the insurance question, for the company which had written the university's policies for twenty years was abruptly discharged.[22]

In 1939, regents Stone and Beal, who had served a combined total of forty-eight years, retired from the board. J. Joseph Herbert, a Manistique attorney, and Harry G. Kipke, the retired football coach, were elected as their replacements.[23] In 1941, Alfred B. Connable, an Ann Arbor and Kalamazoo businessman, was elected to the board. Like Herbert and Kipke, Connable was a Republican. With Connable's election to the board, an alliance among Lynch, Herbert, and Connable began which was to distress Ruthven during the war years and even until he retired. He called them the "minority group."[24] Although there is little in the record to indicate the extent of the disagreements between Ruthven and the "minority group" during those years, the tensions beneath the surface must have tried the patience of the remaining regents.[25]

It was suggested once again to Ruthven that perhaps the regents should investigate purchasing procedures at the university.[26] This prompted Vice President Shirley W. Smith to tender his resignation.[27] Ruthven refused to accept, and he told Smith that he must understand that "the members of our interesting group [the regents] all have different temperaments." Ruthven expressed his hope that he, Smith, and the regents could "continue as a group, at least until better times," for it was important to "do what we can to keep the old boat on an even keel."[28]

During the 1942 fall term, controversy concerning Ruthven's attitude toward the war effort erupted in public print. In contemporary parlance, Ruthven was too "dovish" to suit the "hawkish" regents. The "minority group" of regents told the newspapers that the regents had had a stormy four-hour session, and that further "defeatism" on the part of the university administration would not be tolerated.[29] Ruthven, when called to comment, said that the dispute was only a "minor administrative matter" and "nothing to get excited about."[30] This public disclosure of the board's differences with Ruthven could only be aimed at embarrassing the chief executive.[31]

It seems almost certain that Regent Herbert's successful intervention in the Cuncannon case (cf. Chapter X) must have contributed to the antipathy between Ruthven and the "minority group" of the regents.

President Ruthven was further embarrassed by a bizarre incident involving his former colleague from the university museums, Dr. Carl L. Hubbs. Hubbs was a longstanding faculty member and a prominent ichthyologist. In May, 1943, Hubbs was arrested by Ann Arbor police as a "peeping Tom."[32] Hubbs contended that he had been caught in a compromising position because a previous encounter had left him with an unreasonable fear of the police. Ruthven carefully reviewed the situation and decided that Hubbs should remain on the faculty. However, two of the regents conducted their own investigation and concluded that Hubbs should be dismissed. Ruthven regarded their amateur sleuthing as "amusing." "In my opinion," he wrote a friend, "this is a very poor method of handling personnel problems in the University...."[33] Nevertheless, the "minority group" pressed the issue and the regents, by split vote, resolved: "That Professor Carl L. Hubbs be and is hereby requested to resign, and if he does not resign that he be discharged."[34] Hubbs resigned, but Ruthven issued a formal statement to the board saying that he disagreed with the judgment which made Hubbs' resignation necessary.[35]

With the friction between Ruthven and the "minority group" mounting, it was not surprising that some of the regents wished to replace Ruthven. Ruthven has recorded: "For several months they carried a copy of what was to be my resignation to the meeting hoping to persuade a majority of the Board to ask for it."[36] However, the "minority group" never gained the extra votes needed to replace him. The elections of 1944 pleased Ruthven for, he confided to ex-regent Ralph Stone, he had known R. Spencer Bishop and Ralph A. Hayward for years, and "they have the qualifications of a good regent."[37] Still, as late as 1949, the dissatisfied minority of regents evidently kept pressing for Ruthven's replacement. Then Regent Herbert told Regent Vera Baits that he had wanted a full discussion of the matter for some time, and he added resignedly, "Another academic year will begin, and I am afraid another year lost."[38] In

Ruthven's opinion the board stabilized during the final few years of his presidency, and "again demonstrated in its actions the singleness of purpose, wisdom, and ability which has guided the University during most of its history."[39]

Nevertheless, throughout the Ruthven story, but particularly when the influence of the "minority group" was felt, one is frequently surprised at the regents' lack of understanding of the roles of the various constitutive segments of a university community. The regents were, generally, men of stature, experience, and dedication, but all too often they attempted to govern the university as if it were the more familiar bank, industry, or law firm. The example of Regent Murfin calling for the removal of "communist" faculty members, Regent Lynch or Regent Hemans expecting personal favors, or Regent Herbert overriding the unanimous and legitimate decisions of three faculty committees as he did in the Cuncannon Case did not augment the view that regents are paradigms of wisdom.

In addition to these unhappy examples, there were larger issues on which the president was overruled by the regents. The Hubbs episode was one, and the saga of the Workers' Education Service (cf. Chapter XII) was another. These issues involved important principles. Who, after all, was to make decisions on academic programs and faculty appointments? Ruthven had stated very precisely and very early in his regime that the regents' responsibility was primarily to ensure fiscal stability and to educate themselves to the broad needs of the university. It was not their place to meddle in specific academic or personnel decisions.

In retrospect, Ruthven should have fought long and hard to retain this principle, even if it meant his own resignation. Instead, his protests were mild and his usual reaction was to remain "silent as the pillars of Angell Hall" until the turmoil subsided. There were times when Ruthven, who by nature was a mediator, should have become a gladiator.

He did not, apparently, simply because he loved the university and abhorred adverse publicity. He had pride, but it was more for the university than for himself. "I was under no illusions," Ruthven recalled, "I was just a garden variety president."[40] He did not believe that he was a man of such significance that his university should once again be convulsed by chaos because its president couldn't get along with its Board of Regents.

WORLD WAR II

With the shaky support of a fragmented board, President Ruthven faced the challenge of World War II. Ruthven anticipated the war years with genuine dread, for he had been on the Michigan campus during the first World War, when military training units had totally disrupted the academic program and fifty-seven men had died in an influenza epidemic.[41] Ruthven determined to do what he could to aid the war effort, while at the same time preserving the educational integrity of his institution. He resolved not to allow a repetition of the World War I fiasco.

The university had had a voluntary ROTC unit since the end of World War I. This unit annually enrolled about 1000 men and graduated about one hundred commissioned officers a year.[42] In addition, a Civilian Pilot Training Program was established in 1939. However, Ruthven's determination that new military units not disrupt the campus was evident from the beginning. In April, 1939, the Bureau of Navigation proposed to establish an NROTC unit at Michigan.[43] The president consulted with his faculties and replied that the proposal was "deemed inadvisable," for "curricular adjustments are not entirely satisfactory to [the] University and it has been found quite impossible to provide necessary physical facilities."[44] Rear Admiral Chester W. Nimitz received a similar reaction when he proposed that Michigan students embark on a thirty-day cruise and then attend a ninety-day Reserve Midshipmen's School, for which university course credit would be given.[45] Ruthven and Provost E. Blythe Stason again consulted the faculties and concluded: "The subject matter of instruction does not overlap on any of our required courses, and the type of training does not . . . seem to be the kind contemplated . . . in satisfaction of requirements for our . . . undergraduate degrees."[46] When Nimitz persisted, some units of the university agreed to grant one course credit for the venture.[47]

In the year prior to the attack on Pearl Harbor, the paramount concern of the university community was a bill proposing national compulsory military training for single men between the ages of twenty-one and thirty-six. Congress debated the bill throughout the summer of 1940 and passed it in September, 1940.

When Ruthven realized that compulsory military training appeared inevitable, he began to advocate an on-campus summer

ROTC, for he reasoned that such a program would enable young men to avoid the draft longer and enter the service as officers.[48] He also joined with other educators in urging Congress to allow men to complete the academic year before reporting to the armed services.[49] At the same time, Ruthven took advantage of every opportunity to attack the new law. Speaking at the centennial celebration of the College of Literature, Science, and the Arts, he said that drafting men out of college was a disservice to democracy. To his surprise, Ruthven's remarks received over thirty favorable responses and only two unfavorable ones. "All we are trying to do at the University of Michigan," he wrote such correspondents, "is to say that defense should be accepted in the full meaning of the word, and that we should not unnecessarily sacrifice our gains as free people."[50] Throughout 1941 Ruthven was a forceful antagonist of compulsory military training. "I have been speaking my mind very frankly about the effect of the present Selective Service Act on college students," he told the editor of the Portland, Oregon, *Journal*. "I expected to be very severely criticized for my remarks, but have never said anything, even about the weather, which met with such general approval."[51] Later, Ruthven refused to take part in a discussion with General Lewis B. Hershey, Admiral Nimitz, and President Harold Dodds of Princeton University before the Association of American Universities. Ruthven's secretary wrote the secretary of the Association that Ruthven feels "so strongly that conscription has been bungled and there is so little we can do about it that he would prefer not to take an active part in the discussion."[52] The blandishments of Ruthven and other educators must have had some effect, for in March, 1941, General Hershey issued orders deferring students in certain critical disciplines such as engineering and chemistry.

As war appeared more and more imminent, Ruthven was motivated by fears which caused his position to crystallize. First of all, he worried about the physical safety of his own children (his two sons were draft age) and also for the Michigan students, whom he regarded with paternal affection. The complete text of a Ruthven letter to Rev. William Hainsworth read: "If I knew that the world would stop in its mad rush and listen to me for one minute, I would say just one thing: War under any name is murder."[53] Ruthven also considered war destructive of the humanizing goals he had worked so hard to promote. He told Robert M. Hutchins that he was "trying to convince prominent educators in this country that total

defense must include protection of moral and intellectual values . . .
defense which permits the wrecking . . . of the educational programs
of young people is no defense at all in the long run."[54] He complained to the Secretary of State that the federal government was
apparently willing to spend billions of dollars for defense, but its
support of inter-American cultural programs was minimal.[55]
Ruthven was not proposing an exemption for the country's educational institutions; rather, he thought their greatest service would be
the training of doctors, dentists, engineers, chemists, and teachers
as well as soldiers and sailors.[56] Ruthven did recognize that the
coming war would mean the displacement of students and faculty,
changing curriculums, and war-related research. He accepted this,
though reluctantly. Yet he implored the nation's educators to give
"conservation of citizen resources" equal attention with "conservation of material resources," and he added:

> As the greatest part of the world sinks slowly into the slough of
> barbarism, they should hold up the heads of young people as long as
> possible in the hope that when danger is past it will be found that
> plans for reconstruction have been drawn and that there are some
> persons left who will be prepared to reorganize a society of free men.
> Otherwise there is not much use in trying to win the struggle.[57]

When Japan bombed Pearl Harbor and war was declared,
Ruthven faced the task of speaking to the students about their duties
in wartime. He had never, he confided to Chase Osborn, faced a
task he dreaded more.[58] In typical style, Ruthven urged calm, and
he counseled the distraught students:

> If you honestly believe you will be of more value as a sailor or soldier
> at the present time, you should offer your services at once. The
> University not only will oppose no objections, but will endeavor to
> make equitable adjustments in fees and credits. If, on the other hand,
> you believe more education would increase your value in the strug-
> gle, then with no apologies to anyone, you should remain in school
> until you are called. I would not be misunderstood here. War is
> tragedy. . . . College men must, of course, accept their share as
> Americans have done in past generations. I do not counsel a young
> man to remain in school . . . if his main reason . . . is to avoid personal
> sacrifices. . . . I am asking that in making your decision you examine
> yourselves carefully and take the long view of your country's need.[59]

Shortly after war was declared, Ruthven established a university
"war board" charged with formulating "plans for the adjustment of

the operations of the University to war demands."[60] The war board, which consisted of six faculty and administrators, met daily for several months. One of its first innovations was probably its most significant: in order to accelerate its program, the university's calendar was changed to three terms. This plan, first proposed in January, 1941, was subject to considerable skepticism by the deans but was operative throughout the war.

Major new programs were introduced to the campus. Chief among them were the Judge Advocate General's school for military lawyers, and the army's Japanese language school. Many faculty members began to engage in classified research. By the fall term, 1942, enrollment for men showed a 17 percent decline, and many faculty members began to leave for government service. Still, as Ruthven had hoped, the academic regimen was not appreciably altered, and Michigan continued to function as an institution of higher learning.

By October, 1942, critics of Ruthven's position began to be heard. *The Michigan Daily* published a front-page editorial accusing the administration of insufficient determination in supporting the war effort. The editor urged the students to assume aggressive leadership.[61] A student rally in Hill Auditorium ignited student passions and, after a series of patriotic speeches, Bald reported the campus "agog with the newly aroused interest in war work."[62]

It was against this background that, at the October 1942 meeting of the regents, the following resolution was passed:

> It is the policy of the University to encourage its students to participate actively and patriotically in the war efforts; to aid them in their preparation for war service. . . . Now therefore to assist in implementing such policy there is hereby created a Regents' Committee on War Activities, which committee shall consist of Regents Lynch, Crowley, and Connable to study the war problems of the University . . . and to make its recommendations to the Board of Regents from time to time.[63]

The regents' committee, in a lengthy press release, left no doubt that their group was to be an "action committee." "I'll resign from the committee rather than see it operate in a merely advisory capacity," Regent Lynch threatened. "Michigan can't go on as usual," he added, "when other young people are fighting for their very lives. Education isn't going to be much good if we don't win this war."[64]

Lynch, secretary of the regents' war committee, wasted little time demanding that a "complete survey" of the activities of the university war board be undertaken immediately. He imperiously addressed a series of questions to Ruthven and concluded: "Your prompt reply will assist the Regents' War Committee in its survey preliminary to an evaluation of the entire University of Michigan War attitude and program."[65]

The efforts of the regents' war committee triggered campus support, for following the October meeting of the regents a petition was circulated among the faculty. This petition supported the regents "win the war" policy and condemned the university administration for failing to give wholehearted support to the war effort. Over 150 faculty members signed the petition, and when it was presented to Ruthven he signed it, too, saying, "any loyal American would be glad to sign it."[66]

The Michigan Daily again attacked Ruthven's position, this time more openly. "Students, faculty members and Regents have placed a sizeable share of the blame for our inadequate contribution to the war effort . . . on President Ruthven's own doorstep," the editors charged.[67] The following day *Daily* editor Homer Swander assailed Ruthven's "psychological attitude." Swander demanded fast, aggressive leadership, and he said of the Michigan president: "He has not been able to shake himself loose from his pre-war ideas and methods and he has let the lessons of the last war affect him too much."[68] However, on succeeding days the *Daily* published letters from three students who wrote to defend Ruthven's stand.

Ruthven also received staunch support from the state's newspaper editors. *The Flint Journal,* edited by Ruthven's close friend, Michael Gorman, deplored the action of the regents in smearing the good name of the university and its president.[69] *The Detroit Free Press* called criticism of the university's policy "war hysteria by some super patriots." The editorial suggested that "what the University of Michigan needs is not so much a star chamber guardian of its faculty and president as it does a better board of regents." The article concluded: "Using newspaper headlines to 'try' an educator of the reputation of Dr. Ruthven doesn't strike us as 'cricket'."[70]

Bald reported that "President Ruthven remained calm during all this hubbub. He apparently was convinced that an investigation of the University's activities in furtherance of the war effort would reveal a well-rounded program of cooperation."[71] If indeed Ruthven remained outwardly calm, he was doubtlessly upset by the public row the regents had created. He confided to Howard Mumford Jones that "some trustees and regents are taking a very narrow view of the responsibility of the institutions in these times."[72]

Just prior to the November meeting of the Board of Regents the president delivered his customary address at the annual dinner of the University Press Club, an organization of state newspaper editors. In one of his longest and strongest speeches Ruthven reiterated his resolve:

> Educators, whether preachers, teachers or newspapermen, are traitors if they do not cling to a faith in the ability of man to live in a state of independence, self-respect, and good will, and to activate this faith by the courageous dissemination of knowledge, by the encouragement of thinking even in the face of engulfing emotionalism. . . .[73]

During this speech Ruthven made a special point of deploring the recent incursion of technical curriculums which were prostituting the traditional humanities and "pure science," but he insisted that the universities were doing their part in winning the war.[74] The University Press Club was so enamored of Ruthven's remarks that it passed a resolution declaring: "The Press Club is happy that the University has such leadership in the emergency and extends to Dr. Ruthven good wishes along with its gratitude."[75]

Meanwhile, the university war board drew up a 124-page document detailing its extensive activities and submitted it to the regents' war committee. The regents' committee was apparently satisfied with the war board's efforts, for it "expressed its appreciation of this carefully prepared report which was made available so promptly."[76] The firm backing of the "fourth estate" and the prompt and thorough report of the university war board were probably instrumental in deterring the "minority group" from forcing a showdown over Ruthven's wartime leadership.

Ruthven encountered one other military controversy at the university during the war years, although compared to the battle with the regents it was a mere skirmish. This dispute concerned ROTC commandant William A. Ganoe, described as "self-confident, aggressive with his views, and impatient."[77] Ganoe authorized an article criticizing the university's curriculum for producing "a hothouse, indoor, flabby manhood. . . . Too largely have we succeeded in turning out low-browed gladiators and high-browed anemics," the Colonel asserted.[78] Then he wrote directly to the regents to complain that the university would allow no more than twelve hours credit for ROTC.[79] Ruthven hastened to chastize the Colonel, and told him that his actions did not "contribute to good relations between the University units. In my opinion," wrote Ruthven, "it would have been much better if you had asked for a conference with Dean Kraus and the members of the Faculty Personnel Committee to discuss the matters which concern you."[80] Ganoe, in turn, retorted that he was "genuinely surprised" to receive Ruthven's letter, for "it is accepted practice for a head of a unit in the University to address the Board of Regents directly."[81] Ganoe was later promoted by the army; he left Michigan, and there was no further discord with the ROTC.

As the war continued, Ruthven turned his attention to the role of the post-war university. He felt that the confusing directives of the national government left universities "in the dark" and he asked the federal budget director, "Why, oh why, doesn't the President create a new cabinet position for education? . . ."[82] During 1943, following a visit to England at the invitation of the Ministry of Education and the British Council, he began to extol the virtues of adult education as the best means of meeting the post-war educational demands of workers and ex-servicemen. The president continued his opposition to universal military training in peacetime—then under consideration—and he communicated his opinions to political and educational leaders all over the United States.[83]

Over 32,000 Michigan students served in the armed forces and 520 of them died. In all, the regents granted leaves to 223 faculty members for government service. Much of the classified research at the university was later cited as instrumental in winning the war. By the end of the war, Ruthven had the satisfaction of knowing that the university had made a major contribution to the national defense, while simultaneously preserving its basic reason for existence.

PERSONAL PROBLEMS

As if dissonance with the regents and controversy over the war effort weren't troubles enough, Ruthven was beset by personal problems during the war years. In 1940, he began to be bothered by a palsy which affected his head and hands.[84] The shaking was more pronounced during times of anxiety and, at first, was a source of considerable embarrassment and annoyance to him, for he was a rugged, dignified man who prided himself on always being in control. Public speaking became difficult, and his handwriting was limited to a wobbly signature or a few laborious notes. Ruthven did his best to belittle this unwelcome malady and, courageously, he forced himself to function in a normal manner. Rather than spill a drink, he took his cup or glass half-full and lifted it with both hands.[85] Rather than garble his words, he learned to talk only on exhalations much in the manner of people who have had surgery for larynx cancer.[86] The palsy in no way affected his mind, his ready wit, or his composure, and he learned to control his disease so well that many people who saw him regularly never thought of it as a limitation.

Another personal problem, deeply troubling to Ruthven, first surfaced during the war years. His elder son, Peter, was brilliant, talented, caustically witty, but unable to cope with the world as he found it. Peter Ruthven was an intellectual dilettante who was interested in Islamic art, archeology, and landscaping. He had spent some time at the university's archeological sites in Egypt, and had served briefly on the staff of the Metropolitan Museum of Art. During the latter years of the Ruthven presidency Peter was at home with his parents. On the campus and in the community Peter Ruthven was believed to be an alcoholic and a homosexual. The latter charge was particularly damning, for homosexuality was then an even greater outrage to society and was typically regarded with fear and loathing. Besides, Ruthven and his staff had occasionally dealt with student homosexuals in a stern way.[87] However, in the case of Peter Ruthven, the father stubbornly refused to believe the "vicious, disgraceful, uncalled for, and wholly false rumors . . . circulated about my older son."[88]

Soon after Ruthven retired from the presidency, Peter Ruthven obviously required hospitalization. He was admitted to the Ypsilanti State Mental Hospital. Finally, at the hospital, Peter found his niche in life and became such a helpful force in that institution that the patients and staff erected a bronze plaque in his memory upon his death in 1965. Ruthven was not one to wear his troubles on his sleeve, but one can well imagine his private anguish as he attempted to deal with this tragedy.

Nadir: The War Years

NOTES

1. Jack Brumm to Alexander G. Ruthven, August 26, 1939, Ruthven Papers, box 30, MHC.

2. Ruthven to Karl Litzenberger, July 16, 1939, Ruthven Papers, box 30, MHC.

3. Ruthven to C. C. Little, August 14, 1939, Ruthven Papers, box 31, MHC.

4. Ruthven to James O. Murfin, November 30, 1935, Ruthven Papers, box 18, MHC.

5. In fact, the regents were so loyal to each other that when Regent Murfin was tricked out of the Republican nomination for regent in 1933, a "plan" was devised to bring him back on the board. Murfin was by then the most active and most interested of all the regents, and R. Perry Shorts, a Republican, agreed to resign his post as regent if Democratic Governor William A. Comstock would appoint Murfin in his place. The fascinating story can be pieced together from the Shorts Papers, box 1, MHC.

6. R. Perry Shorts to Edmund C. Shields, January 10, 1933, Shorts Papers, box 1, MHC.

7. In July, 1937, the regents increased Ruthven's salary and expressed their confidence in his administration. He wrote each regent, declaring his gratitude. See Ruthven to Junius E. Beal, July 13, 1937, Ruthven Papers, box 23, MHC.

8. *Who's Who in Michigan,* 1936, p. 174.

9. Ruthven to Charles F. Hemans, October 29, 1935, Ruthven Papers, box 18, MHC.

10. Hemans to Ruthven, November 15, 1935, *ibid.*

11. Ruthven to Hemans, November 18, 1935, *ibid.*

12. Hemans to Ruthven, April 1, 1937, Ruthven Papers, box 21, MHC.

13. Ruthven to Hemans, April 3, 1937, *ibid.*

14. Two years after he left the Board of Regents, rumors concerning Hemans began to circulate around the capitol. It was charged that legislators' votes were being purchased. "Hemans turned state's evidence and it was revealed that in a little black book he had made a record of payments to legislators from bankers, loan companies, racetrack operators, slot-machine owners, and others. Twenty of the defendants were convicted in 1944. In the continuing investigation Senator Warren G. Hooper of Albion, who was about to testify, was murdered. The killer was never found. Total convictions numbered 46 out of 125 indicted." (Willis F. Dunbar, *Michigan: A History of the Wolverine State* [Grand Rapids: William B. Eerdmans Publishing Co., 1965], p. 650.) During the series of trials Hemans suddenly refused to testify, and fled the state. He was later arrested and spent a term in federal prison. F. Clever Bald, *Michigan in Four Centuries* (New York: Harper and Brothers, 1954), pp. 450–51.

15. Herbert E. Wilson to Ruthven, January 18, 1938, Ruthven Papers, box 24, MHC. Wilson was a judge from Indianapolis who had visited Lynch in his home and had been so concerned about the new regent's attitude that he had written to warn Ruthven.

16. For example, on October 20, 1939, Lynch wrote Ruthven (Ruthven Papers, box 31, MHC) and requested that a friend receive a faculty appointment. Ruthven

replied, saying that the man Lynch proposed was not qualified. "In addition to his unimpressive record, he has a very poor command of the English language and certainly could not teach a course." (Ruthven to John D. Lynch, October 28, 1939, *ibid.*) On another occasion, Lynch urged the acceptance of a friend to the dental school. When Dean Bunting replied that the lady in question would be admitted "if it is possible," Lynch stated: "I shall not go into further detail at this time other than to tell you that there are times when it becomes quite essential . . . that the recommendations of a regent be followed without too much detail of the reason being required." (Lynch to Bunting, June 14, 1941, Ruthven Papers, box 33, MHC.) The lady was admitted. (Bunting to Lynch, June 16, 1941, *ibid.*) On still another occasion Lynch complained bitterly to Ruthven of the treatment his son had received from the business administration faculty. (Lynch's son had changed his program of study and had not received full credit during the transfer.) (Lynch to Ruthven, October 2, 1942, Ruthven Papers, box 42, MHC.) The president re ferred the case to the younger Lynch's advisors, then reviewed it thoroughly with them, and reported back to Lynch. The son did not receive course credit. (Ruthven to Lynch, October 3, 1942, *ibid.*)

17. *Proceedings of the Board of Regents,* March meeting, 1938, p. 501.

18. *Proceedings of the Board of Regents,* second May meeting, 1939, p. 938, and annual June meeting, 1939, p. 964.

19. Ruthven to the Regents, letter, June 6, 1939, Ruthven Papers, box 28, MHC. The story is told that, at Ruthven's final Board of Regents meeting, he asked if he might confer Bachelor of Arts degrees upon two of his prized Morgans. The regents, aghast, began to sputter. Ruthven explained that during his tenure as president he had conferred so many degrees on the back sides of so many horses that he thought it only right to confer two degrees on two whole horses. (Ralph W. Hammett to Erich Walter, July 8, 1974.)

20. Shields to Ruthven, February 2, 1939, Ruthven Papers, box 29, MHC.

21. Ruthven to Shields, February 6, 1939, *ibid.*

22. J. R. Sutton to Shirley W. Smith, May 5, 1939, Smith Papers, box 6, MHC. Sutton, the President of the Policyholders Service and Adjustment Co., reminded Smith of their history of amicable relationships and good service, and charged that the university's new insurance company was chosen because one of the regents was connected with it.

23. According to Ruthven, Kipke did not seek to avenge his firing as football coach, and proved to be an able, hardworking, and cooperative regent. Interview, Ruthven, February 10, 1970. See also Ruthven to Harry G. Kipke, December 19, 1947, Ruthven Papers, box 58, MHC.

24. Alexander G. Ruthven, *Naturalist in Two Worlds* (Ann Arbor: University of Michigan Press, 1963), pp. 38–45.

25. Apparently regents Kipke and Shields remained friendly to all parties, and occasionally acted as mediators.

26. Lynch to Ruthven, May 9, 1941, Ruthven Papers, box 35, MHC.

27. Smith to Ruthven, March 11, 1942, Ruthven Papers, box 44, MHC.

28. Ruthven to Smith, March 16, 1942, *ibid.* This interesting exchange is also found in Ruthven's *Naturalist in Two Worlds,* pp. 42–44.

29. *The Ann Arbor Daily News,* October 17, 1942, p. 1.

30. *Ibid.*

Nadir: The War Years

31. Regent Shields noted, "I was very startled to read the interviews of Connable and Lynch in the newspapers and learn that a four hour acrimonious discussion had been carried on about a subject which, if my memory serves me, did not take a minute." Shields to Ruthven, October 30, 1942, Ruthven Papers, box 44, MHC.

32. The story which follows is from the "Hubbs" folder, Ruthven Papers, box 46, MHC.

33. Ruthven to R. Spencer Bishop, September 29, 1943, Ruthven Papers, box 45, MHC. Bishop, a close friend of Ruthven, began a term as regent January 1, 1944.

34. *Proceedings of the Board of Regents,* April meeting, 1944, p. 582.

35. Statement of Ruthven "To the Members of the Board of Regents," May 9, 1944, Ruthven Papers, box 46, MHC. Hubbs joined the Scripps Institute of Oceanography, University of California at San Diego, where he became a world-renowned biologist. *Leaders in American Science,* vol. 8, 1968–69.

36. Ruthven, *Naturalist in Two Worlds,* p. 39. Regent Connable told me that he did not want Ruthven fired outright, but wanted him to become the "Chancellor" so another man could become the chief executive, or "President." Interview, May 6, 1970.

37. Ruthven to Ralph Stone, February 3, 1945, Ruthven Papers, box 50, MHC.

38. Joseph Herbert to Mrs. Stuart G. Baits, June 25, 1949, Herbert Papers, transfer case 2, MHC.

39. Ruthven, *Naturalist in Two Worlds,* p. 45.

40. Ruthven, interview, January 27, 1970.

41. See Smith's *Harry Burns Hutchins,* chs. 22–24, for the best exposition of the university during World War I.

42. Much of the background material which follows is from F. Clever Bald, "The University of Michigan in World War II," unpublished manuscript, 2 vols., 478 pp., MHC.

43. Rear Admiral J. O. Richardson to Ruthven, April 28, 1939, Ruthven Papers, box 35, MHC.

44. Ruthven to Richardson, May 4, 1939, *ibid.*

45. Chester W. Nimitz to Ruthven, August 10, 1940, *ibid.*

46. E. Blythe Stason to Nimitz, August 20, 1940, *ibid.*

47. Ruthven to Nimitz, January 14, 1941, *ibid.*

48. Ruthven to A. C. Willard, September 26, 1940, *ibid.* Willard was President of the University of Illinois.

49. Ruthven to Cyrus J. Goodrich, February 6, 1941, Ruthven Papers, box 34, MHC. Congress agreed to defer all college students until July, 1941.

50. Ruthven Papers, box 37, MHC.

51. Ruthven to Donald J. Sterling, April 9, 1941, Ruthven Papers, box 36, MHC.

52. Ruth Rouse to E. B. Stouffer, August 16, 1941, Ruthven Papers, box 37, MHC.

53. Ruthven to William Hainsworth, July 12, 1941, Ruthven Papers, box 38, MHC.

54. Ruthven to Hutchins, December 30, 1940, Ruthven Papers, box 34, MHC.

55. Ruthven to Cordell Hull, October 3, 1940, Ruthven Papers, box 35, MHC.

56. Ruthven, speech to the Howell Forum, December 11, 1941, "Miscellaneous IV" folder, Ruthven Papers, box 78, MHC.

57. Ruthven, speech to the National Association of State Universities, October 23, 1942, *ibid.*

58. Ruthven to Chase Osborn, December 26, 1941, Ruthven Papers, box 39, MHC.

59. Ruthven, speech in Hill Auditorium, December 16, 1941, "Students" folder, Ruthven Papers, box 78, MHC.

60. *Proceedings of the Board of Regents,* January meeting, 1942, p. 856.

61. *The Michigan Daily,* October 7, 1942.

62. Bald, "Michigan in World War II," p. 91.

63. *Proceedings of the Board of Regents,* October meeting, 1942, p. 58. The "minority group" of the regents included a graduate of Culver Military Academy (Connable) and a past state commander of the American Legion (Herbert). *Michigan Official Directory and Legislative Manual,* 1943, pp. 638–39. It is little wonder that they clashed with Ruthven's war policy.

64. *Ann Arbor Daily News,* October 19, 1942, p. 5.

65. Lynch to Ruthven, October 19, 1942, Ruthven Papers, box 43, MHC.

66. *Ann Arbor Daily News,* October 20, 1942, p. 5.

67. *The Michigan Daily,* October 20, 1942, p. 1.

68. *Ibid.,* October 21, 1942, p. 2.

69. *The Flint Journal,* October 21, 1942, also reported in Bald, "Michigan in World War II," p. 95.

70. *The Detroit Free Press,* October 21, 1942, p. 6.

71. Bald, "Michigan in World War II," p. 96.

72. Ruthven to Howard Mumford Jones, November 6, 1942, Ruthven Papers, box 42, MHC.

73. Ruthven, "Universities Today," November 6, 1942, "Miscellaneous IV" folder, Ruthven Papers, box 78, MHC.

74. In 1945, Ruthven exchanged an interesting series of letters with Russell Kirk, then a sergeant in the army, on the subject of liberal education. Both agreed that there was very little educational value in the technically and vocationally oriented programs espoused by the military in wartime. Ruthven called these programs "education for death." Ruthven Papers, box 52, MHC.

75. Bald, "Michigan in World War II," p. 97.

76. *Proceedings of the Board of Regents,* November meeting, 1942, p. 114.

77. Peckham, *Making of Michigan,* p. 204.

78. Bald, "Michigan in World War II," p. 48.

79. Ganoe's letters to the regents were written on December 8, 1942. See the reference in the Ruthven Papers, box 43, MHC. No actual copies appear in the Ruthven Papers.

80. Ruthven to William A. Ganoe, December 11, 1942, Ruthven Papers, box 43, MHC.

81. Ganoe to Ruthven, December 15, 1942, *ibid.*

82. Ruthven to Harold Smith, January 31, 1942, Ruthven Papers, box 40, MHC.

83. Ruthven Papers, box 49, MHC.

84. The palsy has been identified as a "familial tremor" by Ruthven's physician. It was not, as many on campus thought, Parkinson's Disease. Dr. H. Marvin Pollard, interview, January 13, 1975. Pollard was Ruthven's physician.

85. Mrs. Alan MacCarthy, letter, December 10, 1974.

86. Robert A. May, letter, December 17, 1974.

87. Interview with Erich Walter, January 8, 1975.

88. Ruthven to Vera Baits, July 1, 1945, Ruthven Papers, box 38–4, MHC.

12

Post-War Problems

Early in his museum career, at the invitation of his patron, Bryant Walker, Alexander Ruthven was often a guest at the Huron Mountain Club, a wilderness retreat for wealthy sportsmen. There he rubbed elbows with many of the men who controlled the huge corporations in the state of Michigan, which is perhaps more highly industrialized than any other state. Ruthven was at ease with these corporate giants, for he had a great deal of self-confidence, and he knew that these influential men could be helpful in furthering his career and his museum. To some extent, during his museum days and early in his presidency, Ruthven was a power player, willingly malleable when it came to dealing with his corporate friends.[1] As time went on, his basically democratic character emerged and he found himself at odds with some of the corporate leaders.

He remembered a frustrating evening with his friend "Orm" Hunt, a General Motors vice president, and Charles E. Wilson, president of that company, when he tried to suggest to Wilson that less autocratic management theories would result in better morale and greater productivity. They talked until three in the morning, Ruthven recalled, but he "couldn't make a dent" in Wilson's theories.[2]

Early in his presidency Ruthven and his wife were invited by Henry Ford to attend square dances at Ford's Greenfield Village. Bryant Ruthven knew of these dances:

> Those were, indeed, command performances. I think it's a little hard for someone who didn't experience the times and didn't know Detroit to understand just how much raw power Henry Ford exercised. How many of the affairs Dad and Mother attended, I don't know, but I was aware of a growing rebellion. It began by Dad's leaving the dances early, a rash act in itself, and culminated in his flat refusal to go to any more of 'the damned things.'[3]

Ruthven continued to maintain his ties with Michigan's corporate leaders, for their power was a political reality in the state and the university could not survive in isolation from it. Yet, he was increasingly distrustful of what he saw as abuses of corporate power.

THE WORKERS' EDUCATION SERVICE

One situation in particular heightened Ruthven's resentment: the demise of the Workers' Education Service. The program's untimely end was Ruthven's keenest disappointment during his presidency.

In October and November, 1943, when Ruthven journeyed to embattled England, he observed that a nationwide Workers' Education Service was carrying on an extensive program of educational discussions among laboring groups, even in the discomfort of bombed out buildings.[4] Tutors from the universities were the instructors. In the armed services, too, Ruthven noticed, the fighting men would meet to discuss their role in post-war England. Ruthven, a firm advocate of adult education even as early as his platform statement, was impressed by the English example. Upon his return to Ann Arbor he spoke to the Michigan faculty, telling them that English efforts in adult education had far outstripped the efforts in this country, yet the needs were similar. "Our universities," Ruthven told the faculty, "are still only very timidly looking over the fence at the field of adult education." He urged the educators to accept the responsibility for providing instruction for adults and out-of-school youth.[5]

Adult education was a major consideration of his 1943–1944 *President's Report* as well. He called the common assumption that education is only for the young "deplorable" for it "menaces national safety." Individuals who believe this, he continued, "are poorly equipped to perform the duties of citizenship, for they are inclined to react emotionally instead of reasonably to mutations in their environment."[6]

Ruthven's next step was to confer with Charles A. Fisher, director of the university's Extension Service, and Howard Y. McClusky, who headed the university's adult education program. At this meeting the three agreed that the university should undertake, as soon as possible, a program of education for workers. They further agreed that a statewide committee, to include labor leaders, should be appointed to advise the program. As a final consideration, it was decided that "a full-time person attached to the University staff" should direct the program.[7]

The president's proposal fell on receptive ears in some parts of the state of Michigan. Since 1936, when the Michigan Works Progress Administration had sponsored a small program of workers' education, a few of the social reformers in the labor movement had talked about its revitalization.[8] In 1944, the Michigan legislature voted $250,000 for an "experimental program in adult education" to be organized by the educational institutions of the state. The University of Michigan, well primed by its president, promptly suggested a number of new programs, the most significant of which was the Workers' Education Service (WES).

The purpose of WES was, simply, to train Michigan workers to be better citizens. Workers who had a better understanding of their role, their rights, and their responsibilities, it was felt, would be happier, more productive on the job and in the community and, in the long run, more beneficial to management. To this end, lectures or discussions were held either before or after the regular business sessions of local unions. These courses were taught for the most part by regular University of Michigan professors, although occasionally the instructors were high school teachers or union officials temporarily on the university payroll. Topics were suggested by the workers themselves and included labor legislation, social security, labor's responsibility to society, parliamentary procedure, consumer problems, and collective bargaining. In addition, WES sponsored conferences, films, and discussion forums throughout the state. The director of the nascent program was Arthur Elder, a former Detroit school teacher and President of the Michigan Federation of Teachers, an American Federation of Labor (AFL) affiliate. The activities of WES were to be supervised by a six-person State Advisory Committee composed of two members representing the state, two representing the University of Michigan, and the state secretaries of the Congress of Industrial Organizations (CIO) and the Michigan Federation of Labor.

WES prospered from the start. By the end of the first year, an estimated 40,000 people took part in various WES activities.[9] The following year director Arthur Elder estimated that an additional 3000 workers had participated, and he noted that several other universities had sent representatives to study the Michigan program.[10] Charles A. Fisher, director of the University Extension Service, referred to WES as giving promise of becoming "one of the most significant and interesting developments ever undertaken by the Extension Service." Fisher reported that WES had "succeeded admirably" in gaining the "confidence . . . of organized labor" and "an increasing amount of respect from the industrialists." Fisher was cognizant, however, of "the controversial field in which Workers' Education Service operates" and he stated firmly that "no individual or pressure group can for one moment be permitted to dictate to those who teach in any school or department of the University."[11]

Nevertheless, there were indications that management was growing uneasy about WES. Allen B. Crow, President of the Economic Club of Detroit, represented management's point of view and, as the Workers' Education Service began to attract more and more support from the workers, Crow complained to Fisher of the program's inherent dangers.[12] Ruthven responded for the university:

> The sound program of workers' education which we visualize for the State of Michigan should be equally supported by labor and management and it should have the result of teaching both labor and management the dangers of selfishness, the advantages of interest in the common welfare, and, above all, the fact that no one group has a monopoly on wisdom.[13]

Despite the storm warnings, the president and the university sailed blithely ahead. Ruthven began to attract a national reputation as a leader in adult education, and was named by Governor Harry F. Kelly to the Educational Advisory Committee to develop a statewide adult education program. He became a member of the Committee on International Adult Education, and was elected to membership on the Executive Committee of the American Association for Adult Education. The university announced that, since the state appropriation for WES had expired, it would continue the experimental program from its own general budget.[14] Ruthven expressed the university's backing in a letter to the Secretary-Treasurer of the Michigan Federation of Labor. "This program has proved so successful that it should not be dropped unless it is absolutely impossible to find funds for its support," the president wrote.[15]

By the end of academic year 1947, over 56,000 Michigan citizens were being served annually by WES. The report of the director of the University Extension Service again observed that the Detroit industrial area was the "hottest" in the United States, but he noted that WES was impartial in labor disputes, and Arthur Elder, its director, was "honest, fearless, and intelligent, and . . . has established a program which is unquestionably one of the most forward-looking in the country."[16]

In fact, WES had gained such acclaim that Arthur Elder was called to Washington to present the Michigan program as a model for a federal Labor Extension Service bill then under consideration by Congress. The bill would authorize $10 million (or $30 million, depending on the report) in federal funds to be given to colleges and universities for the operation of special classes for industrial workers. Elder's support of the Labor Extension Service bill was seconded by university regent Alfred B. Connable, who also testified before the congressional subcommittee hearing on the merits of workers' education. Michigan economics professor Z. Clark Dickinson read a similar laudatory statement from Ruthven into the record, and Victor Reuther, Educational Director of the United Auto Workers, added his support. Press reports predicted that the bill would have little difficulty passing Congress. It looked as if the Michigan program of workers' education would serve as the national prototype. It did not.

Management's discomfort with WES was increasingly apparent, and General Motors apparently decided to begin a surreptitious investigation of workers' education.[17] In April, 1948, Adam K. Stricker, Jr., a minor GM executive, enrolled in a WES class taught by Sam Jacobs, like Elder a former Detroit school teacher who had become a union official. During the class meeting, labor pamphlets were distributed.[18] One pamphlet included a cartoon depicting C. E. Wilson, President of GM, applauding vigorously as a huge bull gored prostrate workers. (It was commonly known that Wilson lavished money and affection on his prize bull.) When he saw this pamphlet Wilson was obviously upset, for university regent Charles S. Kennedy reported to Ruthven that he and Wilson had had a "long talk" and Wilson had "already taken some of the questions up with the Governor."[19] Stricker also reported his experiences directly to Michigan Governor Kim Sigler, and then went to Washington, where he testified before the House subcommittee hearing on the Labor Extension Service bill. Stricker presented the labor pamphlet as an example of WES offerings, and he charged that Jacobs was presenting a "Marxist idea of class economics with the support of public funds."

Predictably, in labor-tense Detroit the charges were headlined in the city papers. *The Detroit Times* bannered a front page accusation in red ink: "Charge State Pays For Red Teaching." "Marxist Ideas Taught At 'M' Says GM Aide," read the subhead.[20] Ruthven refuted Stricker's charges as "a distortion of a very small incident," and he said publicly that Jacobs had a good educational background for teaching the course. Ruthven stated privately that Stricker's charges were part of a calculated campaign by GM to kill the national Labor Extension Service bill then under consideration.[21]

GM's Washington testimony and the media headlines had the desired effect for, despite the advocacy of Senator Irving Ives of New York, the Labor Extension Service bill—once seemingly assured of passage—was never reported out of committee.[22] "We cannot tolerate in America such teachings as we have had described today," said Representative Carroll D. Kearns of Pennsylvania after hearing GM's evidence at one committee hearing. "We have to have teachers in our schools that believe in Americanism."[23]

Governor Sigler, who had gained election on a platform of crusading anti-communism, called for a special meeting with the Board of Regents during which he disclosed to the regents the results of a special investigation into WES by the State Police. Media accounts of the meeting varied, but some radio commentators and news editors claimed that Sigler and the State Police had exposed the Labor Extension Service bill as part of a nationwide communist plot to take over all workers' education.[24]

This was too much for Victor Reuther to take, and he wrote publicly to Governor Sigler:

> By the time the simple truth had killed the sorry story, you came along to revive it. You found no evidence of any connection between the University, the course, or the instructor on the one hand and Communism on the other. . . . Yet, you talk darkly of "questionable activity" and of a nationwide plot. General Motors' charges and your hints that the University is involved in a Communist plot are corny, dreamed-up melodrama. Coming from General Motors, the corn is a commercial product; coming from you, the highest government officer in the State, it is evidence of dangerous irresponsibility.[25]

The conspiracy rumors must have touched even Ruthven, for Regent Kennedy wrote: "Be assured that I have not even the slightest suspicion that your colors are red or even pale pink but believe, as do all the rest of the Regents, that they are red, white, and blue, now and forever."[26]

Alexander G. Ruthven of Michigan

Though Ruthven remained above suspicion with the regents, WES and its director did not. The board, at its June meeting, agreed that WES programs then in session would be completed, but that, pending further investigations, no new WES programs would be scheduled.[27] By the end of academic year 1947–1948 the number of citizens served by WES had dropped to 29,181 and, where previously the university's Extension Service director had eloquently praised WES, now the program rated only two terse paragraphs in his annual report.[28]

WES remained in limbo during the summer. For those connected with the program it was a time for soul searching. It was generally agreed that Jacobs, as a union representative, was guilty of poor judgment in dispensing pamphlets so blatantly anti management. Ruthven, wholeheartedly committed to the concept of workers' education, had had previous experience with C. E. Wilson and considered him "arrogant."[29] He did not want to knuckle under to pressure from GM. On the other hand, there is little evidence that the Michigan faculty felt any compulsion to support WES; indeed, Professor William Haber later testified that certain faculty had "a number of questions over a long time concerning the method of selection of teachers, the procedure in launching courses, the contents of those courses, teaching methods and related problems."[30] Two professors closely involved with WES recall that faculty interest in workers' education was, at best, "indifferent" and "apathetic."[31]

A number of letters from off campus urged the president and the regents to reinstate the program. One came from the Acting Secretary of Labor, John W. Gibson, who wrote,

I have been very much disturbed to learn of current attempts to use an incident occurring in one of your classes to discredit the program within the State and also to embarrass the movement to secure the enactment of a national extension service for workers. . . . It seems to me that . . . you are developing one of the most comprehensive programs, a type of program that labor, management or the general public can sincerely support. It is my sincere hope that the university service for workers will continue to operate on an effective basis with full support from you and . . . the Board of Regents.[32]

The executive officers of the university made a full investigation of WES during the summer, as the Board of Regents directed at its June meeting. It is not altogether clear what the executive officers recommended to the regents. Their first report, signed by

Ruthven, Provost Adams, and the three vice presidents, was presented to the regents in September. In essence, this first report of the university administrators equivocated. They agreed that the director of WES had "exercised poor judgment" in selecting Sam Jacobs as an instructor, and that it had been "inappropriate" for Jacobs to distribute union pamphlets. Furthermore, the executive officers said, WES should in the future be more closely allied with the university's Extension Service. On the other hand, the administrators noted that, with the exception of Jacobs' course, there had been no evidence of propaganda, and WES had clearly demonstrated its educational value. They also pointed out that GM had no right to interfere with the program in a manner which disregarded the university's constitutional autonomy. Still, the administrators concluded, if WES had lost public confidence it should not be continued, and if Arthur Elder had exercised poor judgment perhaps he should be dismissed.[33]

However, strong evidence suggests that this September statement did not indicate the real opinion of the executive officers. On October 1—prior to any official action at the October 16 regents meeting—Ruthven wrote to Regent Charles S. Kennedy:

> I did not intend to continue to argue about workers' education. It had always been my opinion that the Regents and the administrative officers could have honest differences of opinion but when the decision had been arrived at we should all cooperate to make it effective. As you know, I believe the Workers' Education Service has done a very good job despite the fact that one mistake in judgment was made. I am convinced that Mr. Elder is thoroughly honest and that he did not stir up opposition to the Regents' action. . . . All this, however, is now quite beside the point. The Regents have come to definite conclusions. . . . I am quite content to let time decide the wisdom of our decision.[34]

In addition, there is an unsigned letter "To the Board of Regents," dated October 15, 1948, and probably written by Provost Adams. The letter states that the executive officers, the president included, "cannot refrain from expressing our conclusions." This letter went on to call unequivocally for the continuation of the WES program and the retention of Arthur Elder. "We believe," the letter stated, "that if the continuation of the program is authorized and Mr. Elder is dismissed, the intentions of the University will be misconstrued and it will not have the support of labor. We believe that, if this should happen, the effect will be as serious as if the program were discontinued."[35]

There almost certainly was a fundamental disagreement between the administrative officers and the regents concerning the future of WES and its director. The regents, under pressure from GM, also probably decided to overrule the president and his staff and dismiss Elder at least three weeks before Elder was notified and the official decision was announced. The equivocal September statement was undoubtedly either pap to please the regents or an attempt by the administrators to defend regental action.

In any case, WES was clearly finished. All that remained were recriminations. G. Mennen Williams, the Democratic candidate for governor, charged that Republican Governor Sigler had "strangled an entire division of the University of Michigan." Williams called it a "devastating blow at academic freedom" and he was quick to point out that not only the governor but all of the regents were Republicans.[36]

Even Ruthven went down swinging. *The Michigan Daily* reported a fighting speech in which Ruthven denounced "self-made Pharisees who . . . have perverted instruction by the insidious method of calling black white, and white black, and accusing by innuendo and false assumptions. Communism is not the only threat to a liberal education," Michigan's president concluded.[37]

At the October meeting the regents agreed to continue WES as an "experimental" program, but to administer it entirely through the University Extension Service. Elder was to be informed that his position was discontinued.[38] A later commission pointed out that neither the regents nor the administrative officers had consulted the State Advisory Committee, the group ostensibly overseeing WES, prior to reaching these decisions.[39] Press releases from the university stressed that WES had always been and still was "experimental" and that administrative reorganization of the program had been contemplated even before the incident in Jacobs' class.

Public reaction was both immediate and intense. "U.M. Fires Teacher in 'Marxist' Row," bannered *The Detroit News*.[40] *The Detroit Free Press* also headlined Elder's dismissal and included a quote from Elder who said that the university administration had no part in abolishing his job. "Only the regents, acting under pressure from General Motors officials, are responsible for this apparent plan to kill off the Workers' Educational Service," Elder declared.[41]

Jacobs' students, including three executives from Michigan Bell Telephone Company, declared that their course had not been subversive and that they would regret any curtailment of WES. Elder received similar accolades concerning WES from all over Michigan.[42] An editorial in *The Detroit Free Press* noted that "criticism aimed at the Board of Regents of the University of Michigan for temporarily suspending workers university extension courses seems to be justified."[43]

Twenty-one members of the "Staff of the Workers Education Service" signed a letter protesting with "utmost vigor" Elder's dismissal.[44] The university received a number of requests, including one from the members of the State Advisory Committee to WES, that Elder be reinstated. These requests were considered by the executive officers and the regents and denied.

On January 18, 1949, the university released a statement to the press that WES would be resumed at the end of the month. E. J. Soop, director of the University Extension Service (Fisher had died), announced that seven organized courses for workers would be held at the Rackham Building in Detroit. The courses would be conducted by members of the regular university teaching faculty. However, Soop's announcement included the proviso that additional courses, to be held in areas most convenient for workers, would be initiated at the request of the workers. But the attempt to resume the program did not satisfy labor. In fact, the program, which had originally aroused the wrath of management, now felt the sting of angry labor leaders. Barney Hopkins, secretary-treasurer of the Michigan CIO Council, said that his organization would not participate in the remodeled WES, a program which, Hopkins claimed, "is cleared only with the General Motors Corporation."[45] Robert P. Scott, secretary-treasurer of the Michigan Federation of Labor, charged: "The new program . . . gives no consideration whatever to the wishes or the expressed needs of labor." He, too, called for Elder's reinstatement.[46] Organized labor then announced a boycott of WES classes and, when University of Michigan instructors appeared at the Rackham Building in Detroit, only one person was present to enroll.

"The difficulties we are now having are with labor rather than management . . . ," Ruthven observed. He professed to be "startled" at the insistence of labor leaders that they should "hire and fire the instructors."[47]

The university was caught between the very forces it had tried to harmonize. Its only option was to bow out as gracefully as possible. On February 7, 1949, the university public relations department released the following announcement:

> In view of the boycott of the workers' education program by organized labor and its effect upon the enrollment, the University of Michigan is withdrawing its program in this field. We regret that the response of the workers for whom the program was designed has not matched the efforts which the University has made to serve their needs. We shall continue to give consideration to the interests of workers in the general programs in adult education conducted by the Extension service of the University.[48]

One regent, as if unaware that GM had coerced the university into abandoning one of its most promising extramural programs, "called upon Republicans to fight in the spring election to prevent labor unions and minority groups from gaining control of the University. . . ." "The caucus," reported *The Detroit Free Press*, "adopted a resolution endorsing Regent Stevens' views and pledged a fight to preserve collegiate freedom at the University."[49]

The short-lived WES was not resurrected by the university, but the controversial program left behind bitter feelings. When a March 11, 1950, editorial in the *Saturday Evening Post* criticized President Truman for recommending the establishment of a national Labor Extension Service, Arthur Elder wrote the President in support of his efforts in workers' education. However, Elder felt compelled to remind Truman: "There is the question of whether . . . the American people can have confidence that our universities and colleges can be relied upon faithfully to administer their trusteeship, in the face of pressures from corporate interests or individuals intent on controlling our educational institutions."[50]

Ruthven, in his reminiscences, referred to the demise of WES when he noted that the university had yielded to external pressures "for the first time in the history of the institution." Ruthven also concluded that "the experience of Michigan would certainly demonstrate to other institutions the probabilities of political interference with courses in worker education in any way critical of management."[51]

It was a sad conclusion to Ruthven's noble experiment. In retrospect, it must be said that Ruthven appeared somewhat naive in underestimating the reactions to WES of first management and then labor. Ruthven the idealist saw WES as the model for educating the nation's workers for higher citizenship, a plan leading to eventual rapprochement between labor and management. It was certainly a worthy goal, but Ruthven's enthusiasm for WES outran his usual cautious political judgment and the program fell easy prey to General Motors. In retirement, he could even laugh about the demise of WES: "I never knew whether the president of the company thought that the pamphlet insulted him or the bull."[52]

TITULAR PRESIDENT

The demise of WES came at a time of rapid change on the campus itself. The crises of World War II were over but, as an aging Ruthven faced the inevitable post-war adjustment, he found that his administrative team was no longer intact. Retirement claimed Vice President James D. Bruce in 1942 and Vice President Shirley W. Smith in 1945. Vice President C. S. Yoakum was asked to devote his full time to being dean of the graduate school. E. Blythe Stason, the youngster in the group, wished to become a full-time law school dean and surrender his responsibilities as provost.

The president and the regents began to search for a younger team. In October, 1944, the regents formed a special committee to "survey . . . the administrative structure of the University."[53] In a letter to the board the committee proposed that the provost should be the key appointment in a new administrative plan. The committee suggested for that post James P. Adams, a former Michigan economics professor at that time Vice President of Brown University.[54] The committee also suggested that law school professor Marvin Niehuss become Vice President in Charge of University Relations, and it was agreed that he would be a liaison between the legislature and the university. The regents' committee decided that this plan, with the addition of a business officer to replace Smith, "would leave the President in the position of counseling and directing the efforts of these men. It would leave him time to work on the longer range programs for developing the University."[55]

President Ruthven concurred with these suggestions, and appeared pleased when Adams, Niehuss, and Robert P. Briggs (Vice President for Business and Finance) accepted the proffered appointments. "I do not believe it is possible to find three men more capable of sharing the administrative burdens," he wrote Regent Ralph Hayward.[56] Adams was forty-eight years old and Niehuss and Briggs were both forty-one.

At about the same time two crucial deanships were filled. Hay-

217

ward Keniston of romance languages replaced the retiring dean of the Literary College, Edward H. Kraus, and physicist Ralph A. Sawyer replaced C. S. Yoakum, who died soon after accepting the full-time deanship of the Rackham School of Graduate Studies. Both appointments met with general faculty favor.

Very soon after the new appointments were announced it became apparent that President Ruthven was giving up many of the responsibilities that had been his. It was announced, for instance, that Clinton P. Anderson, Secretary of Agriculture, would deliver the commencement address, for many years a Ruthven prerogative. When a communiqué went to the University Senate listing university goals, it bore Provost Adams' signature.[57] Indeed, Adams increasingly appeared to be in charge of executive duties that were previously the province of the president. By 1946, Adams was communicating directly and frequently with the regents. When social psychologist Rensis Likert was approached to establish a survey research center, it was Adams who discussed the conditions of appointment. When Professors McClusky and Fisher disagreed about the control of the university's program in adult education, they rested their case with Adams.[58] The minutes of the Conference of Deans show that Adams dominated conversations there. The Ruthven Papers indicate that, as Ruthven edged closer to retirement, Adams was taking the initiative on such crucial matters as faculty salaries and appointment of administrative personnel. It was generally assumed on the campus that Adams was being groomed for the presidency upon Ruthven's retirement.

The post-war changes seemed overwhelming to Ruthven. He felt strongly that the university's enrollment should not exceed 17,000 students.[59] The *President's Reports* from 1945–1946 onward reveal that the president's mind was constantly grappling with the problem of the university's optimum size. Yet, despite the president's desires, the crush of returning veterans, the expanding population, and the growing significance of higher education forced student enrollments to almost 28,000 by 1950.

Ruthven was suspicious of government research because he feared that it would ultimately lead to federal control. He also foresaw a problem for the university if federal projects were not continuously funded. If projects were discontinued or even temporarily halted, Ruthven reasoned, the faculty attracted to Ann Arbor by these projects would have to be assimilated into the regular Michigan faculty. Under those circumstances, he felt, they would be unwelcome parasites. Again, despite the president's reservations, research on the campus blossomed, and by 1951 government and industry were spending over $3.1 million a year on sponsored research at Michigan.[60]

The regents began to talk of a university fund-raising program in the hopes of undertaking special projects which would not be possible from state appropriations. Ruthven was at first skeptical. "I believe that, while we want the University to receive substantial gifts, it would be dangerous to the future of Michigan to set up an organization with the objective of obtaining large sums for general use," he told Regent Ralph A. Hayward. "Whether the organization was successful or not, we might thereby give the impression that in our opinion the State should be expected to have diminishing responsibility for the support of higher education."[61] Ruthven also noted: "I have many times been informed by our alumni that a supersalesman would result in the long run in alumni irritation and in the drying up of support."[62] Nevertheless, a development program was begun, and Ruthven found himself the Honorary Chairman of the Mortimer E. Cooley Foundation, and, later, the chief spokesman for the university's Phoenix Project, a $6.5 million endeavor aimed at exploring the peaceful uses of atomic energy. He later came to believe that an annual giving campaign was beneficial to the university, both in enriching the scope of its programs and in cementing alumni loyalties.[63]

As the Ruthven era at Michigan drew to its conclusion, the president appeared increasingly as the titular leader. Instead of the usual weighty problems of university administration, much of his correspondence dealt with requests for better housing, responses to friends and prospective donors, admission of out-of-state students, and other problems essentially of a public relations nature. He once confided to a zoologist friend of many years:

> As you undoubtedly know, higher education is in a boom period. The University of Michigan seems to be expanding all over the map. These institutions are also changing . . . so rapidly that I am beginning to feel out of place among them. For the first time since I have been in college work I find myself in considerable doubt as to the futures of universities. It is possible to preserve the old values but I am not certain just how this can be done with the increase in size.[64]

The times were beginning to pass the president by and he knew it. He was ready for retirement when it came in 1951.[65]

Alexander G. Ruthven of Michigan
THE RUTHVEN ERA REVIEWED

As he settled back in his presidential chair for the last time he no doubt put another Camel in his ever-present cigarette holder, lit up, leaned back, and began to reflect on the successes and failures of his lengthy regime. He could allow himself some quiet satisfaction because he had been a remarkably effective president for the majority of his twenty-two years. Others were also assessing the Ruthven era for he had served longer than any other president except Angell, and his service spanned what was probably the most trying period in the university's history. What was Ruthven's legacy to Michigan?

Ruthven was the man Michigan needed after the turmoil of the Little presidency. He largely succeeded in maintaining a favorable press and keeping the university out of the papers. His speeches enhanced the atmosphere of prevailing calm he desired for his institution. A Ruthven speech was short and often included a few lines of self-deprecating humor. It was always free from platitudes. He was not an orator, but he spoke directly to the issues in a manner his listeners understood. When reading the Ruthven speeches, one is struck by how seldom his rhetoric outran his reason for speaking. He made no effort to vary his remarks to please a particular audience, but a Ruthven address was couched in nonabrasive terms and nearly always elicited favorable response.

He was available to students and faculty and was never—with the exception of some globetrotting for the Phoenix Project—an absentee president. He dressed conservatively, and avoided drawing attention to himself or his policies. He never appeared to lose his temper or have less than full command of his faculties. When Ruthven sensed that trouble was developing, his first thought was to call the contending parties together. Face-to-face discussion of disagreements, he felt, was a means of settlement far superior to letters or even phone calls. A standard Ruthven practice was to offer a conference to anyone disagreeing with a Ruthven pronouncement. This tactic often resulted in a convert, since Ruthven was particularly persuasive in informal discussions.

Ruthven's methods in relating to faculty promoted harmony. He was adept at changing the station of individuals whom he regarded as potential threats to peace. One thinks of the new positions created for professors Kraus, Reeves, and Bruce, the dismissal of Cabot, or the "distinguished professorships" which enabled the president to replace two deans whose units were not as strong as he desired. Ruthven was patient, particularly with faculty, and rather than attempt to replace the few who were his detractors (for example, Dean Bates or Professor Louis Karpinski) he outwaited them, for they were old and near retirement.[66] When choosing a new dean the president and the provost solicited individual opinions from all professors in the school or college before reaching a judgment.[67] Faculty involvement in this process, in the executive committees, and in the University Senate and Council fostered an institutional commitment.

Ruthven demonstrated a keen appreciation for his place in Michigan's history. Just as there was a yearning for normalcy following two world wars on the national scene, it was natural for the regents to turn to Ruthven following the controversies of the Little regime at Michigan. He represented a stabilizing influence, and as such he was regarded by the regents much as the American public regarded Presidents Coolidge or Eisenhower. It was Ruthven's role to combat the confusion and suspicion which followed in Little's wake. He did this successfully from the beginning—one has only to recall the effect of the masterful "platform statement" on a university community which yearned for positive direction. In contrast with Little, whose long-term effectiveness was impaired because he persisted in speaking out on issues only tangentially related to higher education, Ruthven understood so very well that there were times when tact, discretion, and even silence best promote a university's interest. He was able, during the almost incessant years of crisis, to be the calm, confident, unflappable leader which the times demanded. It was appropriate that, when he was inducted as an honorary sachem into the Michigan honor society Michigamua, he was assigned the tribal name "Peace Maker." Keeping the peace was a sine qua non for Ruthven. One wonders, however, whether his university progressed under his less than charismatic leadership.

One is immediately inclined to ask, though, how much progress was possible during almost ten years of Depression deprivations followed by almost ten years of wartime weariness. One is tempted to say that a president afflicted not only with these national calamities but, in addition, with a contrary Board of Regents for almost ten years did well just to keep himself and his institution intact. On the other hand, one should also keep in mind that ordinary men are not chosen to administer an educational giant such as the University of Michigan. In fact, a common interpretation of history postulates that great men are able to control the direction of institutions despite the events of any given time. To assess progress, this question must be answered: What did Michigan accomplish from 1929 to 1951, and what did President Ruthven contribute to that accomplishment?

Unquestionably, Michigan progressed materially and absolutely. In 1929, student enrollment stood at approximately 13,000; by 1951 it was almost 30,000. The libraries in 1929 contained 718,425 volumes; by 1951 the number had increased to 1,472,837.[68] The faculty had grown to over 1300 by 1951, almost double the 1929 figure of 804. Endowment funds had increased to over $20 million, approximately five times the less than $4 million endowment when Ruthven took office. Ruthven's presidency oversaw construction of the Law Quadrangle, Burton Tower, Rackham Graduate School, Health Service, Administration Building, School of Business Administration, new athletic facilities, and a number of residence halls. Building assets during the Ruthven presidency increased from over $30 million to over $90 million. The annual appropriation from the state legislature was three times as large in 1951 as in 1929. It has been recorded that Ruthven's administration, like that of President Marion Burton, was characterized by unusual financial generosity to the university.[69]

As Allen Schoenfield reported in *The Detroit News Pictorial,* "No similar period compares with Dr. Ruthven's two decades for expansion of the University's physical plant or for the multiplicity of its activities. . . ."[70]

One suspects, however, that these figures, impressive though they are, are not necessarily meaningful. Growth was common to just about all state universities following World War II. The war effort, which heated up the economy, and the return of the veterans assured that. During those years Michigan State College, for instance, experienced phenomenal growth, particularly following John A. Hannah's appointment as President in 1941.[71] The University of Michigan would probably have experienced growth under another president. Furthermore, it must be remembered that Ruthven did not welcome growth per se with open arms; he struggled against growing government contracts and swelling student enrollments.

Perhaps more meaningful measurements of institutional progress would be possible if such elusive criteria as quality of faculty, faculty and administrative morale, faculty compensation, executive leadership, and the university's standing compared with other leading educational institutions were reviewed.

During the summer of 1929 and in the succeeding few years Michigan lost an extraordinary number of renowned scholars. Historian Ulrich B. Phillips went to Yale; Herbert F. Goodrich became dean of the law school at Pennsylvania; engineering mechanics professor Stephen Timoshenko left for Stanford; and O. J. Campbell and Howard Mumford Jones of English resigned to accept appointments at Columbia and Harvard, respectively. Unexpected death felled such academic giants as historian Claude H. Van Tyne, philosopher Robert M. Wenley, sociologist Charles Horton Cooley, astronomer Ralph H. Curtiss, Max Winkler, head of the German department, and deans John R. Effinger and G. Carl Huber. *The Michigan Alumnus* took special note of the unusually heavy faculty attrition.[72] It was a difficult beginning for a president who professed that faculty excellence was his primary concern and whose Depression budgets would not allow immediate replacements.

The 1932 edition of *American Men of Science* listed Michigan as having twenty-nine starred scientists, not including those retired or emeritus. Michigan placed tenth in rank with other universities.[73]

In 1935, *The Atlantic Monthly* published a ranking of universities in order of their scholarly eminence. This report, based on a 1934 survey of the American Council on Education, listed Michigan as having fourteen academic departments of "High Excellence." Overall, Michigan was ranked sixth behind Harvard, Chicago, Columbia, California, and Yale.[74]

By 1947, the Director of Information Services reported that Michigan was ranked fourth (tied with Chicago) in the number of starred scientists. Only Harvard, California, and Columbia exceeded it. It was also reported: "Michigan has more than 200 staff members listed in 'Who's Who in America,' probably the highest percentage of any major large university—more than 20 percent of its regular staff."[75]

Again, one is not inclined to conclude that the university's faculty during the Ruthven era gained stature, or that Ruthven was responsible for such a gain. One can conclude, however, that faculty excellence did not decline and probably exhibited some gains.

Faculty morale is an even more elusive measure of institutional progress. One element contributing to high faculty morale is compensation, and Michigan's faculty did not fare especially well in matters of salary. A 1929 survey of instructors at the university disclosed that the average salary was about $2100.[76] The *Regents' Proceedings* indicate that salaries for full professors in 1929 averaged about $5000. A 1926–27 study of 302 American colleges and universities placed the average salary at $2958 for all faculty at these institutions.[77] One can conclude from these figures that Michigan's salaries were above the national average, but not conspicuously so. Indeed, for a university enjoying a position of national prominence, they were low. Ruthven, in his first *President's Report,* noted with alarm that "the University is in danger of losing its most noted men because of inability to meet even approximately the offers made by other institutions." Other universities, the president declared, had offered some of Michigan's best men "salaries up to two and more times the salary they have been receiving."[78]

The Ruthven Papers disclose that faculty compensation was an ongoing concern. Scholars could tighten their belts during the Depression and be thankful they had belts to tighten and pants to hold up, but following the Depression their expectations increased.

The lower ranks were the first to complain, for their needs were the most acute. The Senate Advisory Committee on University Affairs (SACUA) reported that a number of instructors and assistant professors had trouble subsisting on salaries that ranged from $1500 to $2500 annually. In 1941, a SACUA study revealed, a junior faculty member could expect an annual budgetary deficit of 7 percent.[79] In 1941–42 the average salary for full-time, undergraduate faculty at Michigan was $3805.[80] In 1943–44 the average salary for a full professor in the Literary College was $5606 and the maximum was $7500.[81]

By 1947 the average full-time undergraduate faculty salary was $5060, and the ceiling for full professors was up to $8500.[82] Salaries continued to rise, and the local AAUP chapter responded to a national questionnaire by saying, "In 1948–1949 and 1949–1950 over 90% . . . received selective merit increases."[83] By 1951 SACUA was commending the executive officers and the regents for "initiating plans for the salary increase . . . without pressure from the faculty. . . ."[84] Still, faculty reports indicated that cost of living was climbing even faster than faculty compensation and Michigan salaries compared with other institutions continued to be only slightly better than average.

The record shows little evidence of faculty pressure for other incentives, so presumably they were not at issue during the Ruthven years. Teaching load, for example, ranged from nine to twelve hours in 1935 and from eight to sixteen hours in 1947, perhaps indicative of a slightly increased average work load.[85] On the other hand, faculty sabbatical leaves showed a slight increase during the period 1929–1936.[86]

Surprisingly, despite modest incentives, consistently high faculty morale characterized the Ruthven era at Michigan. One main reason was Ruthven's genuine regard for the ability of professional men to conduct their own affairs.

In the matter of executive leadership, the Ruthven presidency seemed to divide itself neatly into two equal time periods. From the beginning until about 1940, as has been noted, Ruthven was a "mover and shaker."

Then, quite suddenly and almost concurrently, Ruthven collided with two unwelcome and unanticipated obstacles. One was a board of regents which began to question rather than support his policies. The other was World War II. After 1940 he faced the frustration of one unavoidable crisis after another. He was no longer able to control events and, when Provost Adams and a new administrative team took over in 1944, Ruthven became more the titular president than the persuasive leader he had been. This was evident even in his correspondence, for in the final few years of his presidency some letters would remain unanswered for as long as two or three weeks—a practice that he would not previously have tolerated. One suspects that executive credit for the university's post-war progress must go more to Ruthven's administrative team than to the president himself, but, if so, it was an indication of the practicality of the Michigan System he had established years earlier. Still, the evidence indicates that Ruthven remained in the presidency too long. He apparently did not realize that, after World War II, the university's needs had changed, or perhaps he had put so much of himself into the office that he was psychologically unable to surrender it to another man.[87]

Executive leadership, of course, depends not only on the president, but on the quality of his administrative appointments as well. From all indications Ruthven's selections were almost uniformly good. All faculty and administrators interviewed spoke favorably of the ability and dedication of provosts Stason and Adams, vice presidents Smith and Niehuss, and deans Kraus, Sawyer, Anderson, and

Keniston, and most felt that vice presidents Yoakum and Briggs were capable senior officers.

There were cases where Ruthven's judgment could be faulted, but there is also the certainty that he unfalteringly followed his perception of what was right for Michigan. Erich Walter said, "There's no question in my mind that he loved the University. In this sense it was almost as though it were a part of his family. He would have given his own life . . . if he needed to, to have kept this place from having any kind of mortal wound."[88]

One other facet of the Ruthven character deserves mention, particularly at this time of cynicism directed at those in positions of higher responsibility. Ruthven was a man of integrity. Although he was inclined to be cooperative, there is no evidence that he would grant unwarranted favors to anybody. When dealing with students and faculty, Ruthven had little sympathy for a person when he perceived an untruth. Ruthven's own durability was possible because he honored "the facts"; there is no evidence in the Ruthven record of anything less than the truth as he saw it. He was consistent, whether consistency meant telling the same story in the same way to different parties or sticking to a cherished educational ideal over the years. Despite the entreaties of bank boards, Ruthven refused their offers of directorships until he had retired from the presidency. He noted that there could be "embarrassment in dealing with financial organizations with which I am associated" and he pointed out to the president of the Lincoln National Life Insurance Company that "state supported universities are delicate plants which have to be nurtured continually in congenial soil."[89]

On balance, one can only admire a man whose ability, personality, and, perhaps most of all, character saw one of the leading universities in the world through twenty-two of its most difficult years. The trials which confronted Ruthven cannot be too greatly emphasized; bringing the university intact through one crisis after another was perhaps his major contribution. The history of higher education bypasses the Ruthvens of the university world for more glamorous leaders, but Ruthven made a positive and enduring contribution to his university. His main strength was his quiet, yet effective skill in dealing with his major constituencies. All things considered, one would have to place Ruthven in the front rank of Michigan presidents. Indeed, Marvin Niehuss, who has been on the Michigan scene for nearly fifty years, has said that Ruthven was one of the most able and the most underrated of all the university's leaders.[90]

Just prior to a particularly strenuous year, Ruthven told the aged Chase S. Osborn that in times of crisis he drew strength from a proverb taught him by a Chinese friend: "Pure gold does not fear the furnace." "I have no idea that I am pure gold," Ruthven hastened to add, "but if I am sound I will come out all right, and if I am not I will be destroyed, probably for the good of the institution."[91] Ruthven was sound, and his institution has prospered.

NOTES

1. Interviews, Bryant Ruthven, December 17, 1974, and Dr. Theodore H. Hubbell, January 13, 1975.

2. Interview, Alexander G. Ruthven, January 30, 1970.

3. Bryant Ruthven, letter, December 30, 1974.

4. Ruthven, *Naturalist in Two Worlds* (Ann Arbor: University of Michigan Press, 1963), pp. 64–68.

5. Ruthven, speech to the faculty, "Faculty" folder, Ruthven Papers, box 77, MHC.

6. Ruthven, *The President's Report for 1943–1944*, p. 16.

7. Ruthven to Charles A. Fisher and Howard Y. McClusky, memo, December 20, 1943, Ruthven Papers, box 46, MHC.

8. Arthur Elder Papers, Box 19, The Archives of Labor History and Urban Affairs, Wayne State University (hereafter referred to as Labor Archives, Wayne State).

9. *The President's Report for 1944–1945*, University of Michigan, pp. 266–68.

10. *The President's Report for 1945–1946*, University of Michigan, pp. 338–39.

11. *Ibid.*, p. 340.

12. Allen B. Crow to Fisher, March 27, 1945, Ruthven Papers, box 48, MHC.

13. Letter of Ruthven to Crow, April 5, 1945, Ruthven Papers, box 48, MHC.

14. *The President's Report for 1946–1947*, University of Michigan, p. 16.

15. Ruthven to John Reid, May 7, 1947, Ruthven Papers, box 55, MHC.

16. *The President's Report for 1946–1947*, University of Michigan, p. 385.

17. The automobile industry had employed spies before. "G.M., in particular, resorted to labor espionage on an extensive scale. Espionage services were contracted for by the labor-relations division of the corporation, by the personnel directors of Chevrolet and Fisher Body, and by individual plant managers. GM was Pinkerton's largest industrial client; the corporation, according to incomplete figures, was billed for over $100,000 by Pinkerton in 1934 and for over $200,000 in 1935. But GM did not rely on Pinkerton alone; it used at least fourteen other detective agencies and even arranged for some of its spies to check on others of its spies. The company spent approximately $1 million on labor espionage between January 1,

1934, and July 31, 1936." Sidney Fine, *The Automobile Under the Blue Eagle* (Ann Arbor: The University of Michigan Press, 1963).

18. Jacobs claimed they were distributed upon request of the class as examples of union literature; Stricker claimed they were required reading.

19. Charles S. Kennedy to Ruthven, April 27, 1948, Ruthven Papers, box 58, MHC.

20. *The Detroit Times,* May 19, 1948, p. 1.

21. Ruthven to Kennedy, May 24, 1948, Ruthven Papers, box 58, MHC. Also, Ruthven to Senator Taft and Representative Hartley, May 18, 1948, Elder Papers, box 19, Labor Archives, Wayne State University.

22. Irving Ives to Arthur Elder, May 15, 1948, and Elder to Ives, May 20, 1948, Elder Papers, box 19, Labor Archives, Wayne State.

23. *The Detroit Times,* May 20, 1948.

24. It seems probable that the "evidence" from the "State Police investigation" referred to in the media was actually a series of booklets produced by GM. The booklets attempted to link the supporters of the Labor Extension Service bill with communist front organizations. A set of these booklets is in the Ruthven Papers, boxes 81 and 82, MHC.

25. News release, June 20, 1948, Arthur Elder Papers, box 19, Labor Archives, Wayne State.

26. Kennedy to Ruthven, May 26, 1948, Ruthven Papers, box 58, MHC.

27. *Proceedings of the Board of Regents,* annual June meeting, 1948, p. 1326.

28. Ruthven, *The President's Report for 1947–1948,* p. 361.

29. Interview, Ruthven, January 30, 1970.

30. Statement of Haber, April 13, 1949, Ruthven Papers, box 82, MHC.

31. Interviews with Wesley Maurer, February 20, 1970, and Harold Dorr, February 6, 1970. Dorr used an analogy to describe the demise of WES: "If you have a lot of people striking at a snake with sticks, and the snake dies, you can attribute the last blow to whomever you like." Maurer attributed the demise more to General Motors than to faculty indifference.

32. John W. Gibson to Ruthven, August 20, 1948, Ruthven Papers, box 82, MHC.

33. "To the Members of the Board of Regents," September 21, 1948, Ruthven Papers, box 82, MHC.

34. Ruthven to Kennedy, October 1, 1948, Ruthven Papers, box 59, MHC.

35. Ruthven Papers, box 82, MHC.

36. Statement of G. Mennen Williams, October 1, 1948, Arthur Elder Papers, box 20, Labor Archives, Wayne State.

37. *The Michigan Daily,* September 28, 1948.

38. *Proceedings of the Board of Regents,* October meeting, 1948, p. 113.

39. "Report of Commission of Inquiry on the Workers Educational Service of the University of Michigan," an undated report prepared by the Michigan Committee on Civil Rights, Ruthven Papers, box 82, MHC.

40. *The Detroit News,* October 20, 1948, p. 1.

41. *The Detroit Free Press,* October 21, 1948, p. 2. A later *Detroit Free Press* editorial, however, commended the regents for bringing WES more closely under the aegis of the university. October 22, 1948, p. 6.

42. Arthur Elder Papers, box 19, Labor Archives, Wayne State.

43. *The Detroit Free Press,* October 4, 1948.

44. Louis A. Golezynski *et al.* to Ruthven, October 29, 1948, Ruthven Papers, box 82, MHC.

45. *The Detroit Free Press,* January 19, 1949, p. 17.

46. *Ibid.,* January 21, 1949, p. 7.

47. Ruthven to Phillips Bradley, January 31, 1949, Ruthven Papers, box 59, MHC.

48. Ruthven Papers, box 82, MHC.

49. *The Detroit Free Press,* February 1, 1949, p. 15. Regent Kenneth M. Stevens made his remarks at a state Republican caucus.

50. Elder to Harry S Truman, March 15, 1950, Ruthven Papers, box 61, MHC.

51. Alexander G. Ruthven, *Naturalist in Two Worlds,* p. 41.

52. *Ibid.,* p. 41.

53. *Proceedings of the Board of Regents,* October meeting, 1944, p. 705.

54. Adams had previously been recommended for dean by the faculties of Literature, Science, and the Arts, and the School of Business Administration.

55. Letter from the regents' committee on organization to "Board of Regents," November 7, 1944, Ruthven Papers, box 50, MHC.

56. Ruthven to Ralph Hayward, December 1, 1944, *ibid.*

57. "The University of Michigan: A Statement of its Policies," March 1, 1947, Ruthven Papers, box 54, MHC.

58. Ruthven Papers, box 54, MHC.

59. Interview, Ruthven, January 30, 1970.

60. *The President's Report for 1950–1951,* pp. 388–89.

61. Ruthven to Hayward, May 21, 1946, Ruthven Papers, box 52, MHC.

62. Ruthven to Hayward, January 18, 1947, Ruthven Papers, box 55, MHC.

63. Ruthven, *Naturalist in Two Worlds,* pp. 155–56.

64. Ruthven to Calvin Goodrich, March 24, 1948, Ruthven Papers, box 57, MHC.

65. Although Ruthven vowed to the regents that he would not, as Presidents Angell and Hutchins had, serve a single day over the retirement limit, he finally consented to remain in office over the summer of 1951. President Harlan Hatcher replaced him in the fall of 1951.

66. Louis Karpinski was a feisty old mathematics professor who delighted in harangues against administrators.

67. Ruthven to H. L. Donovan (President, University of Kentucky), May 28, 1946, Ruthven Papers, box 51, MHC. The exception to this procedure was, apparently, the appointment of Dr. Albert C. Furstenberg as dean of the medical school. Ruthven appointed his riding companion without consulting Furstenberg's colleagues. Interview, Dr. H. Marvin Pollard, January 13, 1975. After the initial shock, it was agreed in the medical school that the appointment was a good one.

68. Statistics in this section are from the *President's Reports* and from an "Extra" of *The Michigan Daily,* May 21, 1951. The figures differ depending on source; Peckham, for instance, lists enrollment in 1951 as 21,000 and library volumes at two million. (*Making of Michigan,* p. 216.) The differences result from the method of measurement. Some enrollment figures include summer school and extension students; some librarians count each copy of a book as an additional volume.

69. M. M. Quaife and Sidney Glazer, *Michigan* (New York: Prentice–Hall, Inc., 1948), p. 335.

70. Allen Schoenfield, *The Detroit News Pictorial,* January 7, 1951, p. 13.

71. For a comparison of the growth of Michigan colleges and universities, see Willis F. Dunbar, *The Michigan Record in Higher Education* (Detroit: Wayne State University Press, 1963). Ruthven was not happy when the newly-installed Hannah began an aggressive campaign to set a regular season date for the UM–MSC football game and also criticized the university for offering correspondence courses in agriculture. "I will be glad to talk with Mr. Hannah at any time," wrote Ruthven to Regent Edmund Shields, "but I can tell you now that it will do little good because we do not, and never will, speak the same language." (October 16, 1941, Ruthven Papers, box 38, MHC.) Yet within a few years Hannah was sending Ruthven gifts of produce from MSC agricultural experiments and a reconciled Ruthven was working hard to promote interinstitutional cooperation.

72. *The Michigan Alumnus*, Vol. 35, No. 36 (1929) and Vol. 36, No. 23 (1930).

73. Edwin R. Embree, "In Order of Their Eminence," *The Atlantic Monthly*, Vol. 155, No. 6 (1935), n.657.

74. *Ibid.*, p. 655.

75. Memo of A. L. Brandon to *Life* magazine, October 15, 1947, Ruthven Papers, box 58, MHC.

76. Ruthven, *The President's Report for 1929–1930*, p. 20.

77. Trevor Arnett, "Teacher's Salaries," *Association of American Colleges Bulletin*, Vol. 15, No. 1 (1929), p. 9.

78. Ruthven, *The President's Report for 1929–1930*, p. 24.

79. "Special Meeting of University Senate," February 15, 1943, Ruthven Papers, box 44, MHC.

80. "Association of Governing Boards of State Universities and Allied Institutions" questionnaire, June 1947, Ruthven Papers, box 56 (filed under "Visitors"), MHC.

81. *L. S. & A. Faculty Minutes*, 1943–44, 1944–45, p. 998. Ruthven's salary at this time was $20,000.

82. "Association of Governing Boards of State Universities and Allied Institutions" questionnaire, June 1947, Ruthven Papers, box 56, MHC.

83. Papers of the Michigan chapter of AAUP, 1935–59, MHC.

84. "Report on the Economic Status of the Faculty," February 6, 1951, Ruthven Papers, box 64, MHC.

85. 1935 national AAUP questionnaire, Papers of the Michigan chapter of AAUP, 1935–59, MHC, and "Association of Governing Boards of State Universities and Allied Institutions" questionnaire, June 1947, Ruthven Papers, box 56, MHC.

86. 1935 National AAUP questionnaire, Papers of the Michigan chapter of AAUP, 1935–59, MHC.

87. Erich Walter and others suggested that, as Ruthven became more familiar with Provost Adams, he became convinced that Adams was not the man to succeed him and stayed on to prevent the regents from appointing Adams. Interview, February 24, 1970. Bryant Ruthven thought that Florence Ruthven was a factor; she was "terribly proud" of her husband and certain that nobody else could do as good a job. Interview, December 17, 1974.

88. Interview, Erich Walter, February 24, 1970.

89. Ruthven to A. J. McAndless, March 23, 1942, Ruthven Papers, box 39,

MHC. Ruthven went on the board of Lincoln National Life in 1947; he apparently felt that there was no possible question of conflict of interest.

90. Interview, Marvin Niehuss, April 30, 1970.

91. Ruthven to Chase S. Osborn, December 26, 1941, Ruthven Papers, box 39, MHC.

13

Retirement

The retirement president was showered with honors. One May night 3000 cheering and singing students, accompanied by two bands, stood in the rain and serenaded the Ruthvens. The students presented them with a scroll describing their affection and regard, and the president of the student legislature "hailed the retiring president as 'one of the greatest administrators who ever led a University of this size'."[1] That same day the state legislature passed a resolution describing Ruthven as "one of the nation's leaders in education."[2] Two weeks later Michigan State College awarded Ruthven an honorary doctor of laws degree, one of fifteen honorary doctorates he received.

In June, more honors followed. A group of fifty "close friends," led by Earl Cress, President of the Ann Arbor Trust Company, and Michael Gorman, Editor of *The Flint Journal,* presented the Ruthvens with a new Buick. Later that month, 350 citizens of Ann Arbor attended a retirement dinner in the Michigan Ballroom.[3]

Editorials in the state newspapers praised his presidency. *The Ann Arbor News* said:

> In the years to come, if Dr. Ruthven's name ever should be forgotten, his administration of "unprecedented accomplishment" will live on as long as the University exists. To a man who has completed his active career as an educator and administrator, that knowledge must be a comfort and source of satisfaction that few men realize. We bid Dr. Ruthven a reluctant farewell from the University officialdom, and welcome him anew to the citizenry of Washtenaw County as simply—A. G. "Sandy" Ruthven.[4]

In August the Ruthvens packed belongings accumulated over forty-four years. Ruthven, who had accumulated a rare book collection of over 1000 first editions, gave most of his library to the rare book room in the university's General Library. Mrs. Ruthven faced the unenviable responsibility of deciding which furnishings and family heirlooms would be retained for the next household. There was no remorse, though, about leaving 815 South University; it was never a real home to them. In fact, when asked about the move by reporters, Ruthven said, "I have no emotion about it at all."[5]

Exhausted, the Ruthvens left for Frankfort to recuperate, and by October they were moved into their new home, Gordon Hall, an imposing mansion on a hill west of Dexter and only a few miles from Ann Arbor. Gordon Hall and fifty-seven acres had been the spacious home of the late Judge Dexter, and was given to the university just before Ruthven's retirement. With its winding drive, white columns, and great oaks, it looks like a transplanted southern plantation. The first floor was renovated to taste for the Ruthvens, and they and their son, Peter, set up housekeeping there.

At first, retirement was a busy time for the ex-president. He was given an office in the Rackham building on campus, but soon exchanged it for one in Alumni Memorial Hall. There, he was more in the middle of things, and it was easier to keep up his contacts with visiting alumni.

While he was at Gordon Hall, Ruthven made almost daily trips

Students Honor Ruthven (May, 1951)

Gordon Hall

to Ann Arbor, not only to his office, but also to his Morgan horse farm on Geddes Road. His famous Morgans never ceased to delight him, and he enjoyed his reputation as a national authority on the breed. Despite his advanced age, he continued to ride often and, in fact, gave up the sport only after he had passed eighty. The daily operation of his stable was entrusted to "Tex" Talley, manager of Stanerigg since the thirties. Other than riding, Ruthven's main retirement hobby was reading. He read everything from classics to mysteries, and often, when he couldn't sleep, his reading light would burn most of the night.[6] He and Mrs. Ruthven would sometimes attend musical performances on campus for, although neither had musical talent, they enjoyed the glitter of opening night and the opportunity to meet the performers. The arts, they felt, deserved their support.

Retirement was more difficult for Mrs. Ruthven, for she had devoted her life to her husband's career and, other than knitting and reading, she had few interests of her own. She had learned to relish the action of being a president's wife, and retirement caught her unprepared.[7] Although there were now three grandchildren to enjoy, her family was not a close-knit one and reunions were rare.

Her husband was working hard at the role of being an elder statesman. For the first time, he joined a number of organizations outside of university circles. He was elected to the Board of Directors of the Ann Arbor Trust Company, the Lincoln National Life Insurance Company, the Morgan Horse Club, and the Cranbrook Institute of Science.[8]

The most important of these associations to Ruthven was the Ann Arbor Trust Company. Its president, Earl Cress, became one of his few close friends. Wednesday mornings at eleven, without fail, Ruthven would report for his assignment as a member of the trust committee. As usual, he was quiet and did not try to speak on every topic, but his retentive memory and intimate knowledge of the university and its people proved invaluable to the committee.[9]

On campus, he found an unlikely niche. He had hoped that his successor, Harlan Hatcher, might seek his wisdom on major questions from time to time, but a retired president is welcomed by the incumbent like yesterday's news and, not surprisingly, Ruthven was seldom asked for his advice. Ruthven knew better than to volunteer his opinions to the new administration, but nevertheless he fretted to think that his abilities were not used more fully. He found an outlet for his energy in the development council. Late in his presidency he had visited alumni clubs across the country to tell them that the university needed their support for the Phoenix Project. From this one shot fund-raising project he gained an appreciation of the merits of regularized procedures for fund raising in public universities. One of his last acts as president was to create a development council, and place it under the direction of Alan MacCarthy, a professional fund raiser. In 1952 he became a consultant for the council, and was instrumental in its organization and in explaining its purpose to students, faculty, and alumni.

Ruthven found great satisfaction in visiting the alumni clubs. He would always be "their" president, for after a half century as teacher and administrator he was known by all. He, in turn, was blessed with an excellent memory and knew many of them. When it was announced that Ruthven and his wife would attend a gathering the local alumni would go through elaborate preparations. "When I heard that the great Dr. Ruthven would have dinner at my house," recalled Mrs. Donald Bacon, then living in Tucson, "I spent days getting everything just so."[10] Cowboy hats, Indian bonnets, keys to the city, and a variety of citations were pressed on the Ruthvens. Many times the host and hostess were pleasantly surprised to discover that the Ruthvens were unpretentious people. Ruthven never failed to delight the banquet audiences with his self-deprecating sense of humor; this also endeared him to the alumni. His speeches were short and to the point, but he ranged far and wide in informal discussions afterward. One alumnus recalls:

> The place was Buffalo. The occasion, a first district meeting. At the dinner, Dr. Ruthven had been the principal speaker. One of the Buffalo club members had arranged to pick up Dr. Ruthven at 3:00 a.m. and drive him to the station to catch a 4:00 a.m. train for Ann Arbor. When the dinner party broke up I invited Dr. Ruthven to my room as he said that he didn't want to sleep. I had bought a bottle of Martinis for him before dinner and a bottle of Scotch for myself. Both were two-thirds full. So, we ordered a bucket and settled back to enjoy life until 3:00 a.m. The following four hours were filled with conversation ranging from the University, through herpetology, archeology, European politics, Far East politics, the Soviet stance, to the possibility of economic recovery. I had entertained Dr. Ruthven many times before, and had also been entertained by him. I thought I knew the man, but on this occasion I really became acquainted. From that time forward our relationship became one of mutual respect, yes, and admiration.[11]

The Ruthvens made alumni friends all over the country. Many, even today, can cite verbatim conversations carried on with Ruthven years ago. They delight, particularly, in stories demonstrating the humor, warmth, and very human qualities of their president. When the directors of the Alumni Association conferred on him the title "Dean of Alumni," Ruthven regarded it as one of his greatest honors.

In addition to his journeys to the alumni, Ruthven, in early retirement, was frequently asked to be speaker at commencements, banquets, and dedications.

His long-time interest in interinstitutional cooperation found an outlet when commissions were appointed by the legislature to study the futures of Ferris Institute, Big Rapids, and Wayne University, Detroit. At that time there were many who advocated that the University of Michigan should subsume these campuses and establish additional branches as well. Ruthven believed, instead, in pluralism of higher education within the state and thought that other institutions should serve their constituencies exclusive of the behemoth university. The special commissions, under Ruthven's chairmanship, agreed that Ferris Institute and Wayne University should be independent, state-supported institutions.

These institutions, and all public colleges and universities, Ruthven thought, should charge no student fees because "the education of a college student is as much a public responsibility as is the teaching of pre-college boys and girls."[12]

He encouraged the community college movement in Michigan during the 1950s and 1960s, giving support and advice to those responsible for organizing a statewide network of local two-year colleges.[13]

In 1952 Ruthven was named an advisor to the Board of Trustees of Olivet College and later became honorary chairman of that college's fund drive for $10 million. Also in that year Ruthven began an Extension Service course in "Higher Education at Mid-Century," a refresher course for college administrators.[14]

Dean of Alumni

Portrait by John Koch

In 1957, at mid-year graduation ceremonies, Ruthven was presented with his portrait. The portrait, commissioned by the regents
and by Ruthven's friends, was painted by John Koch, a famous
portrait artist who was a native of Ann Arbor and a friend of the
Ruthven family. Koch painted Ruthven in the flowing robes of
office, still robust and alert, and thought that, although the years

238

had saddened him, "his great warmth and humor remained unchanged."[15]

In 1962, Ruthven passed his eightieth year. Many friends and alumni wanted to do something special for him and planned a "Ruthven 80th Birthday Anniversary Dinner" for June 14 in the Michigan Union ballroom. He reminded them that his birthday was April 1 but, being a patient man, he was content to wait for its observance at a time convenient to the committee.[16] Over 500 attended the celebration, and the Alumni Association presented him with a "Gentling" cart for use in the training of his prized Morgans. Ruthven was asked to speak. He began haltingly, and many in the audience wondered if he could continue. Soon, however, he warmed to his subject, a vigorous denunciation of "self-serving politicians." Ruthven lashed out at the representatives of special interests "who for pieces of silver would cheerfully deprive young people of an education by insisting on larger and larger fees."[17] Ruthven closed on a gentler note, saying: "When anything happens twice in Ann Arbor, it becomes a tradition. You gave me a retirement dinner ten years ago and this one, so I will look forward to seeing you all ten years hence."[18] It was a stirring performance, and those who were there never forgot it. "These are things I treasure as memories of a truly great man and a wonderful friend," H. J. "Brick" Mersereau wrote. "No wonder my eyes fill with tears at the thoughts of Michigan."[19]

The eightieth birthday dinner was Ruthven's "last hurrah." He seldom appeared in public after that and preferred, instead, to render his opinions privately. Mrs. Donald Bacon, a close friend and a member of the State Board for Community and Junior Colleges, would often ask Dr. Ruthven's advice. "He would always begin by saying 'I could be wrong, but,'" Mrs. Bacon told the author. "Of course, he never was."[20] Another friend remembers that a Ruthven pronouncement came only after a good deal of deliberation, but when it came it was delivered with certitude, for Ruthven didn't anticipate that anyone would contradict his judgment.[21]

His opinions and stories enchanted his friends to such an extent that they urged him to compile his memoirs. He resisted, saying, "Nobody would be interested in reading about those things."[22] He did not think a biography was appropriate, and he quoted Channing's statement: "Most biographies are of little worth—they are panegyrics, not lives."[23] He also "lacked confidence" in autobiographies, "human nature being what it is."[24] He settled on "random recollections" instead, and his *Naturalist in Two Worlds* was published in 1963. It was typically Ruthven: unpretentious, humorous, candid but controlled, piquant but not biting. He omitted names and dates; the result is a slightly confusing smorgasbord for anyone interested in the history of his presidency. However, the omissions served Ruthven's purpose well; he preferred not to offend anyone and, besides, it was great fun to think of his readers having to guess at the names and times of the incidents to which he alluded. *Naturalist in Two Worlds* is light and delightful. Ruthven's charm shines through every story. Above all, it is the work of a man of wisdom. Any contemporary college administrator would do well to ponder Ruthven's remarks for, despite his modest disclaimer that college administration was only "common sense," he had the key to many problems which still persist.

By the onset of the 1960s, the Ruthvens were old. They had

Reminiscing, 2900 Fuller Road

Four Presidents of Michigan (1969)
Left to Right: Hatcher, Little, Ruthven, Fleming

needed a smaller house and so in the mid 1950s had moved from Gordon Hall to a small, modern one-story house at 2900 Fuller Road, just across from Stanerigg Stables. Their family had scattered: Kate and Larry Stuart spent a good deal of time in Guatemala; Peter was hospitalized in Ypsilanti; and Bryant, with the State Department, was in various Central American countries. They faced the problems common to many elderly people. Lifelong friends had died or moved. Routine travel became a major challenge. Their strength and comfort was no longer sought; in fact, it was sometimes demeaning to be treated in solicitous fashion by well-intentioned younger friends. Even Stanerigg was gone, sold in 1967 to provide the site for Huron High, the city's new public high school.[25] Still, they were together, and for "Buzz" and "Lizzie"—as they called each other—that was everything.

But she was a year older than he, and terribly frail. She suffered a stroke and died in 1968, after seven months in University Hospital. She was eighty-seven.

Now he was alone with his sorrow. At first, he was pathetically lost without his wife of more than sixty years. Gradually, he came to rely more and more on his neighbor, friend, and man of all trades Tex Talley. Ruthven had built the Talleys a little house next to his, and now Tex became chauffeur, shopper, and housekeeper for Ruthven. Ruthven, however, insisted that he would live by himself and that he could do his own cooking. He avoided his son's suggestion that he engage a live-in housekeeper.[26] A small circle of friends saw him often, but he made no effort to broaden the circle and was rarely seen in Ann Arbor. Once in a while he would have dinner with Alan and Til MacCarthy or Jerry Bacon, the widow of Donald Bacon, one of his dearest friends in later years. Often Bryant and "B" Ruthven's children, Alexander II and Becky—both graduate students at the university—would visit to talk and read to him.

Best of all for the lonely man were the regular Sunday morning calls from Earl Cress, President of the Ann Arbor Trust Company. The two of them, occasionally joined by Joe Hooper, Alan MacCarthy, and Lee Kalmbach, would pour a drink, sit back, and let the talk flow free.[27] Topics ran the gamut of trust company affairs, state and local politics and, of course, matters concerning the university. They called these Sunday sessions "going to church." Even within this small, intimate circle where he called his friends by first name he was always "Dr. Ruthven." The homage was accorded because of his former position, his age, and, most of all, his ever-present sense of dignity.[28]

Still, it was a terribly lonely last few years for Ruthven. His son remembers how sad it was to see Ruthven trudge each day to the mailbox only to return with another fistful of junk mail.[29] His eyesight began to fail—a burdensome affliction for such a keen reader. Despite this handicap, he kept a lively interest in current events. Tex read to him from *The Ann Arbor News* and *The Michigan Daily;* he never missed the eleven o'clock evening news; and he continued his love of books by means of recorded readings.[30] He loved to challenge his mind with crossword puzzles, and would complete as many as he could get his hands on.[31]

During this lonely time, in the winter of 1970, I asked Ruthven for a series of interviews. "Of course," he said without hesitating, a twinkle lighting up the dimmed eyes, "I'll tell you all about my mistakes!" There were eight interviews. Each lasted an hour, and each was enjoyable. He was open, friendly, and seemingly uncomplicated. He delighted in the role of raconteur, yet he listened carefully, too. His interests at nearly ninety years of age appeared to include any topic imaginable. There was an air of rusticity—even naiveté—as a natural legacy from frontier Iowa and scientific expeditions in the field. He was immensely likeable. It was easier to think of him as a wise and kindly grandfather than as a man who consorted with magistrates, magnates, and potentates. The detachment of the scientist was always evident, for he neither questioned me about my discoveries nor tried to prejudice the interpretation of events. Either he had long since learned to rein in his curiosity, or perhaps he simply believed that he had done his best and the record would prove it. "I knew I could be wrong, but I didn't see how," was one way Ruthven summed up his career to his friends.

Ruthven was surprisingly vehement on one subject. He called his decision to accept the Michigan presidency the "greatest regret of my life."[32] One wonders why. Part of the reason may be found in an unusually candid letter written to an old friend from museum days, Calvin Goodrich, soon after retirement. "I find now that I get little satisfaction in looking back over the years. I have only done what my conscience dictated but in driving ahead I have failed to make friends and to enjoy life . . . the job has been a lonesome one. . . ."[33] Certainly life is less than fully rewarding when a vigorous, intelligent, personable man feels that he cannot make close friendships because of his position. Another part of the answer is that Ruthven was not able to devote as much time to family as he—and they—would have liked. Finally, there can be no doubt that Ruthven's happiest years were spent in the museum. He resented being removed from a scientific career that had been so fulfilling to him.

But, as his son said, "Nobody was holding a gun to his head."[34] And Ruthven himself acknowledged, "The same organism in the same environment when subjected to the same stimulus will always react the same way."[35] It hurt Ruthven deeply to know what he had given up, but were he to do it all over again, he would have been president of Michigan. His sense of duty, his pride in his ability, and his love for the university would not have permitted otherwise.

Always, during our interviews, there was his air of courtliness, reserve, and dignity. His son thought it to be his strongest quality, and emphasized it in a moving statement about his father's final hour.

"I guess it's natural, being compelled to rethink my association with a person who left us all with such strong memories, that I would tend to sort through those qualities that made Dad to us such a memorable person. Doing this, the quality that comes out foremost in my assessment is dignity. Dad never lost it. It was a quality he never laid aside, never compromised, and he was blessed by the fact that it endured to an age when many men must give it up.

"He even died with dignity. Tex came in that morning to do his household chores and found Dad sitting on the davenport in front of the television. Although Tex noted it wasn't customary for Father to be dressed at that hour of the day in pajamas and robe, he didn't think too much of it. Nor was the protracted silence unusual.

"It wasn't until Tex had been working in the house for over an hour that he realized Dad had died quietly the night before while watching television. We like to think he even managed to go during a commercial.

"Muehlig's funeral home sent a limousine for us the afternoon of Father's burial. . . . It was a lovely winter's day, unusually sunny for Ann Arbor at that time of year. Mr. Muehlig met us at the cemetery and, as he led us to the gravesite, he assured me everything was just as Dad wanted it—no service, no one there but family. . . .

The cemetery was mercifully empty of visitors and reverently quiet. There was the green cloth. There was the gold urn. Behind the urn was a vase holding three yellow roses—his favorite—sent by a young couple he had befriended. And there was the blue sky.

"The four of us stood silently before the grave for several moments, each of us in our own way saying goodbye to him, then we turned and walked slowly back to the limousine. The only comfort that I could salvage from that moment was the fact Father had left this life in as dignified a manner as he had lived it."[36]

Ruthven died January 19, 1971.

NOTES

1. *The Michigan Daily*, May 23, 1951.

2. *The Ann Arbor News*, May 23, 1951.

3. *Ibid.*, June 22, 1951.

4. *Ibid.*, August 17, 1951.

5. *Ibid.*, August 9, 1951.

6. Interview, Mrs. Donald Bacon, January 13, 1975. Dr. and Mrs. Ruthven often stayed overnight in Ann Arbor with the Bacons.

7. Interview, Bryant Ruthven, December 17, 1974.

8. His associations with Lincoln National Life and Cranbrook began in 1947 and 1948, respectively.

9. Interview, Joseph C. Hooper, January 17, 1975. Hooper was a member of the committee and Ruthven's attorney.

10. Interview, January 13, 1975.

11. Jay H. Schmidt to Alison Myers, December 7, 1974.

12. Article prepared for the journal of the Michigan State Medical Society, quoted in *The Ann Arbor News,* January 20, 1971. Ruthven was appointed chairman of the commission to study the future of Ferris Institute in 1949.

13. Interview, Mrs. Donald Bacon, January 13, 1975.

14. This course was one of the first taught by the university's Center for the Study of Higher Education. The Center, under Algo Henderson, its first director, sought to prepare college administrators. It was the first of its kind in the United States.

15. John Koch to Erich Walter, December 4, 1974.

16. Frank J. Ortman to Erich Walter, November 6, 1974.

17. *The Ann Arbor News,* June 15, 1962.

18. H. J. Mersereau to Miss Alison Myers, October 30, 1974.

19. *Ibid.*

20. Interview, Mrs. Bacon, January 13, 1975.

21. Interview, Mrs. Julie Furstenberg Owens, December 18, 1974.

22. Interview, Mrs. Alan MacCarthy, January 14, 1975.

23. Alexander G. Ruthven, *Naturalist in Two Worlds* (Ann Arbor: University of Michigan Press, 1963).

24. *Ibid.*

25. Ruthven sold a little over ten acres to the school district; the remaining acreage was sold to the city for a park. At the same time the Laurence Stuart parcel was sold. Interview, Joseph C. Hooper, January 17, 1975.

26. Bryant Ruthven, letter, November 27, 1974.

27. Hooper is an Ann Arbor attorney; Kalmbach was chairman of the board of the Massachusetts Mutual Life Insurance Company; MacCarthy was the university's development director.

28. Interview, Joseph C. Hooper, January 17, 1975.

29. Interview, Bryant Ruthven, December 17, 1974.

30. Interview, Mrs. Anne Van der Hyden and Mrs. Alan MacCarthy, January 14, 1975. Ruthven, hoping to restore his eyesight, had a cataract operation in 1970, but he never fully regained his eyesight.

31. Becky Ruthven, letter, January 24, 1975.

32. Interview, Ruthven, January 20, 1970.

33. Ruthven to Calvin Goodrich, March 14, 1952, Ruthven Papers, box 63, MHC.

34. Interview, Bryant Ruthven, December 17, 1974.

35. Ruthven, *Naturalist in Two Worlds,* p. 157.

36. Bryant Ruthven, letter, November 26, 1974. Ruthven is buried in Forest Hill Cemetery, Ann Arbor.

Index

Index

Index

Index

Index